African Dance

▼▼▼▼▼▼▼▼▼▼▼▼▼

AFRICAN DANCE:
▲▲▲▲▲▲▲▲▲▲▲▲▲▲

AN ARTISTIC, HISTORICAL, AND PHILOSOPHICAL INQUIRY

Edited by Kariamu Welsh Asante

Africa World Press, Inc.

P.O. Box 1892

Trenton, NJ 08607

P.O. Box 48

Asmara, ERITREA

Africa World Press, Inc.

P.O. Box 1892

Trenton, NJ 08607

P.O. Box 48

Asmara, ERITREA

Copyright © Kariamu Welsh Asante 1998

First Printing 1994
Second Printing, January 1998
Third Printing 2002

Book design: Jonathan Gullery
Cover design: Linda Nickens

Library of Congress Cataloging-in-Publication Data

African dance : an artistic, historical, and philosophical inquiry /
    edited by Kariamu Welsh Asante.
        p. cm.
    Includes bibliographical references (p.   ).
    ISBN 0-86543-196-5. -- ISBN 0-86543-197-3 (pbk.)
        1. Dance--Africa. 2. Dance, Black. I. Welsh Asante, Kariamu.
    GV 1705.A47   1994
    792.8'096--dc20   94-41598
                                                                          CIP

PRINTED IN CANADA

CONTENTS

Acknowledgements

▼ ▼ ▼ ▼ ▼ ▼ ▼ ▼ ▼ ▼ ▼ ▼ ▼ ▼ ▼

This book has indeed been a long time coming. Ideas come fast but the process and conclusion of a project is a slower and detailed operation. So many people come and go during the course of editing this book but they have all made contributions and so in my own way I will try to thank them all. An edited book by definition is a collective process and this book was even more so a collective effort. I not only stand on the shoulders of my ancestors and those that have taught me but I also stand on the ground that they have secured for me.

A special asante sana to Cindy Lehman, Sondra Millner, and Debra Crosby who have proofread, edited, and reread this manuscript. To my dear Rene Yhema, who consistently grows and learns on the job as I include her in dances, manuscripts, projects, and conferences before she can catch her breath from the last project. As always, I do a praisesong for my teacher and mentor, Pearl Reynolds, who lives in me. To the three groups of Kariamu & Co., a lifetime of gratitude. My images on your bodies have reflected our beauty, pain, joy, history, contradictions, and hopes. To Frances, Gaynell, Shawnte, Amma Joy, Rene Yhema, Ashe for embodying my visions, movements, technique, and making it your own.

To Daudi in Arizona, my first born, my continued love, to Khumalo, my second born, love and appreciation for sharing the kitchen table with my manuscripts and papers. Molefi, a special dobale.

Pearl Primus

In Memory of Pearl Primus

(1919–1994)

▼▼▼▼▼▼▼▼▼▼▼▼▼▼▼

Pearl Primus was born in Trinidad in 1919 and moved to New York at an early age. She attended Hunter College and graduated in 1940 majoring in biology and pre-medicine. Primus received a dance scholarship to the New School for Social Research and began to study what were called at the time "primitive dances." Her first choreographed work, *African Ceremonial,* premiered at the Nintey-second Street Young Women's Hebrew Association on February 14, 1943. This was considered her professional debut, and the work received positive reviews. After a ten-month engagement at a club called Cafe Society Downtown, she left to prepare her first solo concert. This performance took place at the Belasco Theater on Broadway in the fall of 1944. This was an extraordinary achievement for a young Black woman in the 1940s. Primus went on to study with some of the great modern dance teachers of that time including Martha Graham, Doris Humphrey, Charles Weidman, Hanya Holm, and Sophie Maslow.

Primus traveled the South observing the lifestyles of the common people, living with sharecroppers, and visiting Black churches . It was that experience that inspired much of her subsequent choreography. Dances like *Strange Fruit* became classics, because of her bold statement of social protest. Some of the other works choreographed by Pearl Primus are *Shango* (1947), *Impinyuza* (1951), *Naffi Tombo* (1960), the legendary *The Negro Speaks of Rivers* (1943), choreographed to a poem by Langston Hughes, and *Michael Row Your Boat Ashore* (1979), which was about the horror of the Birmingham, Alabama church bombings. Primus's choreography chronicled the black experience in the

United States and the traditional dances of Africa and the Caribbean. Primus also worked on Broadway dancing in and choreographing such shows as *Show Boat* (1945), *Caribbean Carnival* (1947), *The Emperor Jones* (1947), and *Mister Johnson* (1956).

Like her predecessor, Katherine Dunham, Primus received the last and largest Rosenwald Fellowship to finance her travel to Africa for eighteen months. In 1949, she was able to visit what was then known as the Gold Coast (Ghana), Angola, the Cameroons, Liberia, Senegal and the Belgian Congo (Zaire). Later, on another trip to Africa with her husband, Percival Borde, she was named "Omowale" which means "the child returns home" by the Nigerians in Yoruba. In 1959, on her second major trip to Africa, Primus was named director of Liberia's Performing Arts Center.

Her work with the National Dance Company of Liberia and her stylization of the Liberian dance "Fanga " earned her that country's highest award, the Order of the Star of Africa, which was bestowed on Primus by the late President William V.S. Tubman.

Primus was married to Percival Borde, a dancer and choreographer . After their two-year stay in Liberia, they returned to the States and formed the Earth Dance Company in the 1970s. In 1976, two of Primus 's dances, *Fanga*, a dance of welcome, and the *Wedding Dance*, were performed by the Alvin Ailey American Dance Theater. The American Dance Festival in Durham, North Carolina, reconstructed Primus's *The Negro Speaks of Rivers* and presented the dance in its Black dance classic series. Primus has taught dance and anthropology at Hunter College, the State University of New York at Buffalo, New York University (where she received her Ph.D. in dance education), and at Smith College where she was a Five College Professor of Humanities. She was honored by President George Bush for her contributions to dance and received the National Medal of Arts at the White House on July 9, 1991.

— Kariamu Welsh Asante

Bibliography

Clarke, Mary and David Vaughan, eds. *The Encylcopedia of Dance and Ballet* (1977); Cohen-Stratyner, Barbara Naomi. *Biographical Dictionary of Dance* (1982); EBA; Emery, Lynne Fauley. *Black Dance: From 1619 to Today* (1988); Long, Richard. *The Black Tradition in American Concert Dance* (1990); NA; NWAT; Patterson, Lindsay, ed.

Anthology of the Afro-American in the Theater: A Critical Approach (1978); Rollins, Charlemae. *Negro Entertainers of Stage, Screen, and T.V.* (1967); Thorpe, Edward. *Black Dance* (1990); Toppin, Edgar A. A Biographical *History of Blacks in America Since 1528* (1971); WA; Wilis, John, ed. *Dance World* ([1967] 1976); WWBA (1990).

Notes

This biography of Pearl Primus originally appeared in *Black Women in America : An Historical Encyclopedia*, Darlene Clark Hine, Ed. (1993), Carlson Publishing Inc., and is reprinted here by permission of the publisher.

FOREWORD

▼▼▼▼▼▼▼▼▼▼▼▼▼▼

Sir Rex Nettleford

The publication of this volume of essays on African dance comes at a time when the world seems willing to search for novel ways of viewing the world, for different ways of knowing, and new bases for social interaction in a world that is fast contracting in its outward reach. This is taking place against a background of old values maintaining their tenacious hold on traditional centers of social, economic, political and cultural power which is still active in the North Atlantic segment of the Planet, even while Japan and the Pacific Rim communities suggest some real shifts in economic and technological areas of influence, if not control.

A core feature of the past half millennium, during which time the "modern world" grew up, is the peculiar relationship between Europe and Africa both on the African continent where colonies were settled or forged in conquest, and in the African diaspora known historically as "Plantation America", with its history of slavery, but more recently extended to such Western European countries as Britain and France, two of the former great colonial Powers.

The lasting consequences of racism and, with it, assumptions about the natural cultural inferiority of "lesser races," continue to plague relations in the changing world despite the cessation of slavery in the nineteenth century and the acceleration of the decolonization process in the twentieth. Cultural resistance and all other forms of struggle against the racism which is still actively denigrating people of African ancestry in Southern Africa, in all of the Americas (including the Caribbean), and more recently in Western Europe, are vital instruments of change in this sense. Armed resistance, polemical self-assertion, cultural action through energetic activity in different branches of the arts (especially the performing arts), and even voluntary surrender by way of co-optation or denial of the co-opted's African ancestral origins are among the many strategies of survival employed by the Africans at home and abroad. The systematic study, analysis, interpretation and diffusion of African cultural heritage by Africans themselves has been late in entering the complex of strategies of demarginalization required by persons of African ancestry if they are to retain and maintain human equilibrium in a world that developed in lopsided fashion to Africa's decided disadvantage.

This volume may well be seen as a timely and potentially important addition to the growing body of literature on the African cultural heritage. That the phenomena involved should invite the range of methodological approaches evident in the pages that follow points to the richness of texture and multi-layered, multi-focal nature of African dance and, indeed, of all African arts. All of the writers acknowledge the mediation of dance in Africa itself by social reality, associated, as the form is, with functions of everyday life and classifiable in terms of those activities relating to birth, puberty and death, war, recreation, initiation, ritual *et al*. This, indeed, makes dance in Africa a traditional source of communication and often "of history re-enacted through movement".

The particularity of Africa's cultural heritage does not, however, rule out the universality of its dance, as colonial anthropology once led Europe and the rest of the colonized world (including Africa itself), to believe. As with the art forms emanating from other civilizations or cultural complexes, it merely means that viewers of African dance need to understand Africa's cultural heritage if they are to understand and critically appreciate in any depth the true meaning and aesthetic authority of what is being seen.

This is no different in the case of either European or Asian dance in all their different modes of expression, that is, whether the mode be traditional, popular/contemporary or classic(al). Girls "running around" the Covent Garden or Lincoln Center stage in tutus and shod in block shoes could be fascinatingly "exotic" in the surface appreciation by non-European viewers unexposed to Europe's cultural heritage. In the same way, muscle-toned, athletic, swirling, writhing, flat-footed and highly energetic black dancers from Africa, or the Americas, are approvingly exotic to unexposed European audiences.

Through colonialism, many Blacks (Africans from the Continent included), are likely to be well versed in Europe's cultural heritage, what with the tradition of mission schools, the proselytizing zeal of the Christian religion, and the all-pervasive force of the master's language and literature for formal instruction and general edification of the colonized or enslaved African. Ordinary Europeans through no fault of their own were not always as well versed in the heritage of the vanquished, and when exposed, were frequently conditioned into negative perceptions. So, African dance for a long time was reported, described and classified as "licentious, savage and heathenistic". The in-depth studies of African dances in this volume should further dissolve such perceptions and reinforce the validity of the continuities of elements of African dance which now inform much that is opportunistically misnomered "Black dance", or inaccurately designated "ethnic dance" in the West. These studies can also help to define and place in context the sort of work in dance-theater to be found in the Caribbean and parts of the United States. For the autonomy of aesthetic logic and cultural consistency has long been denied, and African dance following the way the world has been organized since Columbus accidentally came upon what was to become the center-piece of Europe's manifesto for conquest and world domination.

The acknowledgement of such logic and consistency in African dance still presents difficulties to many in the diaspora where the creolization process, through the cross-fertilization of cultures, defines the existence of all inhabitants and pushes a great number of the cross-fertilized beings and their cultural expressions to stations of confusion as to what, of the ingredients in the plurality are proper and what not, what are superior and what inferior, what are aesthetically acceptable, and what forbidden and so on. Needless to say, in the world of colonizer-colonized the dance and all other artistic expressions of the overlord take precedence over those of the subjugated which have been frozen at the base of some rigid and arbitrary cultural pyramid. There are still those who would not place Katherine Dunham, Pearl Primus, or Alvin Ailey in the "mainstream" of American Dance in which such icons as Balanchine, Martha Graham, Doris Humphrey, *et al.* are made to float.

It is in the nature of the creative arts and, as this volume clearly indicates, to the credit of African dance in particular that such predetermined categories of Eurocentric classification are defied and given short shrift. Africa and Africans have not been short on the complexity of the creative process and the sustainability of what the human being anywhere can produce from the individual and collective creative imagination and intellect.

It is by way of dance and music (the human body and the human voice belong to the human person however bonded or socially oppressed, after all), that Africa continued and still continues to "rule" while others "govern" through the imposition of a Conqueror's language, religion and formal intellectual systems for both perceiving the world and acting (or dancing) in it. Subterranean (or to the Caribbean, submarine), alternatives in the African diaspora continue to battle for accommodation and/or acceptance in a world that is still organized on assumptions of the essential centrality of what is regarded as Western civilization and a supposed predestined peripherality of non-Caucasian cultures.

The on-going study of the African cultural heritage (as is here being done with dance--itself a powerful dimension of that heritage), is therefore a necessary and vital imperative for the continuing struggle for human dignity and cultural certitude of the millions across the globe who actually make up two-thirds of the world but who are otherwise known as peoples of the Third World.

The clearly political, social, and educational functions aside--functions which the West has chosen to isolate into watertight compartments--the studies and analyses in this volume remind the few who may already know and should inform the many who do not, of the intrinsic features of African dance, indicating one possible good reason for its staying power among people of African ancestry in the diaspora and its far too infrequently acknowledged influence on so-called Western "mainstream" dance-art in the twentieth century. The nineteenth century European convention of including blackamoors in Europe's classical ballet offerings found resonances in a number of 20th century works like Balanchine's "Figure in the Carpet". None of this is serious crossfertilization. Rather, one would sooner look to what has come to be called in America "modern dance" and to the sort of "dance-theater" coming out of Jamaica, Cuba, Trinidad and Brazil since the 1950s.

The chapters dealing with both the contemporary influences on African dance in Africa itself and the manifestations of elements of African dance and related arts on contemporary dance in the United States, Brazil, and the African slave populations in the Americas, speak not only of the dynamics of cultural formation but also of the dynamism of African dance.

The emphasis is on volume and mass "so that when a movement comes to rest, we observe a path created by a whirlwind, strong virile and powerful", according to Albert Opoku, the Ghanaian choreographer and scholar who is quoted by Tracy Snipe in his essay. There is an organic relationship to music and particularly to rhythm, hence the dominance of the drum and other percussion instruments. Yet the totality of dance as a microcosm of life makes room for a variety of instruments--wind, string and, above all, the human voice. The call and response feature of the music (instrumental and voice), is echoed in dance-patterns; and the reader will learn from Cynthia S'thembile West that Dianne McIntyre bases her own choreographic style on the use of such elements as "the torso inclined slightly forward with bent knees, flat-footed shuffles, sweeping curves, complex rhythmic runs, circles and shouts". (West on McIntyre's dance)

Such are the elements that have provided sources of energy for the Katherine Dunhams and Pearl Primuses of the United States, the Beryl McBurnies and the choreographers of the Jamaica National Dance Theater Company working in the Commonwealth Caribbean, the Ramon Guerras and Eduardo Riveros of Cuba, the Lavinia Williamses and Leon-Destines of Haiti and the Masters of the (Samba) Halls of Brazil. We must add to these the rich continuities of African dance and music to be found in Brazilian candomblè, Cuban santeria, Trinidad's shango, Haiti's vodun, Guyana's cumfa, Jamaica's kumina, and all of the Caribbean's and Latin and Southern America's creolized festival arts. The African world (at home and abroad), is clearly not in need of raw material for the development and growth of African dance.

A dance-form which challenges the choreographer, performer, audience and formal critic to the fullest understanding of the dynamic shifts in perspective and proportion in terms of scale (varying body structures, for example), volume and the play with texture, is demanding of those who encounter its concentration and the ability to distinguish it from what have come to be stereotypical simplicities in the description of African dance. None of this has been aided either by the trivialization of traditional African dance in parts of Continental Africa and of African-derived dances of the diaspora into accessible fare for transient tourists; or by the commercial adaptations of touring troupes in search of national recognition outside their borders; or of foreign exchange earnings for the depleted coffers of their newly "independent" debt-ridden nation-states. One must rely on the proven inner strength of African dance for self-regulation and maintenance of an intrinsic integrity.

The multi-focality of the visual offering echoed in the polyrhythms of the music; the proliferation of images through repetition; the density of symbols and meanings; the artful mobilization of mass, and the simultaneity of the assemblage of imagery in celebration of the interconnectedness of life as it is lived, are all likely to suffer a quaint reductionism to meet the perceptual needs of city-folks in the West accustomed to their "rationalized" one-way streets, admittedly to facilitate safe and speedy transit.

But modern man's need for safe spiritual transit at end-of-century is leading to a search for modalities to reconnect much that have fallen apart. One may find some clues in the ever-present element of unity in African dance as the volume repeatedly emphasizes. There is unity in the juxtaposition of the secular to the religious, of sacrifice to play, of ritual (in the sense of structured procedures), to improvisation, of the obligatory to the novel, of the naturalistic to the abstract, of tragedy to comedy and sadness to laughter, of this world to "other worlds," of man to woman (virile men dance the roles of women in masquerade without fear of their sexual credentials ever being dragged into suspicion), of ancestral/traditional to modern/contemporary. Adaptations abound. Form follows function and *vice versa*. To traditional Africa, the world is a textured place with many focal points: the unity lies in the sensibility of the beholder making sense of the unruly reality.

Such is the nature of that legacy of the dialectical vision bequeathed by those who were torn from the African Continent to help shape the Americas which are yet to acknowledge that the contribution is of such seminal and elemental dimensions. Westernized Africans back on the Continent dare not lose this vision if only because it faithfully reflects an increasingly complex, though shrinking, world of the 21st century in which contradictions and paradox are the reality. The Africans in their rituals and masquerades at home usually transform thoughts and ideas into spectacle. Abroad in the diaspora their task may well be to transform their spectacles (now manifest variously in the fields of sports and entertainment), into thoughts and ideas. This volume on African dance communicates the challenge by uncovering some basic truths in an objective scientific manner but without ever losing the enthusiasm, spirit and man's essential humanity that African dance, in all its manifestations, both embodies and celebrates.

School of Continuing Studies
University of the West Indies
Mona, Jamaica
April, 1990

TRADITION

African Dance*

▲▲▲▲▲▲▲▲▲▲▲▲▲▲▲▲▲▲

Pearl Primus

Very early in her research the investigator learned that people who truly dance are those who have never bartered the fierce freedom of their souls, never strangled their hunger for rhythmic movement, nor frustrated their joyous physical response to music and song. Furthermore, when such beings dance, for them all time stops; the air draws back and the past, the present and the future merge into a single indescribable jewel in eternity.

When these people truly dance, there can be no observers, for those who seek to watch soon join one of two groups. Either, numbed, bewildered, or frightened by the intensity of their own emotions they subconsciously remove themselves back to their comfortable living rooms and shut out the scene that their eyes unseeingly follow or they are snatched, plucked up by an invisible force and hurled into the ring of the dance, their own heartbeat matching the crescendo of pulsing sound, their bodies becoming one with the sweating dancers.

Our Amai (mother) Pearl Primus joined the ancestral world in October of 1994. She joins her beloved Percival Borde and they can now empower the thousands of dancers that they have taught, touched and inspired. As the South African poet Masisi Kunene says about the dancer "She, The Beautiful Fountain, Dances to the Wind." Ashe! —*Editor*

For them, the magic of all life is experienced! Eternity captured! An initiation! A belief! A voyage into Before and Beyond!

Even as their feet caress the earth, even as their arms defy the waiting air, they know they must someday pay dearly for this freedom. Yet, hypnotized in the ecstasy of dance, they are drawn nearer and nearer to the center of "All Being" and farther and farther away from the harsh paved roads, the carefully planned speeches, the friends who wait on the other side, anxious to share this experience. A hunger consumes them and a thirst to reach the center.

Suddenly inside them there is an explosion, an infinitely silent flash of lightning truth. Everything seems to stop. All the music, all the dance, everything seems to stop. The dancers look around. They peer into the stillness and they know their tongues can never tell what their inner selves now feel. They will be expected to put into words that inner spirit fire which cannot be verbalized, that which may not even be a part of the outward reasons or function or movement of the dance. They know that their bodies will make many journeys over long smooth concrete roads, into high towering skyscrapers. They will sit and speak with scholars, patrons, friends, but their souls will forever remain with the people who truly dance with belief. The investigator belongs to this group.

In this study the investigator refers at all times to dance with belief, for, dance without belief, though often very well done, is without life. According to Edmund Carpenter, even well executed". . . technique cannot conceal that meaningless quality everywhere characteristic of art without belief."[1]

Dance in Africa is not a separate art, but a part of the whole complex of living. Dance is only a part of the whole or the complex. The ceremony is the complex. For the ceremony, the master artists carve and paint fantastic masks. The designers create strange and wonderful costumes. Geniuses draw music from everywhere. Dancers become filled with supernatural power.

African dance is basic, vital! For the investigator it is the source, the well from which she draws inspiration for her creative work. African dance is complete. It ranges from the subtlest and most lyric of movements to the most dynamic, from the most sophisticated choreographed presentations to the simplest. It can defy space in fantastic leaps into the air or burrow into the earth. It does not limit itself to any one part of the body but employs the use of even the most minute muscle. It varies from the slowest and stateliest of court dances to those which move so rapidly the eye cannot hope to register all that is happening. In all, there is the concept of beauty!

> . . . Beauty is primarily in the rhythmic action *per se*, as all regulated
> pulsations are usually perceived as harmonious (i.e., beautiful),
> but also it was "educated" to embrace all elements involved, some
> like anklet-bangles, hand rattles acting with and within the "rhyth-
> mic" itself to confirm and enhance its dominance, others like glis-
> sandos, spins, undulations, countermanding (and finally enriching)
> its value. Composure, smile, body decoration and props, etc. con-
> tributing to beauty each in its own way. As we see it, Beauty (the
> emotions and warmth it generates) is the heart of the matter.[2]

African dance forms are strong, virile and vital with a feeling of dynamic
thrust and resistance. They are exceedingly controlled, having the
power to project the gentle wind or the raging storm. Ranging from the
walk and all its variations, the techniques of the African dance embrace
the leap, the hop, the skip, the jumps, falls of all descriptions and turns
which balance the dancer at the most precarious angles with the
ground. But more than any combination of steps, African dance has an
urgency. The dancer has direction and purpose. The purpose is to
communicate. This is why he can assume the proportions of an ant or
a giant. For him and for his people, the dance is life!

> . . . Dancing is an education; primarily physical it tends toward
> exceeding the limitations of the body as they are experienced in
> every day use. Physical frontiers are slowly pushed back in com-
> petitive emulation. Religious motivations deeply ingrained in the
> necessities of the culture (it is not by chance that dancing is part
> of the sacred grove's curriculum) sustain that tension to go
> "beyond" the possible, men by strength, adroitness, agility, girls
> through agility, deployment of grace, enhancement of beauty.[3]

The dance is strong magic. The dance is a spirit. It turns the body to
liquid steel. It makes it vibrate like a guitar. The body can fly without
wings. It can sing without voice. The dance is strong magic. The dance
is life;

> . . . if spirits challenge gravity by moving on stilts twelve feet in the
> air to dance rhythms in the forest villages of Liberia; if athletes in
> Nigeria can carry nearly a hundred pounds of carved wood and
> shoulder this burden for a quarter of an hour while dancing before

their king; if Dahomean initiates into a society honoring the collective ancestral dead can spin and spin and spin and spin and spin . . . until the very concept of human dizziness begins to lose its force—then anything is possible.[4]

The subject matter of African dance is all inclusive of every activity between birth and death—the seed which trembles to be born—the first breath of life—the growth, the struggle for existence—the reaching beyond the every day into the realm of the Soul—the glimpsing of the Great Divine—the ecstasy and sorrow which is life, and then the path back to the Earth. This is the dance!

People use their bodies as instruments through which every conceivable emotion or event is projected. The result is a hypnotic marriage between life and dance. The two are inseparable. When a child is born, when a person is buried, there is the dance. People dance the sowing of the seed and the harvest, puberty rites, hunting, warfare. They dance for rain, sun, strong and numerous children, marriage and play. Love, hatred, fear, joy, sorrow, disgust, amazement, all these and all other emotions are expressed through rhythmic movement.

> . . . We have war dances, victory dances, stag dances, remedial dances, marriage dances, dances for woman only, mixed dances, dances for the initiated only, dances for the youth . . . We nod our heads, rock our necks, tilt our heads and pause. We shake our shoulders, throw them back and forth, bounce breasts and halt to intone our thanks to Him who ordained that we be alive. We rhythmically hefty shake our rear ends, our tummies duck and peer, our legs quick march, slow march, tap dribble, quiver and tremble while our feet perform feats. "Dance!" What a world of emotions that word calls forth in us![5]

There are also dances which are the exclusive property of certain occupations. There are dances which accompany story telling. Legends and group histories are told with dance and song. Secret societies have special dances. Herbalists, healers, are trained to excel in dance. There are dances to ward off sickness and those to cure illnesses. There are dances to celebrate manhood and those to honor women. There are dances to welcome visitors, and to mark the coronation or stepping into office of a new chief. Any occasion within the life of the group is one for the dance.

The African dancer uses the earth as if it were an extension of the dancer's own feet, as if it were a stage of rubber from which he can bounce to the skies, as if it were a soft bed upon which he could roll and be protected. This love and respect for the earth is one of the main factors of African dance. It gives it a certain vitality and dynamic strength, for it draws up into the dancer the unlimited force and ecstasy of the earth.

The earth is a magic dancer. She lifts her arms and mountains rise. She rolls down gently into the valleys. She hurls herself into space to form the jutting cliffs. In her is birth and death, the From and the Into of all physical forms. The earth is a magic dancer.

The earth and the sky are relatives. The earth speaks to the sky and receives answers through the things which grow upward upon her. The dancer is one of her voices. The dancer is the connection between the earth and the sky. The dance itself requires tremendous technique and imagination, agility and speed, but above all it is the subtle, spiritual communion of the earth and sky through the dancer and the music which makes the dance.

. . . The African dancer not only dances many drums. He plays many patterns.[6]

Who is the African dancer? Does everybody dance? Though everyone in a group does engage in a dance at one time or another, everyone does not dance.[7]

There is a sharp distinction between the trained dancer and the person who "just dances." The person who "just dances" is one who has picked up the dance in early childhood, who has been trained in the dances necessary for his initiation, and who just enjoys speaking with his body. Some of these dance impressively but are still not considered dancers by their people.

. . . Dancing does not come more spontaneously to Africans than "pas-de-deux" . . . to Europeans, the difference between the two areas being that few Europeans are called to ballet schooling while the majority of African youth had to submit to the severe dancing masters who preside, among others, to the compulsory curriculum of initiation.[8]

The professional African dancer is one trained from childhood to be a dancer. Having shown a special aptitude for dance language, he is apprenticed to a master, usually the oldest and most powerful of the dancers. These master teachers employ whatever method they feel is best. Their authority is absolute, their instruction unquestioned. These fierce guardians of tradition are charged with the divine duty to continue group values. They assiduously train not only the physical bodies but also the minds and spirits of those chosen as the dancers for the next generation.

Aside from the rigorous dance training for adulthood, the dancer-to-be learns the traditional dances of his people. He learns them as his ancestors did with exact precision. Then he is encouraged to add to his special talent within the framework of the traditional. He is taught to shade and vary the intensity of projection. But more important than technique, projection, or traditional steps and sequences, the young dancer is taught his purpose, his function. He is told that he is not one, but that he is the entire group. His body is an instrument with which he can speak for his people. This body must not be abused but must be kept in readiness at all times.

> . . . Africans refer to a priceless cultural resource, the suppleness of their dancers, by comparing them to beings who have no bones. To say that a person dances as if she or he had no bones is one of the highest compliments . . . [9]

Among groups in the hinterlands the dancer still holds a high social position among his people. His is the profession of dancing. He is necessary to all ceremonies, all feasts, all occasions that involve the health and well-being of the group. In return for his services, the group provides for his every need. He is the dance. Outside of his own immediate community he is seldom known by his name but by that of his group. He is the chosen representative of his people and as such is responsible for their prestige.

One cannot really speak of dance in Africa without saying at least a few words about costumes and music. Costumes for dance vary from the most elaborate and exotic to the smooth bare body. Some costumes cover every inch of the dancer. Even the eyes are hidden behind nets of straw or fiber. Some conceal their dancers, manipulators for the Spirit World, with elaborately carved ceremonial masks. Some extend the dancer into space by the use of stilts and layer upon layer of raffia. Some bedeck the dancer in coral, gold, ivory and silver jewelry. Some costumes wrap the dancer in the splendid and brilliant velour de Kasai, which is made skillfully from raffia. Some enhance the dark skins of the dancers with cloths of striking colors: red, black, white, yellow, green. Some use whole dresses of sky blue, red, black and white beads and polished brass anklets. Magnificent headdresses towering to the sky are designed to dwarf the dancer's body. In contrast are the bare bodies that gleam like polished ebony, every muscle free, a costume of natural art for the dance.

Besides these there are the hundreds and hundreds of combinations of cloth, raffia, skin, beadwork, feathers, leaves, vines, masks, hair, paint, chalk, wood, metal, claws, teeth, bone and fur.

African music, like the dance is an almost inexhaustible topic. The love of music is matched only by the deep respect the people have for a master musician. This respect is taught as a vital part of the curriculum in the sacred groves. In many cultures the master musician becomes a vehicle through which the ancestors speak to the living. Like the dancers, manipulators of the great masks, great musicians are revered by their people.

As if their bodies, developed through centuries of dance, sunshine and struggle are not enough to portray their feelings, the people create powerful rhythms and songs to accompany their movements.

> . . . Another outstanding characteristic of our outlook is our love for music, dance and rhythm. Our throats are deep with music, our legs full of dance while our bodies tremor with rhythm. The proper subtitle for Africa should have been "Land of music, dance and rhythm." This three pronged phenomenon is indeed the spice of our life. We sing while we hoe. We sing while we paddle our canoes. Our mourning is in the form of dirges. We sing as we pound food grain in mortars. We sing in bereavement just as on festive occasions. Our fables always include a singing part. We sing to while away the monotonous hours of travel. We sing to the strains of our musical instruments. The pulses of our drums evoke in us song responses. We sing under moonlit nights. We sing under the canopy of the blue sky. Gramophone record music entrances us not because it's foreign or something out of the way, but just because it's music. With us music, as also dance and rhythm, is a relishable obsession.[10]

Although there are many dances which are performed in silence, i.e., certain hunting dances, some dances connected with magic and some associated with secret societies, dance in Africa is usually accompanied by music. A brief survey of music making devices would reveal that everything capable of making sound is used. These range from turtle shells, seeds, spiders' webs, gourds, pebbles, sticks and metal discs to the great drums, harps, flutes, gongs, horns, bells and xylophones. Music is created by bracelets rubbed together and wet arms striking the sides of sweating bodies. Great carved paddles dipping against strong river water, dried elephant ears fanning open clay pots, puffed out cheeks tapped with fingers, bands clapped together, feet stamping on the earth all make music for the dance.

Special care is taken of music-making devices for ceremonial dances.

> ... Accompanying instruments: rattles, drums etc. are treated with reverence, eventually prayed upon, sometimes blessed by priests; their components: wood, skin, raffia, vine, pegs etc. are not haphazardly chosen. Conditions of use or storage are respected.[11]

It is believed that the greatest drummer musicians are not those who "learn" to play the instrument but those "born for the purpose"—divinely inspired. In their hands the drum becomes a voice, sweet, soothing, teasing, laughing or sharp, commanding and powerful. The great drummers say, "We do not play the drum. We are the drum." The investigator believes that someday there will come an inspired artist musician who will listen to the thousand sounds in Africa and capture them for posterity in a great symphony.

> ... There is rhythm in the winnowing and pounding of grains, there is rhythm in the gait of our women folk; there is highly developed rhythm in coition, there is rhythm in the groan of a sick person, there is complex rhythm in the milking of a cow, there is rhythm in pulling a drawnet to the shore, there is rhythm that beggars description in the beats of our tomtoms, there is rhythm in almost everything we do.[12]

To understand the African dance adequately, one should have some knowledge of African religions, for in the ecstasy of a religious experience the dancer becomes a god-form and the body frees itself of its structural limitations. Legs, bodies, arms, heads may move in seemingly impossible counterpoint. But, like costume and music, this is a subject for another discussion.

Notes

* Reprinted with permission by the author from her dissertation entitled "Masks in the Enculturalation of Mano Children," from New York University School of Education, Nursing and Arts Profession. The investigator referred to throughout the dissertation is Dr. Pearl Primus.

1. Edmund Carpenter, "Collectors and Collections," *Natural History*, New York, LXXXV.3, (March 1976): 60.
2. Roger Dorsinville, *The Regulated World of Hinterland Dancing*, Monrovia, (1970): 58.
3. Dorsinville 6.
4. Robert Farris Thompson, *African Art in Motion*, UCLA Art Council (Berkeley and Los Angeles, California: University of California Press, 1974): 14.
5. D. K. Chisiza, "The Temper, Aspiration and Problems of Contemporary Africa," Nyasaland Economic Symposium, July 18-28, 1962.
6. Robert Farris Thompson, *African Art in Motion*, UCLA Art Council (Berkeley and Los Angeles, California: University of California Press, 1974): 16.
7. In discussing dance training for dancers, Roger Dorsinville states in *The Regulated World of Hinterland Dancing*, Monrovia, 1970: "It is the expatriate African who gave birth to the 'spontaneous' musician and dancer. He reacted by singing and dancing to the pressure of exile, finding solace in that expression medium because there were none other, meeting friends—securing companionship—through that communication medium—he knew none other—than he had to live up to the expectations he had created in the world around him."
8. Roger Dorsinville, *The Regulated World of Hinterland Dancing*, Monrovia, (1970): 1.
9. Robert Farris Thompson, *African Art in Motion*, UCLA Art Council (Berkeley and Los Angeles, California: University of California Press, 1974): 9.
10. D. K. Chisiza, "The Temper, Aspiration and Problems of Contemporary Africa," Nyasaland Economic Symposium, July 18-28, 1962.
11. Roger Dorinville, *The Regulated World of Hinterland Dancing*, Monrovia, (1970): 20.
12. D. K. Chisiza, "The Temper, Aspiration and Problems of Contemporary Africa," Nyasaland Economic Symposium, July 18-28, 1962.

TRADITIONAL DANCE
IN AFRICA

▲▲▲▲▲▲▲▲▲▲▲▲▲▲▲▲▲

Doris Green

In the raw, traditional African dance is the integrated art of movement that is controlled by her music which is governed by her languages. African dance is not like any other form of dance. Its relationship to music, thereby language, is what chiefly distinguishes it from any other art form. According to Bebey, it is not an exaggeration to say that without African languages, African music would not exist.[1] Therefore, the logical deduction is if African music would not exist, then African dance would not exist.

African dance, based upon the spoken language, is a source of communication through which it is possible to demonstrate emotion, sentiment, beliefs and other reactions through movement. Therefore, there are as many styles of African dancing as there are different ethnic groups and languages. Because of the great number of different ethnic groups and languages in Africa, it would be impossible for me to give examples of each. However, I will concentrate on a few from various areas in Africa to give the general style of dancing of a particular people in different areas of Africa.

According to Keita Fodeba, unlike other forms of dance, African dance is not detached from the lives of the people, but is a spontaneous emanation of the people.[2] African dance translates everyday experiences into movement. In an interview with Maurice Sonar Senghor (1971), this theory was supported when he revealed that before a dance can be created, an event or happening must occur.[3] Therefore, one can conclude that Africans dance about everyday experiences or happenings or events in their lives which they choose to remember. The event could be of great historical significance, such as war, famine or the independence of African nations, or of everyday significance such as birth, puberty or the pounding of maize to make a meal. There are a number of factors that can have an effect on the style of dance and instrumentation. The themes of the dances can be drafted from many sources, such as legend, war, politics, cult, ritual or history, to cite a few.

According to A.M. Opoku, the Ewe people, while migrating from Dahomey (Benin), to their present homeland in Ghana, were guided by a bird.[4] Therefore, incorporated in their dances, one can see the movement of the bird's wings in the movements of the dancers arms in dances such as Gakpa, Agbadza and Atsiagbekor, to name a few. In another legend, namely, TCHITELELA of southwest Angola, in the writings of Domingos N'Guizani, if an eagle flies over a village and casts its shadow on the children, it is believed that the shadow will steal the souls of the children.[5] In presenting the dance TCHITELELA on stage, the opening scene has the children imitating the movements of the eagle in flight. The entire dance-drama evolves around the appearance of the eagle; the mothers racing to protect their children; the hunters searching for the eagle; the killing of the eagle; the return to the village; and culminating in a celebration where everyone rejoices. In the aforementioned dances, there are stylized body and arm movements that depict a bird in flight.

Another factor which can have an effect on the dance is the environment. One of my cultural informants, Chris Olude, Artistic Director of the Nigerian Traditional Troupe, supported this theory in his raconte that all traditional Nigerian dances can be traced to rituals, history, religion, animals, cults, wars and environment.[6] To view how the environment affects the style of dance, one can use the Masai people of Kenya, East Africa. The Masai people live in the Rift Valley area, consequently, they do not have many trees and animal hides to make drums. Therefore, Masai people do not use drums to accompany their dances. They use Africa's oldest instrument, the human voice. Their dances consist of a series of jumps accompanied by chanting. Their jumps are done in a vertical plane, straight up and down as opposed to side to side or front to back. The absence of drums somewhat limits the development of rhythms and polyrhythms. From my research in Africa, I found that the Masai style of jumping is less complicated than dances in West Africa that consist of a series of jumps accompanied by drums. The Masai concentrate on one kind of jump, from both feet to both feet with some gestures in a vertical plane, whereas, dances of West Africa, namely Thie Bou Dienne and Sabar of Senegal, concentrate on all five types of jumps:

> Jump (from both feet to both feet); leap (from one foot to the other foot); hop (from one foot to the same foot); assemble (from one foot to both feet); and sissonne (from both feet to one foot).[7]

These jumps are done with a multitude of gestures and in the vertical, horizontal and sagittal planes. During my research of African dances, I observed that in this region of West Africa, where drums are the accompaniment for the dance, those dances that are characterized by jumping use oppositional gestures of arms and legs which can be followed in the musical pattern. In the East African region, among the Masai and Pokot people, drums are not the accompaniment for the dance. Although here the dance is characterized by jumps, it tends to use very few gestures of the arms.

Body segmentation is another characteristic of traditional dances found throughout Africa. From my observations, it is more complex in West Africa, and is most noticeable in the movements of Akan dances employing complex arm, hand and foot movements together with head, facial and eye expressions. The body among the Pokot and Masai people of East Africa is carried in a place high position, whereas the Basukuma people (Tanzania) have a tendency to use a forward high body carriage. An exciting observation is the carriage of the body of the Wamakonde people (Tanzania and Mozambique), particularly in their puberty dance, which is backward high.

All African dances do not look alike even when they contain the same movement. When I first went to Africa, I had a perplexing question—"Why are there so many pelvic contractions in African dances?" This movement, pelvic contractions, was used in all categories of dances—war, religious, recreation and puberty. Puzzled by this movement, I demanded an answer and found that many of my younger cultural informants did not have a plausible answer and had accepted the answer of a "sexual notion" to explain the existence of this movement. My retort was "if so, then why does it appear in your war dance"—to which there was no response. Relentlessly, I continued to ask this question. When I asked older (first generation) cultural informants, they related movement to instrumentation of the dance. In Nigeria, Chris Olude stated that secondary rattles are worn on the body in many dances.[8] These rattles must be moved in accordance to the music. If the rattles are worn on the waist, then the dancer has to move the waist. Moving the waist will produce a "pelvic contraction". Therefore, one will see pelvic contractions in various categories of dances. This answer was the general response by first generation cultural informants, while second generation cultural informants often did not have an answer.

Another interesting movement of the waist is found in Ghana in the dance "Bamaya". According to A.M. Opoku, the Bamaya dance is about a man who was hungry and did not have money to buy food. Therefore, he decided to steal some. Food is generally found where women are, so he decided to disguise himself as a woman to gain easy access to the market where he stole a chicken. He was caught and unveiled.[9] This event (happening) was one the people chose to remember so they created a dance, about it, which is performed by men. The men adorn themselves in skirts with frills around the waist to imitate the movements of a woman's hips, and there usually is a female singer who acts as a "crier", the one who alerted the authorities of the theft.

Dances have also been created to commemorate everyday activities. In Cote d'Ivoire (Ivory Coast), among the Bete people of Daloa, there is a dance called "Ziglibiti" which is about the pounding of corn, called "bitico" in the Bete language. Recorded in their folklore, is the story of women who were pounding "bitico" (corn). Bete men were passing by and remarked that the bitico was pounded so fine that it resembled sugar, "sucre" in French. The Bete people substituted the "s" with a "z," mispronouncing the word as "zucre." The final pronunciation of the French word for sugar became "zigli." The word "bitico" was shortened to "biti." Therefore, "Ziglibiti" is a melange of two words which describe corn that was pounded so fine that it resembled sugar. The dance, Ziglibiti, as performed in Daloa (1988), is about pounding corn and is characterized entirely by the rapid stamping action of the feet throughout the dance. Rattles are worn on the ankles which must be moved in accordance to the music. Again, this supports the theory that wherever the secondary rattles are worn on the body in dance, that is where the movement will be concentrated. This dance was popularized by Ernesto Dje Dje and is now a standard dance performed throughout Cote d'Ivoire.

According to Dr. Emeka Nwabuobu, work movements ultimately become the movements of dance.[10] In the Sokoto State of Nigeria, live the Birnin Kebbi people. They fish and farm as their main occupations. Consequently, they have many dances which concern fishing and farming. The fishing dance entitled "Su", commemorates annual fishing festivals. The dance has two parts—a ritual to clear the water and purify it for an abundant catch. The second part concerns the actual movement of fisherman into the waters. In the fishermen's dance "Rawar Masunta," women who claim descendency from fishing families perform this dance. The women hold cloth in their hands. This cloth represents the fishing net which is cast into the water. In order to cast the net successfully, a certain stance is developed which is the stance used in the dance. The body is carried in a forward high position and the hands imitate the collecting of fish. The hands are thrust into the water, forward low position of the arms, and slowly drawn to the waist, trapping the fish between the hands and body as they are gathered. Nwabuoku (22), also discusses the action of shaking found in many dances of the Birnin Kebbe people. The word "rawa" means to shake. Therefore, a person whose teeth chatter due to exposure to cold is actually called "rawar haba," the action of dancing of the jaw. Other actions such as planting, digging and mixing mud to make bricks for a house are all actions of work which ultimately become the main movements of dances associated with work activities.

Other common place daily activities such as eating can also be seen in the dance Thie Bou Dien, which is the national dance of Senegal as well as being one of the main food dishes—fish and rice. The manner in which the hands and arms are used to gather the rice in the hand, form a ball and then toss it into the mouth are depicted in the movements of the right arm of the dance. The movements described are for the right hand only as the left is not used in eating. In the dance, the left hand usually holds the costume, sometimes acting as a time-keeper, while the right hand does the majority of the actions. Lenjengo a popular dance in the Mandinka regions of Senegal and Gambia has arm movements similar to those of the wings of a bird that makes its home in the Casamance area of this region.

The most exciting correlation between common place activity and dance is the movement of the blades of a fan which is depicted in the dance "Ventalateur," popular in Senegal. The women bend forward middle and move only the backside, imitating the blades of a fan. Some women are so agile that they can stop the movement, put it in reverse, then accelerate with one blade only moving only one cheek.

This dance recently surfaced in Black America as the "BUTT", but the Senegalese have been performing it for years.

In the area of Senegal and Gambia, viewing the dances of the Wolof, Serere, Mandinka and Diola people, one can see that the majority of their dances consists of a series of all five classifications of jumps. For the greater part, they do not perform group dancing as we know it. Although many dancers perform, it is done in a friendly competitive basis where one dancer enters the ring, or Bantaba, an area cleared for dancing, dances for a few minutes and is challenged by another dancer who takes over and becomes the center of attraction. This action of competitiveness is repeated for hours with the drummers playing for each solo dancer. When the dancer is exceptionally good, comrades and onlookers will give the performer money. The Wolof dancers tend to use their arms in an alternating fashion, while the Mandinka and Diola tend to be more symmetrical with both arms performing the same movement. In this area there are also dances of possession and dances that are used for the purpose of exorcising evil spirits and curing the sick. A popular dance of this nature is called "N'Deup".

In the SeneGambia region, we also find the Peulh acrobats, whose dance routine includes many movements found in the recent rage called "Breakdance," and "Pop". They begin with a face-off of the performers in the hand spin, where the elbow of the supporting arm is pressed in the pelvic area as the body spins around. The back spins of the Peulh routine usually ended in a neck stand. All of these movements were performed expertly by Abdoulaye Diallo, of the National Ballet of Senegal, in October 1971 at the Brooklyn Academy of Music. His routine brought the audience to their feet with applause. The best performance on the head was rendered by Samba Diallo Fula. He literally did a head stand and propelled his body, while in a head stand, off the floor in a slight jump on the head. He literally sprang across the floor on his head, a feat which has not been equaled to date.

Self defense movements seen in the martial arts are commonplace movements found in Nigeria among the Korokoro dancers. This dance is performed by men and consist of many kicks and arm thrusts which is said to demonstrate how they meet their opponents in war. This type of martial art movements can also be seen in the Capoeira dance which is derived from dances of Angola.

In the regions of Ghana, Ivory Coast, Togo, Burkina Faso, Benin and Nigeria, group dancing is more common that competitive solo dancing found in Senegal and Gambia. The group dances are performed in lines or circles, with the circle being more prominent in recreation dances and the line formation prominent in war dances. In my estimation, dances in the above-mentioned areas concentrate on body segmentation, with one segment moving in opposition to another segment of the body. I also find the foot movement in this area is varied, often acting as the timekeeper beating out the pulse of the selection with their feet. In dances such as Agbadza, Atsiagbekor, Gahu and Kadodo, the feet acting as timekeepers is clearly evident. In dances such as Ziglibiti of Ivory Coast, the tempo of the dance is established by the feet in conjunction with the bell.

What the dancer wears while dancing is another factor which can shape or mold the style of movement seen. For example, if the dancers wear heavy boots, then the association or dynamic quality is not "light and airy", but one of forcefulness. In Isicathulo (the boot dance), the Zulu people of South Africa exploit the percussiveness of the boots by clicking the heels together and slapping the boots with their hand producing distinct rhythms. Surely if this dance was done barefooted, it would not have the same forceful dynamic quality, but a lighter quality similar to "Ham Bone". In the dance "Takai" of Ghana, the dancers carry an iron rod, wear leather boots and a Betekele ensemble (flowing robe and trousers with the elongated seat). As the dancer pivots, the robe and pants flow, creating a design in space similar to an umbrella that is opened and then twirled. The dance is percussively pulsated by the stamping of the feet and the striking together of the iron rods. Without the attire and iron rods, the dance would lose its flowing dynamic quality and percussive intonations. Dressed in a Betekeli outfit, secondary rattles on the waist could not be effectively used, nor could pelvic contractions. They would be totally hidden by the Betekeli robe. The Takai dance is a group dance performed in circles and not a dance of individual competition.

Dances which celebrate puberty are popular throughout Africa. Under normal conditions, they are performed after a person has successfully completed the rites of puberty. These rites are generally given in seclusion in bush schools or youth camps. The Wakwele people of Tanzania have an initiation dance called "Bigililo." According to Washa Ng'wanamashalla (1970), when a girl, called Kigoli before puberty, notices her first menstrual flow she makes an alarm by yelling to attract her parent's attention. After the alarm is heard, a group of neighborhood women will perform the Bigililo dance for one or two hours in praise of the coming of age of the soon to be new initiate, who is now called Mwali. While the dance Bigililo is being performed, the initiate is escorted into her parents house to begin the first stage of seclusion. At this time her mother will take a new piece of white cloth and place it under the initiate to collect the flow. The stained cloth is kept in safe custody until after the first flow is over. At a certain time all young girls who have attained Mwali (blood status), will go into seclusion in the bush.[12] They are secluded shortly after the first menses so they will not come into contact with men and have sexual contact. Among the Wakwele people, it is an unforgivable offense for a girl to become pregnant outside wedlock. They will emerge from seclusion on the day of Kuchezewa Ngoma when the Bigililo dance is again performed. This dance is accompanied by singing. There are no instruments used except the secondary leg rattles. Each dancer carries a fly whisk and an axe.

I have said all this in order to expose the reader to the raison d'etre of puberty dances. It is hoped that when the viewer sees such dances, they will be more informed. For example, when scarves or handkerchiefs are seen in puberty dances, they will not be described for the design made in space, but for their significance to the dance. In "Tokoe", a puberty dance of the Ga-Adangbe people of Ghana, scarves are affixed to the index finger of the dancers. The dancers flick their wrists so the scarves move in accordance to the flicking action. The scarves are used throughout the dance; they are waved, furled, and unfurled. The significance is not the design in space, nor the color, but the actual alarm, which can be seen in the waving of the scarves as the alert that the girl has come of age. The passing of a scarf through the palm shows that the scarf is being presented as evidence, proof of the coming of age. In certain villages, the menstrual cloth must be shown to the woman who will conduct the girl into bush school.

The first of anything always has a special preference in one's heart. Sindimba was the first dance I learned on the continent of Africa. I recall the circumstances under which I was attracted to it. It was in the Siku Kuu Ya Saba Saba Festival (1970) in Tanzania. The Wamakonde people has just warmed up their drums when I heard the most intoxicating rhythm played on the Liganga drum, a double headed (alto) drum. I was awe-struck, totally mesmerized by each drum rhythm, combined with a subtle movement of the left hip. I began to move my feet patterning the dancers. The lead dancer twice came over and stood in front of me; both times I stopped moving my feet and he returned to the arena. The third time he came over, he pulled me out of the chair and placed me among the dancers. I danced with them. After the dance, they all embraced me. Unfortunately we could not talk because we did not share a common language. After leaving the ceremonies, I told Washa of the experience and he arranged for me to study with various Wamakonde groups where I learned to play the music and the dance.

Sindimba is a puberty dance which is performed after successful completion of the rites of initiation which are administered in seclusion in bush schools. In the Sindimba dance, performed by both boys and girls, emphasis is placed on the hips, which are accentuated by a wrap of additional material tied around the hips of the girls. The boys wear looped fringes that hang from the waist of the shorts, and play a vital part in shifting of the hips. The dance is accompanied by a host of musicians including marimbas, rattle and drummers, led by the Ntoyi drummer. Each of the drums is played with sticks with the exception of the Ntoyi master drum which is played by hand. As I learned in the "shama", a place cleared for dancing, the cry "Wa Nembo" (drummer's call), translated as "Are you ready to dance?" The dancers responded by shouting "Elo"! translated as "We have cast off our youth, and are ready for the adult world." As I stated in both the film Sindimba (1971)[13] and the pamphlet, NGoma Sindimba,[14] the master drummer puts the dancers through a series of different routines, always returning to the main movement, a subtle emphasis on the left hip, initiated by the knee, while the torso is in a backward high position.

Another type of dance popular throughout Africa is the mask dance. In the western world when one thinks of a mask, one thinks of a covering for the face, a protective screen or a disguise. The masks in Africa come in many sizes shapes and forms, namely "cap", "helmet" and "full body". The cap mask rests on the head with side fringes and coverings; the helmet type covers the entire head similar to a helmet; and the full body mask completely covers the entire body from head to foot. Although the mask is not a living object, it has a psychological significance which might be considered as a psychological disguise. When the person adorns the mask, he is transformed into the spirit or being he is representing. The identity of the mask wearer is not revealed according to secrecy of tradition. It is on record that during ceremonies, women, uninitiated boys, and girls are not permitted near the mask wearers in order to keep the identity of the masked performers secret. African masks have many different functions, creating variety in form, types and designs of the masks. There are masks associated with funerals. According to Pascal James Imperato, the Dogon people of Mali celebrate a special death anniversary called DAMA.[15] The Dama is held every two or three years to honor people who have deceased since the last Dama. In this ceremony, there are approximately seventy-eight different masks, the tallest of which stands approximately twenty feet tall and represents a house. It is called "Sirige". Other masks in the ceremony include Kanaga (Bird), Staimbe (Woman), Pulloyana (Peulh woman), Dyommo (Rabbit), Na (Bull), Tena-tana (Stilt walkers), Walu (Antelope) and Bede (Young girl). The Sirige mask is the last mask to enter the dance arena. The purpose of the masks is to usher the souls of the deceased to their final resting place.

To go into details of the numerous mask dance figures throughout Africa would be beyond the scope of this paper. Therefore, I am going to list a few of my favorites. In Nigeria, we have the Egungun and Gelede mask societies. The Gelede masks are characterized by a helmet which has three tribal marks on each cheek, identifying it as belonging to the Gelede society. Gelede is a fertility organization, more commonly known as the society of old women or Iyale. Men dance this dance in order to placate women (Iyale), or witches as they are called, because in the spirit world they possess supernatural powers. These powers can sometimes be destructive. If there is a drought, epidemic or famine, it is said to have been caused by the destructive powers of Iyale. The dance, Gelede, is then performed to appease Iyale so that she will withdraw and the spell from the affected town or village. From my research notes, I have pictures of men dressed as women carrying figures of babies on their backs. They are holding a fly whisk in each hand as they masquerade in the Gelede festival. The Gelede festival is also performed annually in December.

Egungun is essentially an ancestral society which governs relationship between the living and those who have passed on to the spiritual world of the ancestors. These masks perform at funerals and at the annual festival of Egungun. The masks themselves have many shapes and forms. There are those made from yards of material, solids, stripes, patchwork panels and different African prints. These materials are fashioned into elaborate costumes that conceal the wearer. Some have faces made of contrasting cloth, depicting various characters such as village chief, animals or spirits. In performance, these figures strut and rearrange the clothing (yards of material) to reshape their image. The Yoruba share a common cultural cluster with Benin (formerly Dahomey), where there are enclaves of Yoruba people who migrated to various places in Benin. A festival depicting this cultural cluster is called "Igunnuko". These mask figures are made from cloth structured in a series of pill boxes mounted one atop the other covered with side fringes. As the dancer stoops, his figure diminishes. This figure also grows as the dancer stands and becomes extremely tall when the dancer wishes. Because of their tall shapes, it is said they can intercede with the heavenly world to ask for rain.

In Cote d'Ivoire (Ivory Coast) some of my favorite masks are Zaouli, which is a helmet mask, and the headdress of the forest dancers, which is an elaborate cap mask with side fringes or hairs. The mask is a network of braids and weaves crowned with stalks or shoots of different colored triangular poms-poms. These masks cannot change their form or structure in performance. The dance activity is essentially fast movements of the feet dictated by the rhythm of the drums for the Zaouli figure; and head movements for the forest dancers. These masks are a regular feature of many cultural troupes in Cote d'Ivoire. Other favorites are masks of the Dan people, Senoufo and Poro. There is a mask figure clad in a khaki colored material from head to toe which appears at funerals. Each of the figures carries a drum which they play in cadence.

Other interesting masks are the masked dancers of Tanzania and Mozambique, namely, Isinyago and Midimu, discussed in an article of the same title by J.A.R. Wembah-Rashid.[16] Mr. Wembah-Rashid defines mask as any disguise or covering that is intended to transform the wearer once he adorns it. Masks that cover the face are called "midimu". Masks that cover the entire body are called "isinyago". In the Makua language "isinyago" can be defined as beast or animal. The performance of these masked figures occur on a lunar cycle, being performed between quarter and half moon and always at night (38).[17] Most of the masks represent animals or beasts common to the area. There is a fire dancer called Chipalamoto. There is a shared cultural cluster of the Wamakonde people of Mozambique and Tanzania. The Wamakonde people from Mozambique exclusively use the helmet type mask (41).[18] There are also masks called female mask which depict pregnancy. The movements of the dance are slow and sluggish depicting the agonies of pregnancy (41).[19] This mask is usually accompanied by a male masked dancer presumed to be the husband. This mask is called Amwalindembo—young pregnant woman. The Wamakonde people prefer the facial mask and often use stilts. The stilted mask figure is called Midimu ya muha (42).[20] Midimu dancers also perform when boys and girls come out of seclusion from their initiation camps. After the masks are used, they are returned to the hiding place and are destroyed by fire.

Mask dances occur throughout Africa, but by definition, I have not seen a masked dancer in Ghana. However, in the Volta region of Hohoe there is a figure called "Kakabotovi" which has a painted face as a disguise with body covering. This figure comes out and mingles with other performers. His purpose is to ward off and scare off.

Cowrie shells also serve as body coverings or masks among the Bambara, Kissi, Peulh and Senoufo people during their initiation dance. Oddly enough, the cowrie shell was first used as money in Africa. Certain instruments, such as the Sekere rattle of the Yoruba people of Nigeria were decorated with these shells and only royalty permitted to play this instrument. How the cowrie evolved from a common currency to ornamental status is not known. In Ivory Coast, there is a puberty dance where the entire body is covered with cowrie shells and the movement of the dancer produces its own percussion which sounds like a multitude of rattles being shaken.

Liana covered dancers present an aspect of the full body covering as a mask. Liana is a substance similar to raffia and looks like "hay". The dancer's entire body is covered with this material and resembles a haystack, a term I coined for these hay figures, in my early days of research. Some of the more popular haystack dance figures are the JOBAI of Sierra Leone and Liberia; GBINI, of the same region, and KOUMPO of Senegal. The Jobai figure is often called a devil in Liberia as it is referred to in the article, "The Making of Liberian Ballet", by Roger Dorsinville,[21] who is originally from Haiti and serves as the editor of "Nouvelles Editions Africain" in Dakar, Senegal. A feature of these figures is that they have the power to grow and diminish during performance. The Gbini as described in the article "Men's Masquerades of Sierra Leone and Liberia" by William Siegmann and Judith Perani[22], is a dance figure of layered unbleached raffia with a pill box structure atop. The spirit of the masquerader is said to be a great monster from the forest which the Poro captured and now use to control women and non-initiates.[23] The Jobai figure truly looks like a huge mound of hay. It has a basket woven pill-box cap which sits atop the figure. This cap has projections around it. The body of the Jobai dancer[24] is covered with clear raffia on a rattan frame. This hay figure can go completely flat just like the "Koumpo" figure, then regain its shape. It jumps and swirls around the dance arena and is exciting to watch.

The Koumpo dance figure is also made from undyed raffia or liana. The Koumpo has a stick that emerges from the top of the costume. The stick is pointed to the floor and rests on the ground when the dancer twirls around. It is not necessary for the stick to be placed on the floor for the dancer to twirl. The image that the observer sees when the dancer twirls is symbolic of trees or branches swaying in the wind. When the dancer twirls fast, it gives the appearance of a windmill of hay moving in a continuous circle until the dancer decides to change direction. At times, the Koumpo figure looks like the spokes of a spinning wheel—a spiralling helical body. It is associated with harvest, has a playful spirit, and also has the ability to go flat and then regain its massive appearance. Different colored raffia can be used to create a rainbow helix of different hues when the dancer twirls. This came into being when the Koumpo, of the National Ballet of Senegal, costume was too worn to be effective. As a friend of the Company, I was asked what could be done to restore the costume. Realizing that we did not have the exact fibers used in the costume, I suggested raffia; showed them samples of different colored raffia, thus a new multi-colored Koumpo dance figure emerged. Other dance figures that are made partially from raffia with face masks and upper torso clothing of fabric are plentiful in Ivory Coast among the Dan (Yacouba) people. Among the Mandinka people, we find the grassy roots figure called Kankuran. Among the Bambara people, we have the popular Tyi Wara headdress figures.

Stilt dancers are also prominent masquerade figures common in various regions of Africa. Some of my personal preferences are Chakaba of Senegal, Gambia and Guinea; and the charming "Gue Gblin" of Ivory Coast. My first encounter with these towering masked figures was in the late fifties and early sixties with Guinea Ballet. These towering figures were called Gods of the Sacred Forest and actually frightened some of the younger people in the audience. There are several functions of the stilt dancer in African folklore. Because of their height, they act as mediators between the world of the living and the spiritual world of the ancestors, and are able to ask for special favors, such as rain to save their crops from the drought. It is also said that they mediate disputes among the living when all else has failed.

The Chakaba figure can be found in West Africa in several countries from the coast of Senegal to Mali. These stilts vary in height ranging from five feet to ten feet. Chakaba wears a headdress with side fringes. His body is clothed in an African print costume that covers the body to the top of the stilts. The legs of the stilts are covered in the same material that covers the body. Some Chakaba wear a fiber or raffia skirt and carry a whisk. There are those Chakana that have only one leg. It is mystifying to see this figure enter the dance arena on one leg, then all of a sudden spring up on the stilted leg. Some of these stilted figures not only dance, but jump rope.

The Gue Gblin stilt figure of the Dan (Yacouba) of Ivory Coast can be found in the regions of Dan, Man, Mahou, Karadjan, Danane,

Biankouma, Touba and Seguela. This figure has a black headdress with a plume of animal skin, topped with feathers projecting from the headdress. The headdress has red side fringes and the face of the mask is black, with a corded black tassel in the nose area. Gue Gblin wears a black and white stripped costume with matching pants that cover the legs of the stilts and carries a black whisk in each hand. He is accompanied in dance by sets of triple-headed Sangba (Djimbe) drums and slit-lot drums. His dance routine is somewhat acrobatic and agile for a stilt figure.

In conclusion, one can see that there are many styles of dances in Africa, as numerous as the different ethnic groups. Dances can be as simple as games like "Ampe", where young children jump, clap and then extend one leg in an odd and even situation. This routine reinforces counting. There are other dances where the general rule is that the feet must not be moved too high about the ground, such as dances found in Uganda, namely "Endongo". This dance is performed by women who throughout the entire routine, maintain their upper arms a degree or two below side middle, and their lower arms in a side high position with the hands facing inward and outward. The motion of the dance is located in the hips, which are accented with different materials that are tied around the waist and cover the hip area.

Dance is a way of life for African people and is associated with everyday activities. Dances can be grouped into categories such as birth, death, puberty, war, recreation, initiation and ritual. Dance in Africa is always accompanied by music which ranges from handclapping and singing to massive orchestras of instrumentation. Dance is so vital in the everyday lives of people, that in Ghana if you are a chief and cannot dance the way of your people, you can be dethroned. Dance in Africa is a way of life, a source of communication, and history reenacted through movement.

Notes

1. Francis Bebey, *African Music A People's Act* (New York: Lawrence Hill & Co., 1975): 122.
2. Keita Fodeba, "The True Meaning of African Dance," *UNESCO Courier*, Jan. 1959: 20.
3. Personal interview with Maurice Senghor, Director General of Theatre National Daniel Sorano, Dakar, Senegal, 1971.
4. Personal interview with Albert Mawere Opoku, Director of African

Dance, University of Ghana at Legon, Legon, Ghana, August 1971.
5. Domingos N'Guizani, "La Pedagogie de la Choregraphie," thesis Conservatoire National de Musique, de Danse et D'art Dramatique, Republic of Senegal, (1986): 6.
6. Personal interview with Christ Olude, Artistic Director of Nigerian Traditional Dance Troupe, Lagos, Nigeria, 30 July 1971.
7. Ann Hutchinson, *Labanotation* (New York: Theatre Arts Books, 1970): 79.
8. Olude interview.
9. Opoku interview.
10. Emeka Nwabuoku, "Dance As a Mirror of Human Condition," *Dance Notation Journal* 2.1 (1984): 18-30.
11. Nawabuoku 22.
12. Personal interview with Washa Ng'Wanamashalla, Regional Cultural Research Officer of Tanzania, Dar Es Salaam, Tanzania, July 1970.
13. Doris Green, *Ngoma Sindimba*, Brooklyn 1971.
14. Doris Green, *Ngoma Sindimba*.
15. Pascal James Imperato, "Contemporary Adapted Dances of the Dogon," *African Arts* 4.1 (1971): 28.
16. J.A.R. Wembah-Rashid, "Isinyago and Midimu Masked Dances of Tanzania and Mozambique," *African Arts* 4.1 (1971): 38.
17. Wembah-Rashid 38.
18. Wembah-Rashid 41.
19. Wembah-Rashid 41.
20. Wembah-Rashid 42.
21. Roger Dorsinville, "The Making of Liberian Ballet," *African Art* 4.1 (1970): 36.
22. William Seigman and Judith Perani, "Men's Masquerades of Sierre Leone and Liberia," *African Art* 9.3 (1976): 43.
23. Seigman and Perani 43.
24. Seigman and Perani 45.

Works Cited

Bebey, Francis. *African Music A People's Art*. New York: Lawrence Hill & Company, 1975.

D'Agri, Paul and Doris Green. *Ziglibiti*. Research conducted in Daloa among Bete people, 1988.

Dorsinville, Roger. "The Making of Liberian Ballet." *African Art*. 4.1 (1970): 36.

Fodeba, Keita. "The True Meaning of African Dances." *UNESCO Courier*, Jan. (1959): 20.

Green, Doris. *Ngoma Sindimba* (film), Brooklyn: 1971.

——. *Ngoma Sindimba*. Brooklyn: 1972.

——. *Ziglibiti*. Research as Fulbright lecturer to Cote d'Ivoire, 1986/7.

Hutchinson, Ann. *Labanotation*. New York: Theatre Arts Books, 1970.

Imperato, Pascal James. "Contemporary Adapted Dances of the Dogon." *African Arts*, 4.1 (1971): 28.

N'Guizani, Domingos. "La Pedagogie de la Choregraphie." (Thesis) Conservatoire National de Musique, de Danse et D'art Dramatique, Republic of Senegal, 1985/86.

Ng'Wanamashalla, Washa. Regional cultural research officer of Tanzania. Interview. Dar Es Salaam, Tanzania, East Africa, July, 1970.

Nwabuoku, Emeka, Dr. "Dance As A Mirror of Human Condition." *Dance Notation Journal*. 2.1 (1984): 18-30.

Olude, Christ. Artistic Director of Nigerian Traditional Dance Troupe. Interview. Lagos, Nigeria, 30, July 1971.

Opoku, Albert Mawere. Director of African Dance, University of Ghana at Legon. Interview. Legon, Ghana, August 1971.

Seigman, William, and Judith Perani. "Men's Masquerades of Sierra Leone and Liberia." *African Art*. 9.3 (1976): 42-47.

Senghor, Maurice. Director General of Theatre National Daniel Sorano. Interview. Dakar, Senegal, 1971.

Sindimba. Siku Kuu Ya Saba Saba Festival. Performance, Dar Es Salaam, Tanzania, July 1970.

——. Field research conducted as a recipient of C.U.N.Y. Faculty Awards 1970 and 1971, produced film and pamphlet on the Sindimba dance. (See Green, Doris).

Wembah-Rashid, J.A.R. "Isinyago and Midimu" Masked Dances of Tanzania and Mozambique. *African Arts*. 4.2 (1971): 38-44.

A PANOPLY OF AFRICAN DANCE DYNAMICS

▲▲▲▲▲▲▲▲▲▲▲▲▲▲▲▲

Esilokun Kinni-Olusanyin

The dance to drum (and other percussion) is a potent and vitalizing element of African culture. Although diverse instrumentation, as well as singing are commonly involved, drumming and dancing are almost synonymous projections—as ardent, driving rhythms, pungent complexities of form, and consonant, articulate expression.

This work shall focus upon the dance-choreography to one genre of drum—the cylindrical, double membraned, snared talking drum, as it is practiced in Yoruba and Nupe cultures. The performance of dance and drumming in the masquerading, ceremonial context and as more secular choral stage presentation shall be considered.

Dance Drum

Among the Yoruba, this class of drum is found in selected areas, along with the more commonly placed instruments (Kinni-Olusanyin: 1980); but among the Nupe, this music is enjoyed with more widespread popularity. Both the Yoruba and Nupe employ it basically as a ceremonial music for deities and royalty, marriages and burials and formerly for war. The Nupe also have associated "sets" of professional dancers who activate drumming for allied purposes. It also is played for collective farming and all kinds of processional involvement (such as weddings), ground leveling at funerals and assorted social engagements.

It is important to note that this type of percussion is ancient and fairly common to African dance music. The Turks played a similar instrument before the conquest of Constantinople (1453). From there, it subsequently was borrowed by the European military, utilized by its marching band, became known as the snare or side drum, and was eventually introduced into classical music (1706).

Although there have been independent developments of this drum by the Yoruba and the Nupe, the two bear striking similarities of construction (very little of which may concern us here). Besides being cylindrical, double membraned and squat in appearance, the single or double snare gives the drum a more crisp, snappy, rattling or buzzing, and reverberating quality, when played on their goat skin heads. In contrast to its hollow sound, brass bells may be placed around the rim of the lead talking drum, to add a jingling effect. A curved stick with a flattened tip is used. Consorts among the Yoruba consist of up to five instruments in graduated proportions, whereas the Nupe play two or three sizes simultaneously and display large ensembles of eight or so men. The "master", or controlling drum is used to play all the leading roles, the improvisations, the proverbs, and the dictates for dancing.

The technique of playing any drum is almost as relevant to the kinetic response of the dancer, as are the rhythms and dynamics. On this type of drum, the one hand (left), one stitch (right) method and/or the bare hands may be employed. But generally, the rear membrane is cuffed and slapped (left). It also may be chopped by the side of the hand and muted by the wrist. Beats for the left hand almost serve the effect of an accessory to the stick method—much dance phrasing being based to the resultant one line or combination rhythms of the two. The stick may be allowed to rest upon the head to mute sound. Otherwise, it makes a sharper or more explicit vibration than does the left hand, which plays both membranes. Correct ear training and dexterous, discriminate twisting of the wrist are the criteria which determine the superior drummer. This instrument is capable of producing the loudest, most thunderous and shattering volume of all percussion— hence its onomatopoeic name in some languages (*bembe* in Yoruba). The ethos that the writer derives from it is of a strong, aggressive, authoritative principle.

The snared drum is played mostly by professionals who have a muse, and protective patron of the arts (Kinni-Olusanyin: 1980), but priests who perform for themselves during some ceremonies, claim over objections, to surpass the *beau ideal* standard of the professionals. Of course, the musical arrangements established by the two differ somewhat. A fine portion of the drummer's visceral aesthetic is perceived as an intoxication by music whenever the environing atmosphere integrates with the performance ideal in the recherché execution of a composition. The professional musician therefore feels inebriated by the mystical aspect of his deity which then electrifies him. In this manner, the drumming genius is similar to both 'white heat' which inspires and sustains the individual in the act of creation—and to a psychic or spiritual transformation which the artist undergoes in order to achieve an extravagant utopian plateau. (The special praise name of the muse [in Yoruba] is Ayan Agalu: Ayan mounts—is high and mighty on—possesses on or by the drum.)

The male or female priest who plays for his own deity has a similar experience, except that he (or she) becomes charged by a more collective generation of spiritual forces. The dancer as priest, might move still further, to the point where he sustains the "attitude" beyond the musical experience, to the extent that he metaphysically can enact the deity itself, by dance, pantomime, song and speech, onto a protracted level of openly prophesizing and philosophizing. That is, he enters the common state of possession whereby the human body merely is a vehicle for the deity to "ride"—hence the expression "horse of the godhead", for such an involved individual. In masquerade dances, the horse alternately may move into and out of such a state every few minutes, or may, once the masquerade is applied, maintain the possessed state throughout the performance. The "high" or fully possessed priest (dancer) presents a ritual aesthetic just as does the impassioned occult drummer.

Dance

There are a few distinctive movements that the snare drummer suggests to the dancer that when combined in number and form, reveal a certain style, which is captured by the most conversant performers. Let us examine a Nupe, professional female choral dance team as designed by an aged and prominent woman, which performs not only for the Emir, but in theatrical appearances throughout the land.

The seated leader introduces her subject by an extended extempore song. The sole male singer sits on the floor to her right and from time to time utters phrases or interjections in a clear and strong nasal voice. Behind the choreographer stand mature women, who sing the

31

responsorial and dance. A pubescent girl stands to the left of them. About eight drummers sit to play throughout on two levels: loud and exceedingly loud (fortissimo); their change in dynamics corresponding to the increase in dance momentum, wherein they are forced to "get down" more intensely. Of several distinctive dance styles to snare drum, this kind of group presents that one which is *restrained* and *supersubtle*.

As the principle stands to begin the movement, her dancers follow, dipping and sliding along the floor to the rhythm of a subordinate (not master) drum. The women's short steps give them the appearance of gliding. The dance soon becomes very dramatic and sensuous, more so than were it tuned vivaciously, the syncopated cross-rhythms quickly being built up. The modulation of rolling hips from side to side, backward and forward; the shifting of torso from side to side, is emphasized by large laps of cloth which are draped over the lower body. But the girl, herself, instead of rolling and performing the exquisitely smooth use of the torso and hip, executes a "chicken switch", which is very marked and sharp. It presents a startling *contrast* with a strikingly different dynamic from the women. Likewise, she always is placed in front of, or behind the others. By mid performance, the dancers are acting for themselves, i.e., they have lost their self- consciousness and obviously feel free and inspired in their work. Although the dancers approximate the same movements to each other, they are not at all precise in spatial outline (but definite in timing)— which is a powerful example of the way in which different bodies *artistically* interpret the same *well-executed* movement in African dance. Their nuances still blend into the overall concept of fluid body pattern, not withstanding another aesthetic, in which a more crack, exacting martial approach to spatial boundaries is preferred. The music, however, implies something not quite expressed in this dance of dignity and decorum; that is, the "break loose" which may be reserved for more intimate settings. In this imaginative choreography, the angular, inverted V-shaped placement which has been fashioned, is fired by a moving forward and change of place, until it flows into a single line shuttling crosswise, backward and forward—and finally to the counter clockwise circle. The arranger always takes a prime position in the construction.

The snare drum (henceforth referred to as *"bembe"*) dances are characterized by other drums to dance movements. The passage may be smoothly applied—and it may be marked. There may be many quick, rapid footsteps, followed by a pause and pose; after which bends and turns are created. The arms almost always are extended forward and parallel for a while and/or one after the other. There are swift, deft

32

moves, quarter turns and short phrases. But most of all, emphatic pulses of the music are marked by visceral statements.

Although there is a particular masquerade dance most typical to *bembe* drumming, the flamboyant Egungun collective ancestral spirit also may take it in those areas where the music is conspicuous, if the Egungun emanates from an Ayan professional lineage. Otherwise, in a very few areas, there are specific and colorful masquerades called Egungun *ilu bembe*, (Egungun for the *bembe* drum), which react to this music exclusively, the point is made here because the natural and functional music of Egungun follows quite different instrumentation, called *bata* [Kinni-Olusanyin; forthcoming].

In the Egungun, *bembe* is yet another example of dance substyle, which may be illuminated here. If the Egungun is dancing in the crowded house, the movements, of course, are more restricted than those in the open, where the masquerader may romp and leap around. He may only be aroused to stand to dance at all, when the drum talk is very provocative. He walks from one place to another to bless the company and to perform. He may dance in place or take very few steps or leaning forward, heavily shake his shoulders from side to side, shake his waist with a great curlicue, and engage in frequent pelvic rocks, punctuating in space on strong drum pricks. The masquerader might spring up and down—and jump to syncopated rhythms (syncopes are observed), as well as rise on the toes in order to land on the remainder of the foot. Out of a metre either of twelve or eight fast pulsations, the fifth often is accented in the overall snared drum dance: 1-2-3-4-5-6-7-8-9-10-11-12!

The ritual dance-masquerading attended by a snare drum (of independent development), in both the Yoruba and Nupe is of the deity Igunnu, or more properly Igunnu-Ndako-Gboya (the masquerade itself), also called Igunnuko, meaning Great Gunnu, deity of fertility and good health, who always brings rain, dissipates epidemics and quells anti- social behavior. The originally Nupe Igunnu has flourished in Yorubaland for not less than one hundred years, taken South at the instance of both male and female, both Yoruba and Nupe. Its secrets have remained the property of its affiliated families. It is the style, rather than the form of the two displays which has been maintained! (Let it suffice to say that the Igunnu is *not* an Egungun as has been published, although it certainly is a deity in masquerade (Abraham 1958: 258 and *Nigeria Magazine*).

This splendid masquerade, itself, appears exceedingly tall, twelve feet high or often more, and domical, with several graduated tiers of panels, streamers, or tassels, in white color with red trim; with several alternating colors, or even a striped effect. Underneath the panels may be any multicolored and designed materials which are revealed when the Igunnu moves, and causes the panels to shift or wave. Near the bottom of the masquerade is circular skirting of any color, which must widen when he expands his dance steps. A train may be attached, therefore covering the entire human body.

Among the Igunnu's most notable characteristics is a sudden extension of height—and also an opposite and extreme lowering to the ground. Igunnu tilts, bends, widens and contracts; twirls, swirls, bounces, stands upside down and assumes numerous positions. He performs conjuration and athletic feats as well. With finesse and adroit maneuvers, the Igunnu, which is constructed of cloth, avoids becoming wet, throughout the heavy rain which falls at some point during the outing. Masquerades of this structure of movable form, also are known to be enacted among the Igala, the Igbo (where it is elaborately decorated with carved figurines), and the Efik and the Ibibio from east of Yoruba and Nupelands. No doubt, there is some relationship between these forms in their technique of construction, they are all ritual masquerades. Just how the singular manipulations in space (to be described below) are achieved is a trade secret among the confederation of priests. Another readily observable feature is the wide range of movement which, with grace and elegance, is coaxed out of the masquerade. Its tented structure is not a hinderance, but rather presents more a marvel in contrivance of zestful dance to precisely timed music.

The public portion of the Igunnu dance is controlled by several functionaries who organize the strategy of a festival. Briefly, the Idaso (Ndaso), high priest, governs the *lakara*, that is, any masquerade. He also trains the singers and other participants. The Iyalomo, a woman, may be responsible for the all important praise singing, while the Saba is the priest who translates, or interprets from the za Nupe speech of Igunnu. He also leads, commands, sings to and constantly bombards the masquerade with a profusion of praises.

The legitimate performance of Igunnu always attracts a large crowd and the streets, even highways, are blocked by the authorities to allow an uninterrupted flow of ceremony. As many masks as possible (that is, family members who are available to support them, at least seven), appear either simultaneously, or in order of seniority. The play is considerably heightened by the appearance of the chief masquerade, which may be taller and a bit more elaborate than the others. He has his own following and embellishments, such as huge bodies of lush, leafy branches carried by men and is more spectacular than the others. He is joined by his lesser Igunnu comraderie.

Some other personalities in the exhibition include children who bear clay pots of potions (herb water) on their heads; men who brandish whips of tree limbs and who wrap palm fronds around their heads and/or hang them from their waist in a band, and paint their faces in splashes of color, especially red, white, and yellow, on the cheeks and forehead.

Singing is performed mostly by women, but is taken up by men, whose songs usually differ and who sing at appropriate times, such as while in or exiting from the *igbale* (esoteric grove). The song form is a short, often simple and syncopated antiphonal-responsorial (call and response), consisting of three to five notes. Songs and epideictic orations to other deities commonly are interspersed with Igunnu's own encomium. Praise songs to the Idaso priests also feature.

Instrumentation consists of the snared *bembe* drums, often two in number, *baabo* ritual gourd rattles with external strikers of cowrie and *dunkun* (duku) pot drums. The *dunkun* drums normally are played in the grove and in seated position, thus are not used when the ensemble is highly mobile.

The *bembe* drummers flank the mask and, by means of drum language, direct and critique Igunnu and the others in the prevention of precarious actions, such as going astray or falling. The various rhythmic-tonal patterns also suggest the particular kinds of steps and runs (circles, side to side, etc.), the directions, the spiraling, sinking, swaying and bouncing that are characteristic of the deity in masquerade—besides its instrumental panegyrics; its coordination with the singing and playing of the standard fare which is idiosyncratic to the Igunnu manifestation.

The *bembe* drum is significant in Igunnu performance not only for its quality of interaction with the masquerade, it is also such a common feature that many view it as symbiotic to it, but because the professional drummers themselves (in the various areas where Igunnu exists) insist that it is their most compelling musical form!

Outlined below is the compacted structure of a selected, high spirited, Igunnu ceremony.

A single *bembe* drummer, wearing a cowried vest, moves through the village bearing a stylized gait, swaying and inclining to the side, somewhat reminiscent of the demeanor of the masquerade whose peculiar rhythms he is playing to announce the forthcoming event. From the *igbale* emerge the Igunnus costumed in circular rows of fringed red, yellow, orange and then pink, which are supported by a long length of figured *ankara* (manufactured cloth in African prints). The masquerades are assisted by a boy, who shakes a small gourd rattle of internal strikers. The Igunnus squeal and yelp; and spiritedly stamp their "feet" as they move from house to house, while excited children reply by shouting, *"Esogbe"* (one of Igunnu's appellations). The masquerades dip downward and shift upward, at will. Whenever Igunnu turns to reverse his direction, the children fall back and scamper away.

In the early afternoon, the *bembe* and *dunkun* drummers assemble and sit under the largest shade tree, to unfold a protracted prelude. The chorus of women stands to their right. The choragus holds up a type of *iganawasa* (symbolic wand) throughout the episode. Across from them, two lines of women who have marked their faces with red lines on one side and white on the other, wear *asoke* (hand woven cloth) wrappers and a series of multicolored beads criss-crossed from the neck to the waist. They face each other to dance in unison and to sing, as well. The whooping Igunnus who, upon being re-called from the grove, by the outer music, enter the arena from behind the houses. They are led by the bare-chested Saba, who wears an asoke wrapper and holds an animal horn in the left hand and rattle in the right. The dignitaries, who have been sitting directly across from the drummers, intermittently dance with the Igunnus—and are proffered due respect by the masks' *kunle*, by means of bending all the way over, so that the "head" of the device touches the ground. A short pair of identical "twins" dance in synchronized duet; and another couple, one of whom steps much faster than the other, provides a polyrhythmic scheme to counterbalance his partner. The incentive to dance is increased by the tonal magnitude and impact of the music. The Igunnus shorten and roll on the earth, only to rise and twist energetically, while growing taller and taller. The wizardly "footwork", which is observable as movement underneath a gown, is in contrary motion to the streamered "body". The Saba, who incessantly mandates Igunnu to swivel, to spin, to lean from side to side, to shrink, to stretch, even to widen, by the verbal designs of his attributes, is ably conducted by the drummers who render the *ne plus ultra* to Igunnu in euphony. The singing women poetically induce him to continue the dramatic spectacle with the stated dancers, who also alter their choreography with each musical discourse.

As the dancers eventually glide away single file, the masqueraders are free to retire to their cloistered wood, later followed by the drummers, who will further express the significance of Igunnu in the serene and blissfully secluded enclosure, the *igbale.*

Igunnu has been displayed out of context in performances of state arts council's festivals and in music dramas, by theatre companies, such as the late Duro Ladipo's *Oba Koso,* which dramatizes the exploits of the famous deified Yoruba king Sango (the composer also was a priest of Sango). There, the masquerade symbolizes Sango's familiarity with the Nupe, his inheritance of Igunnu and his personable first wife, Oya, also a Nupe, who figures rather prominently in the production, as she does in Yoruba mythology. In *Oba Koso,* the masquerade is staged during the court scenes and moves very subtly and in place. Although three masquerades are in view, two of them operate with no one inside, while only the third one is borne by a man. This exemplifies part of the mysterious qualities of Igunnu. The person of the masquerader is an Idaso priest, who must perform many sacrifices before he is able to displace the masquerade in function and locality. The correct and proper preparation, before the presentation of ritual material on stage, is an important consideration for all concerned; the director, the performers and even the audience.

Summary and Conclusion

The aesthetic of "dance to drum" stands at the apex of African performing arts. Of the profusion of forms and styles in existence, however, the question which arises, is the content analysis of its overall framework—the separation of the important independent elements and then their re-union as a *workable* whole. This must be done without neglecting the subsidiary and imperative appurtenances (high rituals, other instrumentation, costuming, properties, etc.), of the specific subject at hand.

Whether as secular stage dance, ritual theatre or religious ceremony, the snared drum dance has its own sub-styles of projection, which are dependent upon the situation and the precise disposition of the music. Our few examples serve to illustrate how the dance to drum actually operates, without which, the soul of the dance itself becomes a weak and wandering spirit.

The initiation of Nupe choreo-music institutions has led to the blooming of certain conventions of movement which creatively result in sensational modes of output—a peculiar idiom of the snared drumming experience.

The lavish and exuberant Yoruba Egungun aggregate which has a "phraseology" of its own, lends but another dimension to the choreo structures which radiate from the central snare accompaniment when and where Egungun bembe is performed.

Moreover, Igunnu, one of the few masquerading Orisas produced as a towering, paneled or fringed structure, readily responds to potent singing, rattling and drumming in performance. This phenomenon possesses both physical charm and the efficacy to positively affect fertility, precipitation, and other mundane matters—hence his implantation in Yorubaland from the northern Nupe.

Because the Igunnu rite is, in itself, a mixture of Nupe ceremonies (Gunnu, Ndako-Gboya and sometimes Tsoede), the snared talking drum is intimately associated with it. This drum is of a genre which exists in Western Africa in several regional varieties, crossed into the Ottomans and infiltrated European music to become labeled the modern side or snare drum. This instrument, however, which is played mostly by professionals and by priests in Yorubaland, is of indigenous technology, rather than that of the Nupe (as must be conceded by evidence from traditional sources). The *bembe* talking drum is employed to accompany, survey, caress, indulge and fulfill Igunnu in performance. On *bembe* are played the motifs which identify and attract the sacred character. This dynamogenic relationship between music and dance-masquerading of the spiritual is a symmetrical, consonant concert of sound and animated movement, color and form, which is an analogue to the rectification and purification that the community receives upon its extended and dedicated application.

Works Cited

Abraham, R. C. *Dictionary of Modern Yoruba*. London: London University Press, 1958.

Blades, J. *Musical Instruments Through the Ages*, ed. A. Baines. Middlesex: Penguin, 1966.

Johnson, S. J. *The History of the Yorubas*. Lagos: C.S.S. Bookshop, 1921.

Kinni-Olusanyin, E. "The Enshrinement of Drums Among the Yoruba," *Occasional Publications of the Department of Theatre Arts*, II, No. 1, 1980.

—. "The Question of the Professional Musician . . .", *Occasional Publications of the Department of Theatre Arts*, III, No. 1.

—. "The Classic *Bata* Dance: Its Ritual," ed. Adelugba, D., Soyinka Anniversary Publications, Vol. II, forthcoming.

Nadel, S. F. *A Black Byzantium*. London: O.U.P., 1942.

—. *Nupe Religion*. London: Routledge, Kegan and Paul, 1954.

Nzewunwa, N., ed. *The Masquerade in Nigerian History and Culture*. Port Harcourt: University of Port Harcourt Press, 1983.

TRADITION
AND CONTINUITY

AFRICAN DANCE:
TRANSITION AND CONTINUITY

▲▲▲▲▲▲▲▲▲▲▲▲▲▲▲▲▲

Robert W. Nicholls

African traditions demonstrate that dance can be a significant psycho-social device able to penetrate many aspects of human existence. By commemorating such events as the passage of seasons and life-cycle transitions through life experiences are dramatized and made more meaningful. The paradigm presented by traditional dance in Africa is a challenging one that has global relevance. Sociologists who have examined the problems of alienation and other social ills that accompany industrialization, point out the need for ritual in the lives of individuals. As life in modern society becomes increasingly technical, the need for increased participation in affective and aesthetic areas becomes apparent. Dance, as a functional sociocultural tool on the African model, could play a part in a cross-cultural "affective renaissance." The evidence shows, however, that modernity is having an adverse affect on traditional dance. Critical social changes are leading to the demise of many traditional customs which engender dance. Oral traditions are fragile, and experiences, insight, and methodology that have sustained African communities for generations could well be lost to future generations. It is advisable therefore, that relative to traditional African dance, an agenda of cultural conservation be planned.

Africa has undergone far-reaching changes in the twentieth century, many of which have had an impact on dance. The cumulative impact of various modernizing agencies, such as education, mass media, religion, and urbanization, has eroded the indigenous culture, and tradition makes little impact on modern priorities. Educational processes are often faulted for making little reference to indigenous sociocultural ecology. The mass media are narrowly based, have a large percentage of foreign program content, promote an urban bias, and are insensitive to the different needs and cultural particularism of rural dwellers. Moreover, interaction with pop culture by the young has created a generation gap. For the adult population also, aspects of consumerism have proved a potent lure, stifling participation in the African cultural milieu, especially among modernized urban dwellers.

The intrusion of alien values and life-styles on indigenous cultures is described by Friere as a "cultural invasion,"[1] while folklorist Alan Lomax (1977) talks of a "grey out" in which the many "little" cultures give way to, or are becoming absorbed by, an incoming dominant culture.[2] The effect of sociocultural change on traditional dance in Africa impacts in diverse areas. Christianity, for example, discourages traditional dance and has failed to acknowledge, with the exception of the Aladura-type churches (free churches in Nigeria), that dance in Africa is a means of expressing spirituality. Pop culture has also served to displace traditional dance by providing new contexts and new forms. The influence of Western thought has now limited the functions of dance to mere recreation in many African cities.

In Africa, the decline of traditional art means more than a loss of entertainment or a diminishing of aesthetic. Indigenous cultures are functional social instruments which have been developed over the centuries to meet practical needs. In non-literate societies art forms contain a mosaic of information and skills for coping with a variety of environments, many of which are extreme. They serve not so much as an artifact—an end in itself, but more as a process—a means to an end. For the Igede of Nigeria's Benue State, music and dance contribute to the integration of society by expressing social organization, validating institutions, perpetuating values, and promoting group solidarity. As a link in a chain of activities directed to some specific goal, music and dance have been central to African rural economies. One result of the loss of traditional culture in many rural communities is that the mode of production has been stripped of its energizing forces. Although basic farming technologies have remained unaltered for centuries, the social institutions that have orchestrated those technologies and shaped them into a dynamic force, have been eroded. Impoverishment in many rural areas in Africa can be directly attributed to the decline of traditional culture of which music and dance is an integral part.

Occurring simultaneously with the decline of traditional dance at the level of the village community, are efforts initiated by African governments to foster a cultural revival at the national level. Due in part to a nostalgia for a classical past, but primarily to develop a national sense of cultural identity, many countries have sought to showcase their traditional dances. An example of this effort to strengthen national unification through traditional culture is provided by Nigeria where the government sponsors an All-Nigeria Festival of the Arts. This rotates between different states so that people of different religions, customs and languages (about 1,200 competed in the festival of 1972) can meet to perform their traditional dances and music. This interest in cultural revival also finds expression in the formation of national dance theaters and touring troupes of trained professional dancers. Dance troupes from Senegal, Benin, Guinea, Madagascar, Ivory Coast, Niger, and Cameroon have travelled all over the world, often with direct or indirect assistance from their respective government. Sometimes different ethnic groups are merged, as with the Mali national troupe, which is a synthesis of the Peulh, Senufo, Dogon, Songhai, and Bambara peoples. Although recognizing the value of these efforts and the artistic endeavor involved, it can be noted that superficial similarities between these contemporary neotraditional dances and their historic antecedents often disguise fundamental differences between them.

Characteristics of African Dance

By untangling the threads of culture, tradition, and history that create Africa's dance heritage, it is possible to deduce the characteristics of authentic traditional dance. The paradigm that this provides is in depth and range, broader and more far-reaching than we are familiar with. In pre-Christian Europe, dance served ritualistic purposes and as late as the 12th century, clerics performed "Carole" dances in English churches at Christmas. Since that time, however, dance in the European tradition has been primarily a secular activity engaged in for recreation or entertainment, embracing such factors as physical exercise, exhibition of skills, emotional expression, aesthetic enjoyment, courtship and partner selection, inter-personal communication, and cultural continuity. All of these factors are featured in African dance, but more significant functions are also included.

It is frequently argued that there is no "art for art's sake" in Africa. Although this is an overgeneralization, it emphasizes the extreme functionality of African art. Kwakwa points out that the organization of traditional African dances was motivated not only by theatrical, but also by sociological, historical, political, and religious considerations. He emphasizes that this identification is crucial to an understanding of dance in Africa, these being the most important factors that differentiate it from the "Art," "Creative," or "Contemporary" dances of present-day Africa and also from the Classical Ballet and Contemporary Modern Dance of the West that are performed primarily for the entertainment of others.[3]

Dance in Africa retained its ritualistic character into the 20th century. Within the ritual context, dance is one among an amalgam of activities aimed at the realization of a predetermined goal. Among the Akan of Ghana, religious ceremonies sometimes take the form of plays which go on for several days. But although a puberty festival, for example, may last five to seven days, the dance activities rarely go beyond the first couple of days. A sense of pluralism is manifested during ritual festivals by the dynamic interaction of multiple elements. It is customary to integrate dance with other arts, with music, drama and oratory, as well as with various forms of visual display such as masks, body paint, and costumes. Leg or wrist rattles are often worn to enhance the percussive quality of the performance. Traditional dances tend to be participatory in nature, since the audience and the performers usually belong to the same community everyone is involved. The dance arena is created by the spectators who reinforce the dancers by shouting encouragement, ululating, clapping, joining in on choruses, and vocalizing responses. The role of audience and performer is often interchangeable, and, depending on the occasion, the ranks of the spectators might be broken by an individual eager to demonstrate his or her own dancing skills. Due to their multi-dimensional character, the integration of different art forms, and the lack of rigid distinctions between performers and audience, traditional dance performances might be described as "whole theater."

There is nothing haphazard about the timing of ritual festivals, for human life was organized to symbolically echo natural cycles. Traditional African cultures recognized that continuity of experience is dependent on periodic renewal, consequently, and the underlying theme of most ritual ceremonies is regeneration. The Ngas of Nigeria's Jos Plateau, for example, believe that the moon regulates the rhythm of all life. At the turn of the year an astronomer-priest symbolically shoots the moon with a spear and engenders the new year. Many important festivals are related to agricultural processes such as sowing, harvesting, or the arrival of the rains. Throughout Africa, music and dance are closely integrated with ceremonial life, as Nketia points out, the "union of sound and action" is of supreme importance whatever the context, "There must be drumming and dancing at the funeral as at the festival."[4] Most African groups have some form of annual thanksgiving such as the Ebi-Woro New Year purification festival of the Ijebu Yoruba, or the "New Yam" Festival of the Idoma of Nigeria. "Odabra," an Idoma word meaning "yams in abundance," is danced by boys about ten to sixteen years of age. The dance steps express the hunger that is past and the joy in the sun and rain that bring a bountiful harvest.

Other ceremonies relate to the human life-cycle and the rituals of passage by which an individual moves from one stage of existence to another—naming ceremonies at birth, initiations, marriages, title-installations, and funerals. Dance is used to give meaning and significance to these important occasions:

> A child becomes a member of a community at his naming ceremony; an adolescent is initiated into the responsibilities of adult life; a woman moves from her paternal home to that of her husband's family; an elder receives a recognition for his services in the form of a title; a member of the community joins the world of the spirits; at none of these times is an individual left alone to bear the emotions which accompany these critical changes. The members of the community carry him through the crisis with appropriate ceremonies which contain the emotion of the moment in music, song, and dance.[5]

Dance symbolism is essentially appropriate to occasions of renewal, for according to Hanna, "Dance metaphorically enacts and communicates status transformation in rites of passage, death ceremonies, curative and preventative rites."[6] Referring to the funeral dances of the Dogon of Mali, she states, "death creates disorder; but through the dance, humans metaphorically restore order to the disordered world."[7] The overt purpose of an Igede funeral ceremony is to transform the deceased into an ancestor. The masquerades, as emissaries from the ancestors, dance to signify the acceptance of the deceased's soul into the ancestral realm. Thus, the change in status receives divine ratification. The funeral, although commemorating a death, is a celebration of life. It honors the achievements of the deceased in his lifetime and affirms the continuation of the community in the midst of trauma.

In addition to seasonal festivals and rites of passage that recur at somewhat predictable intervals, other ceremonies such as curative rituals, exorcisms, preventative rites, and divinations, are performed when the situation demands. The Masabe dances of the Tonga of Zambia are performed by women to exorcise mischievous, possessing spirits. The Azande of southern Sudan use divination dances when hunters repeatedly fail to make a catch. Similarly the origins of the Adzogbo dance of the Ewe of Ghana was as a divination dance through which war leaders would predict the course of an upcoming battle by interpreting the movements of young male initiates. Dance acts as healer during curative rituals involving the diagnosis and treatment of the physically and mentally ill. Rites termed "drums of affliction" that include dance, are performed by the Ndembu of Zambia, while Afruja dances are used by the Igede to treat persons suffering from mental illness. On being cured the former patient joins the cult responsible for the cure and participates in subsequent curative rites. As a form of preventative medicine, dance in Africa is recognized as a valuable form of exercise. In the past when tribal wars were relatively common, dance was used to prepare young men both physically and mentally for battle. Coordinated team dances taught them the necessary control and discipline, while forceful music and patriotic song texts provided motivation. Nketia states that the music of Akan warrior ensembles provide a "high spirited music and a lot of messages of incitement, encouragement and direction." He describes the drumming as "stirring." This effect is achieved by "peculiarities of style such as the unpronounced or seeming lack of metrical symmetry in some of the drum combinations, and the independent pace of drums and songs."[8]

The functionality of African dance has led Hanna to proclaim that, "In traditional Black African cultures ... dance is less an 'art' than a 'craft.'"[9] In any functional art, including African dance, the form of the art product is subordinated to its adaptation to a specific purpose, and cannot be understood without reference to this purpose. For example, in some African societies, members of professional organizations—hunter, farmer, and fisherman guilds—perform specific dances which reflect the economic life of the community and include mimetic re-enactments of occupational gestures. Among the Vai of Liberia and the Akan of Ghana, hunters' dances contain elaborate dramatizations of the hunt. Dances associated with the Chisungu nubility rites performed for Bemba girls of Zimbabwe, mimic such common domestic chores as grinding maize and collecting potatoes. The principle male dance of the Dakakari of northwest Nigeria is based on the movements involved in hoeing yams. Dancers wear decorated loin cloths with a "tail" attached to the rear. The "dancing" of this tail accentuates the hoeing movements. The dances of the Dakakari's Hausa neighbors also include pantomime of occupational activities: "The Makera dance illustrates the hammering of blacksmiths, the Nama Hausa mimes the action of the meat sellers, and the Ruwan Gwandon Kifi illustrates the work of the fisherman in casting nets and using spears and fish traps."[10]

Within a ritual festival the sequence and character of the component events are determined by purposes relative to the larger world view. In other words the *why* of the festival—in terms of its sociocultural context, determines the *what*—in terms of the form of the activities that take place. African dance, as an avenue of expression closely related to the themes and purposes of a particular occasion is, in effect, *context determined*. A fertility ceremony from southeast Ivory Coast that commemorates the seasonal arrival of the rains, demonstrates this point. Its cultural purposes permeate every aspect of the ceremony and influence the content and form of the dances performed. Within a dance circle comprised of the whole village, various dances that express the themes of the occasion are performed by dance groups of different ages and sexes. These include a performance by four little girls who "danced almost squatting on the ground, holding their tiny aprons in one hand, and scattering imaginary seeds with the other," and a "pantomime of the copulation of various beasts and birds" by "strangely dressed old men."[11] In this ceremony every action is not only relevant to larger agricultural cycles, but, in that it ceases with the first drops of rain, it is specific to about two hours in the year. For the African, dance is a mode of communication which utilizes gestures and movement to convey information, and as such, is a major educational vehicle. Repetitive dance sequences introduce children to traditional patterns of behavior. During initiation ceremonies that introduce adolescents to adult society, dance communicates messages about respect for self and others, physical coordination and mental poise, standards of conduct, and cultural integration. Within communal rituals, forms of dance theater become the medium by which the world view is made salient to the community. Nketia has outlined some of the dance vocabulary of the Akan:

When a dancer points the right hand or both hands skyward in an Akan dance, he is saying, "I look to God." When he places his right forefinger lightly against his head, he means, "It is a matter for my head, something I should think seriously about, something I should solve for myself." If he places his right forefinger below his right eye, he is saying, "I have nothing to say but see how things will go." When he rolls his hands inwards and stretches his right arm simultaneously with the last beats of the music, he means, "If you bind me with cords, I shall break them into pieces."[12]

The Agbekor dances of the Ewe relate the history of how the Ewe fought their way to that section of Ghana where they now live. It is a highly standardized dance and the drummer must change his patterns continuously because they are correlated to each element of the dance choreography. The dancers stylize their movements in keeping with the language of the drums and the meaning of the dance. "Several dancers try to describe the situations of war: 'Get down and be ready' or 'Go forward slowly; stop and watch right and left, and go forward again' or 'If I get you, I'll cut your neck'."[13]

Most African dances are integrated into specific social situations and the appropriate dances performed on each occasion. As such, they are reproductive—before one can participate, one must know the dance movements and the drum rhythms with which they are coordinated. In addition to being context determined, African dances are usually event specific. For example, dances performed at Dangme puberty festivals are only performed on that occasion and their form is determined by the purpose of the ceremony, in this case the adult women conveying to the girls some of the functions of womanhood:

> Dangme girls of Ghana ... are taught the Otofo dance which is said to symbolize the utmost in femininity—the simple and delicate foot patterns; the gentle thread of the feet on the ground; the deliberately controlled swing of the arms along curved paths; the slight tilt of the neck to the side and the slightly downward cast of the eyes—are said to teach the girls how a woman should walk and behave.[14]

The music of the calabash horns of the Ogirinye warrior ensemble are only heard publicly in Igede at the funeral of an Ogirinye association member.* At this time Ogirinye members take turns to honor the deceased by performing solo dances. The arrival of the Ogirinye masquerade is pure theater. He does not dance but simply runs at full speed through the meeting ground to the burial place. His speed represents that of a skillful warrior, who is so fast that he can hardly be seen, and by extension death, who also appears unexpectedly among the living. The funeral ceremony contains fundamental values relative to kinship, tradition, and the Igede perception of life and death. In common with other African oral traditions, Igede ideology is not simply theoretical or contemplative, but lives within the actions by which it is expressed. The medium, in effect, becomes the message. Values are conveyed through the performances of the various music and dance associations to which the deceased belonged. The dances of the Aitah masquerade with its large wooden mask, machete, and shaggy costume of raffia, serve as finale to the funeral. Responding to the cajoling of the talking slit drum, which is symbolically the voice of the ancestors, the masquerade's movements express the qualities of a great warrior: vigor, determination, and fearlessness.[15]

Dance in New Contexts

Throughout most of Africa, Christianity has served as the vanguard of modernity; as it spreads, indigenous religions and the arts they generate decline. Islam also is a proselytizing religion which contributes to the fragility of African indigenous cultures. According to Schadler, indigenous African religion has been the inspiration for the arts: "A union of cult, life, and religious ritual ... makes possible the creation of arts and crafts that ... embody a transcendental force." He maintains that this aesthetic union can only continue as long as the underlying belief system survives. He attributes the decline of traditional arts to "changing beliefs and growing secularization in general,"[16] and states "Minority religions everywhere face hard psychological pressure from mass religious and ideological movements."[17] He predicts, "in the foreseeable future the identity between cult and art is expected to disappear almost completely."[18]

Ethnomusicologist Alan Merriam was in the village of Lupupa Ngye, Zaire, in 1959-60 and again in 1973. Of all the changes that occurred in his absence, the most significant was in the area of religion. In 1959-60 Christianity had made little impact, but by 1973 it had made significant inroads into Lupupan life. This had led to an abandonment of traditional festivals, especially those attached to Lupika, a fertility deity represented by a large carved wooden figure identified with general well-being, the fertility of the women and the land, and protection against catastrophe. A schism was created between the young and the old when the village's only Lupika figure was sold to an art dealer in the 1960s. While the elders lamented the loss, the young argued that Lupika was the devil. The disappearance of traditional ceremonies has resulted in a decline of adult dance and music activities. Merriam notes that of the four prominent musicians residing in the village in 1959-60 only one was still active in 1973, and *he* had relocated to an urban setting.[19]

Because some free churches incorporate the African propensity to worship through dance within their services, arguments have been made that this represents one of the most significant examples of traditional dance retention within modern African society. Free churches, called Aladura in Nigeria, and which include the Cherubim and Seraphim and the celestial churches, arose relatively recently as alternatives to established denominations which failed to adequately administer to the need of the congregation to reach spiritual ecstacy in the holy dance. Drums which are banned in more conventional churches, feature significantly in Aladura services.

Spirit possession and African dance are sometimes discussed as if these terms are interchangeable, and undue emphasis has been given to indicators of possession such as "speaking in tongues" and catalepsy. Although possession dances exist, they are only one type of religious dance, and one that is practiced by a small, specialized segment of society and are considered exotic even in Africa. The calabashes that the Hausa Bori dancers carry on their heads, for example, are the embodiment of spirits which "mount" the heads of the dancers. While possessed, the dancers can prophesy and perform feats considered remarkable by the Moslem Hausa. Possession consists of a form of controlled hysteria and the erratic movements are probably governed by spontaneous responses rather than culturally preserved dance patterns. Gorer (1949) maintains that the M'deup possession dance of the Wolof of Senegal is not particularly elegant or varied, consisting of small shuffling steps and a violent jerking of the arms and head. Although the Igede masquerades that dance at funerals embody ancestral spirits, the behavior of the masquerade do not parallel the behavior that occurs in possession cults. The masquerade's behavior is extraordinary but it is controlled. On those rare occasions that a masquerade dancer shows signs of being out of control, he is quickly captured and de-masked.

In the course of social evolution, a modernizing, urbanizing people need to see reflections of their emerging new identity mirrored in their popular arts. With the diminishing significance of traditional dance in urban areas, new forms of dance music were created in response to the citizenry's need for recreation and entertainment. The Highlife is typical of these popular new dances. While many traditional dances are specific to particular events within an ethnic subgroup, the new dances were part and parcel of a large, all-embracing, heterogeneous culture. The Highlife is essentially a hybrid music which emerged in West African urban centers in the post second world war era, as an African response to European ballroom dancing. A combination of Western musical instruments and African drum ensembles provided a new and exciting dance music. It was originally oriented towards "polite" society and, untypical of traditional dances, was danced by mixed couples, but with stance and movements which were decidedly African. Highlife rhythms are a synthesis of various dance rhythms associated with traditional ceremonies. Adowa rhythms, for example, previously associated with Akan funerals in Ghana, are an important ingredient of Highlife.

Both the Highlife of West Africa and the "Congo" music of Central and East Africa have evolved into authentic popular music styles which include the Lingala music of Zaire and the Makoosa from Cameroon. This music reverberates across the African continent and the beat of a new Africa is unfolding to its tones. Like Pidgin English and Creole dialects that are fast becoming the unofficial African Linga Franca, such music replaces a village identity with a national, regional, or continental identity, while retaining a universal African sound. Comparable to the Calypso of Trinidad, many Highlife lyrics contain valid social commentary and by any definition is a functional "people's" artform. Such music represents however, a new departure from traditional forms and must be differentiated from the ritual dances from which it evolved.

In an effort to upgrade the role of indigenous arts, many African countries have engaged in a cultural revival since obtaining nationhood. This is normally done through organizations such as National and State Councils for Art and Culture. Typically, the Councils organize competitive dance festivals coinciding with national holidays or official national functions. Rather than a tribute to tradition, many of these cultural festivals are simply exercises in official pomp and pageantry. A cultural show usually takes place in an urban sports stadium where a rectangular stage is erected. While the rank and file occupy regular stadium tiers some distance from the stage, privileged dignitaries are comfortably seated under the protective canopy of a V.I.P. Pavilion. Participating dance troupes are often required to perform one after the other in quick succession before officiating judges, with an allotted performance time of only four to five minutes each.

Although dances staged within cultural arts festivals are based on traditional forms, they have been uprooted from their customary social context in time, place and motivation. Sometimes they are significantly modified to suit the imagined tastes of the metropolis. Costumes are often changed and sometimes new musical instruments are added to the original ensemble. In some cases two or more unrelated dances are merged together on the grounds that they are similar, or school children perform dances which in the villages are restricted to older youths or adults. Although cultural revival dances contribute to national goals and provide encouragement to dancers, they fail to meet the criteria of authentic traditional dances, and might best be described as *neotraditional*.

For many modernists in Africa, Art is seen as a frill, an inducement to consumer enterprises such as tourism. Thus, exploitation of traditional dances can be found in cabaret acts performed for tourist or night club audiences. These audiences generally have little understanding of the genre, or of traditional aesthetics and are not concerned about the authentic employment of masks, dance gestures, or drum passages in dance. The voyeur stance of tourist towards the performances they observe in their search for local color, has often been cited as a cause of the decline in cultural and artistic standards. It is argued that under the corrosive effect of tourism, the culture of the host country is commercially exploited and becomes devalued, and consequently the local inhabitants lose dignity performing for the benefit of goggling strangers. Examples of the degeneration of African dances are found among the ubiquitous nightclub acts based on indigenous performing traditions but with large helping of razzmatazz—fire-eaters, snake charmers, topless dancers—thrown in for good measure.

Creative dance theatre makes no pretense at traditional authenticity. Working within a Classical or Art tradition, they recognize that traditional dances cannot be accurately reproduced in a staged metropolitan environment. Instead, they value innovation, and, using traditional themes and imagery, are able to create a new and different genre. Duro Ladipo's dance-drama *Oba Koso*, for example, successfully combines dance, music and speech to advance the plot. The dance theater of the Ori Olokun Company of Ife, who represented Nigeria at the 1971 World Festival of Arts in France, also operates within this genre. With choreography by Peggy Harper and featuring dancers Peter Badejo and Ladago Ogunedele, their performance of *Alatangana* is based on a myth of the Kono people in Guinea, which explains death as the original state of being on which life superimposes itself fleetingly. Interestingly, *Purakapali and the Moon Man*, is not based on African mythology but on a story from the Tiwi people of Northern

Australia. Where they survive, creative dance companies provide new directions and new audiences for African dance.

A Comparison of Contemporary and Traditional Contexts

The traditional role of dance in African communities can be contrasted to the new directions dance has taken in today's African society. Live performances include government organized cultural competitions, cabaret entertainment, and dance theater. Neotraditional and contemporary modern dance are performed by specialist artists, on a raised stage, for the entertainment of heterogeneous audiences. This contrasts to the participatory nature of dance in the traditional context where community members create the dance arena and play an active role in the performance. Recreational dance using recorded music occurs at dance parties and discos, which in addition to popular African music such as Highlife, features non-African pop (mainly Black American music) and Caribbean Reggae and Soca.

While the primary role of modern dance is recreation and entertainment, traditional dance has a functional orientation aimed at the realization of social outcomes external to the context of the performance, and its characteristic gestures and locomotion are determined by the sociocultural purposes it fulfills. Although a neotraditional revival dance may retain the external form of a ritual dance, divorced from its formative context, it provides a replica of the original, but one that no longer serves the same sociocultural function. The separation of form and function is observed in the process of artistic trivialization that is occurring throughout Africa, from Ritual Art-to-Folk Art-to-Tourist Art. Each stage represents a loss of authenticity, a loss of aesthetic quality, and a corresponding loss of historical significance and cultural relevance.

Historically, dance is embedded in the ritual activities of specific communities and a hypothesis can be made that in Africa, the arts, including music and dance, are appraised by the same aesthetic criteria that are applied to the larger world view. In traditional Africa, life was not compartmentalized as it is industrial societies. Barriers between sacred and secular, work and play, technology and artifact were not rigidly defined. The arts were not specialist pursuits set aside from everyday life, nor were artistic principles unique to the discipline. Hardin discovered that among the Kono of eastern Sierra Leone, aesthetic criteria are directly related to the principles which people use to organize their lives in general.[20] Relative to dance, Hanna maintains that "what we perceive as aesthetic factors are intermingled and designed for practical applications in the economic, political, social, and religious spheres of life."[21] Chernoff emphasizes that the values which inform the African musical sensibility embody philosophical and ethical traditions, and that relationships in music are comparable to relationships between people.[22] In discussing Chernoff's theories, Riesman states: "What is exciting about this analysis is that we see playing the music as participating in a relation, and that relation expresses in music the qualities of feeling that Africans value in the conduct of social life itself."[23] In Africa, musical values and social values are interconnected, and in a sense, music and dance provide a microcosm of the world view. As a consequence, full participation in a dance performance requires initiation into cultural conventions beyond the mere translation of drum texts or interpretation of dance gestures. Working knowledge of the cultural calendar, social structure, esoteric lore, and socialization processes, may also be necessary. Participation in traditional dance in effect demonstrates the extent of an individual's enculturation.

In the traditional context, dance extends further into the life of the community and, on the level of the individual, the density and frequency of dance experience is greater, involving intimate and symbolic interaction with peers and community members at regular intervals throughout the life-span. Harper studied the different dances of a single Yoruba village, that of Ipele in Owo district of Western Nigeria and revealed that there was a great diversity of dances with distinctive functions. She names five ritual dances (Ire Orisa, Agherebe, Igede, Laghalogbo, Egungun), two dances expressing official authority (Olosorope, Ogagago), three distinctive dances for various age groups (Igharo, Arile, Igbade), two occupational dances (Arokogo, Ida), three funeral dances (Igogo, Bembe, Olomarse), two dances performed at marriages and naming ceremonies (Totogiri, Ajabure), and six recreational dances (Ireso, Gbedu, Arab, Are, Akula, Ayu). Although Ipele village need not be taken as a typical traditional village, this conservative estimate of twenty three diverse dances, each with its own live music and distinctive functions, is nevertheless impressive.[24]

The age range of participating dancers is also greater in traditional communities than in modern society. In the traditional context most sections of the community are involved in some aspect of dance. Elders are revered as living archives of traditional music and dance. The Igharo dance guild of Ipele Village in Harper's research, is for men over the age of sixty-five years who perform the Gbegberekutu dance at the Ero festival when the initiation of a new member is celebrated. In

Igede, young children are considered the personification of innocence and their participation in dance is necessary for some rites of purification. In the past, a dance known as Adiya (dance queen), was performed by two young virgins, one dark in complexion, the other light in complexion, as part of the New Yam Festival. The two girls were transported to the dance arena on a mat, in order that their purity would not be defiled by contact with ordinary ground.

Special efforts are made to establish formative links between music and movement early in the Igede child's life. Babies are rocked and patted when mothers sing to entertain or soothe them. One popular game entails the mother tossing the infant into the air as she sings *"Apwu eji pwu ka gbaji ka uhe"* ("You can't yet reach, yet you're jumping up"). As children grow, adults encourage them to learn skills that will supply the future society with accomplished performers, and more of a child's leisure time is spent in drumming and dancing than with any other form of recreation.[25] Other factors possibly contribute to adult encouragement of children's dances. Among the Igede, as in other African groups, a belief in reincarnation depicts life as a continuous cycle routinely interrupted by death. Le Moel suggest that adults among the Bobo accord importance to children's imitation of adult ritual because of their cyclical sense of time[26]: in a sense these children are the parents' own ancestors.

The result of this positive reinforcement is that by the time the Igede child is about seven years old, he or she has developed a high level of expertise in music and dance. As youngsters of any society whose play involves the imitation of adult activities, Igede children meticulously observe the required form. The adult musical groups have their infant counterparts, where the children arrange themselves around three tin-can drums, which substitute for the three membrane drums— *ubah, egbong,* and *okpirih*—of the adult group. Confronted by a six year old Igede boy who could beat out complex rhythms on a tin-can, I conceived that acquiring rhythmic skills is comparable to learning a language and that similar cognitive aptitudes are employed. Children are socialized informally into language and can learn more than one with relative ease. At a later stage learning a language, or mastering a rhythm, can only be achieved by much intellectual effort.

On his return to Lupupa Ngye in Zaire, Merriam noted that although adult dance activities had declined, children's dance activities had increased, primarily in connection with school performances organized under the loose rubric of the Boy and Girl Scouts.[27] This illustrates a trend that seems to be occurring throughout Africa. In the name of national preservation of culture, formerly serious cultural practices are relegated to the status of children's play. Studies of children's games in Europe make an interesting comparison. It has been shown that childrens' culture—games, nursery rhymes, ditties and dances—carry vestiges of archaic cultural forms that have disappeared in adult society. Could this be the direction that Africa is heading?

When children develop a high level of dance attainment through participation in traditional dances and games, there is always a danger of this skill being frustrated when there is a lack of continuity in cultural dancing in childhood and in their lives as young adults. Although vigorous participation in hymn singing may serve as a partial substitute for dance, the Igede of Nigeria make a distinction between singing and dancing. Hymns, lively though they may be, remain simply songs to the Igede and do not satisfy the need for creative performance contained in Igede dance traditions. One young lady, a member of a teachers' college choir, explained to me that she joined the choir when she felt she was too old for her childhood Ogbete dance association.[28] Due to the generation gap, the towns and cities exert a powerful attraction to the young as harbingers of modernism and mobility unencumbered by old and outdated ideas. As if the lure of Western trappings and bright lights is not enough, the cessation of meaningful dance stimulus just when young men and women reach adolescence, may encourage them to enter bars and parties that feature modern disco and pop music. Away from the supportive influences and moral guidance of the communal setting, there is a danger that they can develop a loose and careless lifestyle, risking unwanted pregnancy and sexually transmitted diseases. Whatever the case, a fissure between modern and traditional life- styles.

An Agenda for Conservation

Ethnomusicologist, Bruno Nettl reminds us that, relative to African music and dance, an urgent sense of preservation is not a new phenomenon:

> In the 1950s, a movement developed within the field of anthropology, conveniently labeled "urgent anthropology." It recognized modernization's imminent destruction of societies, cultures, and artifacts and emphasized the need to concentrate anthropological resources on their preservation. ... For a long time and until very recently, much of ethnomusicological fieldwork could be placed in this category—propelled by this sense of urgency.[29]

56

The trouble with preservation is that its focus has been just that, "preservation" when "conservation" is needed. Conservation implies continuity within a living tradition, while preservation is limited by archival considerations. Preservation activities have been discipline-based and oriented to the academic community rather than to the indigenous art-producing community. Art Historians, Social Anthropologists, Dance Ethnologists, and Ethnomusicologists dissect a culture and extract only that which is relevant to their discipline. A mask in a museum, a musical recording, a photograph or text in a book may all be interesting or appealing in their own right, but such fragments cannot realistically represent the holistic experience from which they were derived.

Perhaps there is a challenge for the Dance Ethnologist here. What we document and how we record is being called into question. The recognition that in Africa, dance is conterminous with the music that accompanies it and the visual art that embellishes it, implies that an interdisciplinary approach would be the most fruitful. Research demonstrating the inter-relationship of dance, music, and the visual arts is needed. Ideally, a set of criteria to examine African performance as an integrated experience could be established. Cinematography has yet to emerge as a vehicle for serious ethnographic study but could be an important medium for documenting African dance in the traditional context. Although a motion picture cannot capture all the facets of a performance, unlike still photographs or tape recordings, it can capture the visual momentum of dance. Phil Ravenhills's films of Senufo, We, and Guro masks of Ivory Coast, and Lester Monts' films of the Vai of Liberia provide good examples of dance documentaries using the motion picture medium.

In addition to documenting the external form and character, the *what* of dance, it is equally important to record underlying determinants in terms of context, functions, social milieu, ritual themes, symbolism, and other factors relative to *why* a particular dance is performed. Arguments made in the area of ethnomusicology that propose that an objective documentation of musical behavior is needed and that this takes precedence over the subjective analysis of musical products are relevant. Koetting argues that ethnomusicologists spend too much time "spinning out theories about what *we* hear and what *we* see in our transcriptions, and we spend too little time digging beneath the surface to discover what the African carriers of tradition conceptualize and hear."[30] Nettl concurs and states: "We must find ways to preserve and record the conceptions of music and musical behavior. This in fact is more urgent ethnomusicology than the continuing preservation of the musical artifact alone."[31] The urgency that Nettl conveys is fueled by the realization that in the process of degeneration the first casualty is the *original context* of the music and dance performance. He states:

Of the various components of musical culture, the music itself—the sound—changes least rapidly; behavior changes more quickly, and the concept of music—of what music is and what it does ... changes perhaps most rapidly, or at least before the other components.[32]

Nettl argues that in a study of African conceptualizations of music and dance behavior, the role of the individual performer is paramount: "In studying the role of the individual performer, we should work with him intensively, as an individual performer to the position of "expert" and the corresponding devaluation of the scholar's role to that of "student," is not always an easy adjustment. Even African academics are reluctant to reverse roles with rural performers who usually have a low social status. Unless the skills of the traditional performer are sincerely appreciated by the African intelligentsia, however, the future of traditional music and dance looks bleak. According to Bebey, only the continued encouragement of African carriers of tradition can insure the conservation of traditional music and dance:

African music will have no future if we ignore the musician who creates it. The musician needs to be constantly reminded that his music is essential. ... The musician has an extremely important coordinating role to play, not only as far as production and evolution are concerned, but also in the use of his art and its integration into modern African life.[33]

Bebey explains that the activity of an individual musician cannot be divorced from the cultural milieu from which he hails: "The participation of whole communities is the only way to guarantee the authenticity of the music whose preservation and development is at stake."[34]

In recent years a school of thought has arisen that advocates that anthropologists and other scholars who study the cultures of traditional peoples, should be accountable to the people they study. The scholarly tone and specialist focus often renders feedback of research findings, obscure to the ethnic community. Nevertheless, the interest shown by a prestigious outsider generally reinforces communal pride in local art products, as Nettl affirms: "There is no doubt that ethno-musicologists, simply by displaying their interests in certain kinds of musical phenomena, have stimulated the societies they study to keep up, develop, ... and preserve musical phenomena."[35] Merriam's activities in Lupupa Ngye provide an example of this point. Merriam discovered that Nkolomoni, a Lupupa xylophone maker and player, lapsed into inactivity during Merriam's thirteen year absence, apparently because his pair of xylophones had been sold. Merriam did not discover the reason for Nkolomoni's long period of retirement and "why he did not undertake to either train youngsters in the traditional apprenticeship system or to make good players of amateur xylophonists."[36] However, when Merriam commissioned a new pair of xylophones for him, "Nkolomoni returned both to making and playing with avidity; indeed he was supremely delighted to be making music again."[37] Another demonstration of the value of outsider encouragement of local performers is provided by the experiences of Bob Haddad in South Peru. Haddad, owner of a small recording company specializing in ethnic music, recorded the dance music of Paucartambo village in 1983-84 and in 1986. In 1988, when he attended the local Mestiso festival, he took with him some of the finished albums. The proceeds from albums sold at the festival were used to revitalize the "Panderos" (the Bread Bakers' Dance) by commissioning masks, costumes, and instruments. The Panderos was a popular local music which had lapsed into disuse due to lack of funds.[38]

Posing an alternative argument, Nettl outlines the downside of outsider intervention, in which a flagging musical custom is isolated and artificially preserved:

> Preservation meant, no doubt, the intrusion of a collector, fieldworker or scholar who tried to persuade people that they should not change their ways, that it was incumbent on them to retain their preindustrial and possibly primitive practices. This intrusion was often resented by people who wished, in fact, to change their way of life and felt that it was necessary to change their music as well.[39]

This scenario reinforces the need for a "conservation agenda" as opposed to mere preservation, for as Bebey emphasizes: "As far as music is concerned, the preservation of ancestral forms is meaningless unless it is part of a genuine development program."[40] To be authentic, indigenous arts must be rooted in historical traditions *and* in present-day life. True authenticity cannot be achieved by preservation alone, since this leads to stultification. Is a transformation of traditional forms possible; one that provides new, alternative contexts for dance and accommodates modern needs but does not lead to degeneration? Some scholars in Communication Studies have examined the utility of "folk media" for disseminating information to bring about improvements in rural areas. According to this rationale, African artistic resources could be matched to developmental goals; and music, dance and song could help to educate rural inhabitants in the ways of agricultural and community development. If new but equivalent contexts are created for dance, the underlying aesthetic sensibility will survive. In the service of development it could stimulate constructive activities and educate the rural population by providing new orientation and motivation.

Notes

* An album of Igebe music recorded by the author will be available on the *Music of the World* label, New York, in the Spring of 1989. Ogirinye, Aitah, Ogbete and other music ensembles will be included.

1. Paulo Friere, Pedagogy of the Oppressed (New York: Herder and Herder, 1970).
2. Alan Lomax, "An Appeal for Cultural Equity," Journal of Communication.
3. Patience Abena Kwakwa, "Traditional African Dance Forms: Context, Role and Meaning," Centre for Nigerian Cultural Studies, Ahmadu Bello University, Zaria, Nigeria.
4. J. H. Kwabena Nketia, Drumming in Akan Communities in Ghana (Lagos: Thomas Nelson, 1963): 174.
5. Peggy Harper, "Dance," The Living Culture of Nigeria.
6. Hanna, (1987): 121.
7. Hanna, (1987): 113.
8. Nketia, (1963): 110.
9. Hanna, (1965): 49.
10. Harper, (1976b): 158.
11. Gorer, (1972): 38.
12. Nketia, (1974): 208.
13. Chernoff 84.
14. Kwakwa 4.
15. Nicholls, 1984.
16. Schadler 153.
17. Schadler 155-156.
18. Schadler 153.
19. Merriam.

20. Hardin.
21. Hanna, (1965): 49.
22. Chernoff.
23. Riesman 110.
24. Harper, (1976b): 154-155.
25. Nicholls, 1985.
26. Le Moel.
27. Merriam, 1974.
28. Nicholls, 1985.
29. Bruno Nettle, (1985): 12-13.
30. Koetting, (1986): 58.
31. Nettl, (1985): 18.
32. Nettl, (1985): 18.
33. Bebey, (1985): 140-141.
34. Bebey, (1985): 140.
35. Nettl, (1985): 18.
36. Merriam, (1974): 52.
37. Merriam, (1974): 52.
38. Haddad, personal communication, 1988.
39. Nettl, (1985): 12.
40. Bebey, (1975): 138.

Works Cited

Bebey, Francis. *African Music: A People's Art*. New York: L.Hill, 1975.

Chernoff, John Miller. *African Rhythm and African Sensibility*. Chicago: University of Chicago Press, 1979.

Friere, Paulo. *Pedagogy of the Oppressed*. New York: Herder and Herder, 1970.

Gorer, Geoffrey. "The Functions of Different Dance Forms in Primitive African Communities." *The Function of Dance in Human Society*. Ed. F. Boas, Dance Horizons, 1972.

Hanna, Judith Lynne. "African Dance as Education." *Impulse 1965: Dance and Education Now*, 1965.

——. *To Dance is Human: A Theory of Nonverbal Communication*. Chicago: University of Chicago Press, 1987.

Hardin, Kris. "Aesthetics, 'Arts,' and the Cultural Whole." Paper presented at the Seventh Triennial Symposium on African Art, U.C.L.A., 1986, April 4.

Harper, Peggy. "Dance." *The Living Culture of Nigeria*. Ed. S.O. Biobaku. Lagos: Thomas Nelson, 1976.

——. "Dance in Nigeria." *Dance in Africa, Asia and the Pacific: Selected Readings*. Ed. J. Van Zile. MSS Information Corporation, 1976b.

Koetting, James. "What Do We Know About African Rhythm?" *Ethnomusicology* 30.1 (1986).

Kwakwa, Patience Abena. "Traditional African Dance Forms: Context, Role and Meaning." Seminar Paper. Centre for Nigerian Cultural Studies,

Ahmadu Bello University, Zaria, Nigeria, 1979.

Le Moel, Guy. "Les Activities Religieuses des Jeunes Enfants chez les Bobo." *Journal des Africanistes* 51.1-2 (1981).

Lomax, Alan. "An Appeal for Cultural Equity," *Journal of Communication* (Spring), 1977.

Merriam, Alan R. "Change in a Zairian Village." *African Arts*. 7.4 (1974).

Nettl, Bruno. "The Concept of Preservation in Ethnomusicology." *More Than Drumming: Essays on African and Afro-Latin American Music*. Ed. I. V. Jackson. Westport, Ct.: Greenwood Press, 1985.

Nicholls, Robert W., "Igede Funeral Masquerades." *African Arts*. 17.3 (1984).

——. "Music and Dance Guilds in Igede." *More Than Drumming: Essays on African and Afro-Latin American Music*. Ed. I. V. Jackson. Westport, Ct.: Greenwood Press, 1985.

Nketia, J. H. Kwabena. *Drumming in Akan Communities in Ghana*. Lagos: Thomas Nelson, 1963.

——. *The Music of Africa*. New York: W.W. Norton, 1974.

Riesman, Paul. "The Person and the Life Cycle in African Social Life and Thought." *African Studies Review*. 29.2 (1986).

Schadler, Karl Ferdinand. "African Arts and Crafts in a World of Changing Values." *Tourism: Passport to Development?* Ed. Emanuel de Kadt. New York: Oxford University Press, 1979.

AFRICAN DANCE: BRIDGES TO HUMANITY

▲▲▲▲▲▲▲▲▲▲▲▲▲▲▲▲

Tracy D. Snipe

Dancing is an expression of a physical, psychological and spiritual state of being that enables people to give meaning and context to their greatest joys, hopes, frustrations, fears or sorrows. This expression contributes to a sense of wholeness. Diversity is the key to African dance which can be as spontaneous as moving to the beat of an intoxicating highlife rhythm, or may involve an elaborate rite of passage performed for centuries in celebration of the community. In either scenario, there is a sense of beauty and life in the dance. To dance is to live. In Africa, dance forms a vital bridge between the dead, the living and the unborn.

Although African dance may be entertaining, it functions primarily as a cultural and artistic expression of the community; in Africa the notion of art for the sake of art is a foreign concept.[1] An effort is made herein to form a thematic link between the socio-cultural, aesthetic, religious, contemporary and political aspects of dance primarily from West Africa, although references will be made to dance in the "New World." Ultimately, such an analysis is invaluable because it enables people to establish a deeper understanding on both the intercultural and interhuman plane which entails cross-cultural benefits, advances multiculturalism and at the least, avoids miscommunication with regard to art, culture and politics.

The Socio-Cultural Function of Dance in Africa

Dance can be defined as cultural behavior in the sense that "... a people's values, attitudes, and beliefs partially determine the conceptualization of dance as well as its physical reproduction, style, structure, content, and performance ... " (Hanna, 1979, p. 3). This definition provides a valid way of interpreting dance in Africa where there are more than 1,000 ethnic groups (Hanna, 1983, p. 47), and each group has its unique culture and specific dances that celebrate various events related to the history of that group (Hanna 1983, p.47). Needless to say, it would be difficult to categorize all African dances on a rigid classification system due to the sheer number of ethnic groups. Instead, dance may be viewed as a mirror of the culture of the different peoples of Africa.

Dance as a ritual ceremony and occasion is characteristic of most societies in sub-Sahara Africa (Laude, 1978, p. 13). Pearl Primus notes that dance rituals in Africa express the very heartbeat of communal living and is an accurate mirror of the psychology of the people (Primus, 1946, p.15).

> The true African dance is basic in subject matter: birth, death, puberty rites, marriage, hailing a new chief, discovering evil spirits, detecting criminals, praying for rain, sun, strong children, good harvest, good hunting, victory in warfare, success in love, revenge, protection of the gods, honoring the ancestors, and play ... (p.15).

During ceremonial occasions, and also when contemporary African dance ritual is performed, the role of the drummer is of fundamental importance. Drumming is one of the most honorable professions in traditional African society (p. 15). The drummer can be given as much esteem as the griot for his knowledge and repute. Accordingly, "he is at once a historian, a courtier, a creative artist in sound, and an entertainer of the highest caliber" (Opoku & Bell, 1965, p. 25).

To emphasize the importance of the drum, the drummer is usually placed in the center of the circle (Gorer, 1972, p. 23). Although the drummer may initiate the dance, there are also times when the dancer tries to impose his rhythm on the drummer, who in turn competes to regain control. Sometimes dancers wear beads and bracelets to act as accompaniments when they move in rhythm to the drums. This creates an intricate interplay between the dancer and drummer and adds to the variety, quality and spontaneity of the dance which the audience enjoys. In fact, spectators who are moved by the dancing and drumming feel a need and right to participate.

This practice reinforces the integrative aspect of dance in Africa, incorporating other art forms such as drama, oral poetry, and music, including the choral ensemble. From a cultural viewpoint, the resulting rich and splendid ceremony composed of dancers, musicians, poetry, costumes and masks serves to give the community a replica of itself in the natural environment (Opoku & Bell, 1965, p.1). The integrative aspect of dance is exemplified at the Sigi Festival held by the Dogon. The Dogon people of Mali are known for their striking geometric masks. They hold mask dances to console the dead for their loss and to accustom them to their new status (Pern, 1982, pp. 94-95). At the Sigi or Third World Festival, which the Dogon hold every sixty years to celebrate those who live, their oral poetry is recited. These ceremonies are considered to be significant landmarks in the sequence of days, contrasting with the monotonous routine of daily occupations. Time takes on an almost mystical meaning during these occasions (Laude, 1978, pp. 15-16).

When a ceremonial dance is described as an historical event as is the case with the Dogan in Mali, the performance space must be explained because of its influence on the dancers. The ceremony occurs in a set aside space in the main square of the village where daily life can be observed (Huet, 1978, p. 16). In this instance, the design of the circle in dancing patterns is of tremendous choreographic importance. The symbol of the circle is primordial because it represents the image of the infinite structure of the family and village (Turenne, 1985, p. 33). Even when contemporary African dance ritual is performed in the concert hall where the audience has the opportunity to observe distinct dance styles, the circle sometimes manages to retain a high profile.

Aesthetics of African Dance

On the whole, the style of dancing in Africa is dynamic and demands stamina as well as economy of movement. For instance, in Africa the dance expresses the volume or mass, "so that when a movement comes to a rest, we observe a path created by a whirlwind, strong, virile, and powerful" (Opoku & Bell, 1965, p. 1). Each society emphasizes different parts of the body such as the eyes, hands, feet, neck, shoulders, belly, ribs and toes (Warren, 1972, p. 26).

African dance also involves repetition with an emphasis on the earth. This emphasis on repetition reveals that the community is attempting to express the perceived stability of its environment. That the majority of the dances are focused into the earth emphasizes its importance because men and women till the soil to survive and at the time of death, their remains are laid there to rest. Dancing in the Orient also relishes the centrality of gravity and the earth (Clarke & Crisp, 1981, p. 67). In contrast the idea of ballet is to defy gravity. The type and style of African dance are affected by the geography and the natural habitat of the people (Turenne, 1985, p. 33). Some of the territories along the western coast can be distinguished by the undulations of their movements. This brings recollections of the sea which is a prominent force in their lives. In territories where agriculture is practiced, the inhabitants often use their feet when dancing. The feet are anchored on the soil while the arms move toward the earth (Turenne, 1985, p. 33).

African dances can also be mimetic (Gorer, 1972, p. 24) drawing from nature. Men viewed animals and the environment itself with admiration and respect. For example, warriors made dances that would reflect their inward thoughts and outward reactions when confronted by the enemy. Dances of this nature were made to imbue the warrior with the courage and strength to face the challenge that lay ahead (p. 24). In this particular instance, African dance shares some features with native American dances. Just as the colonialists forbade many dances, including the war dance, the United States government forbade the war dance of the native Americans (Clarke & Crisp, 1981, p.21).[2]

Although some dances appealed to specific groups like the warriors, the young and old alike dance in Africa. It is not uncommon to observe 8-16 individuals of the same age and sex dancing in unison (Gorer, 1972, p. 23). Children are taught the critical awareness of body aesthetics, and how to express a wide variety of emotions like anger, grief, sadness, love, and hatred through dance with the accompaniment of songs and drums (Thompson, 1974, p. 1; Opoku & Bell, 1965, p.1). Moreover, from infancy to adulthood the young are taught the spiritual or secular significance of a dance, and so form an acute dance consciousness that is retained throughout life.

Dance and Religion in Africa and the "New World"

To appreciate the religious aspects of African dance, it is necessary to comprehend the role of religious practices, such as ancestor worship and ritual, primary components of African dance. Ritual in religious practice is primarily carried out through song, story and dance, then resulting in possession (Emery, 1972, p. 49; Warren, 1972, p. 6).

Slavery in the "New World" provides a powerful example of the transcultural influence of African ritual dance. The slave population included Ashanti, Congolese, Dahomean, Ibo, Koromantin, Yoruban and other groups primarily from West Africa. They brought many aspects of African culture with them to the "New World," including the Voodoo rites and their accompanying dance from Benin, formerly called Dahomey (Emery, 1972, p. 49). The dehumanizing act of enslavement which sought to de-Africanize these people could have resulted in the complete loss of respect for their culture and identity. How a distinctive African artistic form such as dance emerged is miraculous when one considers the magnitude of the linguistic, cultural and physical adjustments the enslaved Africans had to make to survive and insure their identity in the "New World."

To convert the enslaved Africans to Christianity meant that they would have to be treated with some remnants of humanity, but Christianity forced Africans to deny many aspects of their heritage, such as polygamy, ancestor worship and dancing. Despite these obstacles, even in the more restricted Protestant churches of North America, the dances of Africans were revealed in shouting ceremonies in church (Emery, 1972, p. 120; Primus, 1946, p. 387). On a parallel note, Geoffrey Gorer notes that the women in the "Church of the Holy Spirit" performed a dance strikingly similar to the m'deup and spoke "in tongue" afterwards (Gorer, 1972, p. 27). The m'Deup was a trance dance most commonly performed by women in Senegal. Some groups in Senegal, like the Wolof, had come to accept some aspects of Western culture as early as the 19th century; nevertheless, the Wolof had been converted to Mohammedism for many generations (Gailey, 1989, pp. 552-553).[3]

In contrast to the Protestant church in North America, the more liberalized and less disciplined Catholic Church in South America permitted the slaves to retain many of their Africanisms which affected their dances (Emery, 1972, p. 15-16; Blassingame, 1979, pp. 47-48). The people combined aspects of Christian and African religions as they danced. Within the three main divisions of the Haitian Vodun, thousands of Loas exist, because each family could incorporate its dead ancestor into the form of a Loa in a manner similar to which Catholic saints were canonized (Emery, 1972. p. 58).

Voodoo is still practiced in New Orleans as well as in the West Indies. In most instances only those who have been initiated can participate in the voodoo ceremony and possession is the aim of drumming and dancing (Emery, 1972, pp. 49-51). Voodoo ceremonies are not merely pastimes, nor are they based on "black magic" or superstition. These ceremonies are times of intense physical, emotional, and spiritual outpouring which enable the worshippers to establish contact with the ancestors and a higher being. The anthropologist-dancer Katherine Dunham who studied and participated in voodoo rituals in Haiti eloquently writes

> There is something in the dance of religious ecstasy that has always made me feel that through this experience man might come into his own, be freed of inferiority and guilt in face of whatever might be his divinity (Emery, 1972, p.58).

Shango, a religion originating in southwestern Nigeria, is closely related to Voodoo. Dances to Shango, the Yoruban God of thunder and lightning, are found in those areas of the "New World" where Yoruban religions have remained intact like Brazil, Cuba, and Trinidad (Emery, 1972, pp. 60-61; Thompson, 1974, p. 191). The main object is still to induce possession. Fernando Ortiz, an expert of Afro-Cuban music, dance and religion, states that dances to Shango among other gods "'in which phallic pride is exalted and movement to onanism and sexual copulation are imitated, are nothing more than survivors of ancient magic dances to bring rain and fertility to the land'" (p. 70). Though Africans did not acquaint sex with sin, these dances were characterized as sinful by the early missionaries because of their limited knowledge of the customs and heritage of the Africans.

Contemporary Cross-Cultural Aspects of African Dance

Traditional African dance is commonly passed down from one generation to the next within a group for religious, social and/or ceremonial purposes (Asante, 1985, p. 402). However, in some instances, modernization and change have helped to spark creativity in some traditional dances which have become more secularized. One of the most popular contemporary dances in West Africa is the highlife (Hanna, 1976, p.164). The highlife comes from Ghana and has its origins in the funeral dance known as the adawa performed by the people there (Spencer, 1945, p. 109). Its graceful movements mimic that of an antelope from which the dance got its name (Opoku & Bell, 1965, p. 38). The highlife combines Western ballroom dancing, which was learned from the British, with styles and movements of indigenous secular African dances (Hanna, 1976, p. 165).

It is virtually inconceivable to speak of the highlife dance without noting the considerably rich highlife music. Highlife music originated in Ghana and Sierra Leone and is one of the most popular and potent forms of music in Africa (Graham, 1988, p. 76). Ronnie Graham writes "highlife can be considered a fusion of indigenous dance rhythms and melodies and western influences including regimental music, sea shanties and church hymns, which first emerged in the coastal towns of Ghana in the early years of the twentieth century" (p. 76). Some early instruments include the harmonica, guitar and accordion. Some of the more popular imported instruments are the jazz and Latin drum, saxophone, trumpet, trombone, bass and vibe (Hanna, 1976. p. 166). Though some highlife numbers are instrumentals, most of them include vocals in vernacular, pidgin, English or English sung by male voices; nonetheless, females also sing in highlife bands. Today it is still possible to observe people dancing the highlife in nightclubs and at bars in West Africa (See Hanna, 1976, p. 164).

The concept of dance fusion or the blending of seemingly distinct dance styles (African, modern and ballet or any derivative of the three) is on the increase in the dance world. According to Jean Laude, contemporary artistic movements in the West are now striving to establish connections to ritual celebration where art is not distinguished from life, to bring a deeper communication between mankind and the universe (Huet, 1978, p. 19). Africa is bound to be affected by these changes because of the role that the arts play in this society even though such changes may provoke some criticism and controversy.

In 1977 Maurice Bejart, choreographer and artistic director, helped to establish the school Mudra-Afrique in Dakar on the premise that dance could be used to connect distinctly different cultures (Acogny, 1980, p. 86). Initially, Belart was supported by UNESCO and the Calouste Gulbenkien Foundation as well as by the former President Leopold Sedar Senghor of Senegal, though in other circles Bejart's actions were interpreted as a form of cultural imperialism. From a creative and artistic viewpoint, a movement of this nature can serve to make dance an even richer and fuller mode of expression. The blending of elements from distinctive individual cultures in areas like dance-art can be seen as the beginning of an attempt to fashion a universal culture. However, a careful attempt must be made to preserve the distinctive elements of African dance and its culture in this process.

In an amazing feat, a distinctive community of African-Americans who live in the Sea Islands have managed to retain Africanisms in their speech and dance (Twining, 1985, p. 463). These islands are virtually isolated off the coasts of South Carolina and Georgia and extend almost 400 miles from the southern border of North Carolina to the northern border of Florida. According to one theory, this group of people are the descendants of slaves from Angola; thus Gullah is a term sometimes used to denote these people as well as their language, although Geechee is the word most frequently used to describe this population of approximately 250,000 African-Americans (Burros, 1988, p. C. 1.). Their language, which sounds distinctly West Indian, is essentially a mixture of African languages and English. Since dance shapes the values and socio-political vision of a community, there should be a movement to preserve the dance of the Gullahs as their isolation ends.

African Dance—The Political Context

Dance can be viewed as political. Allen Cloves suggests that creative approaches traditionally confined to artistic expression must be admitted into our daily activities whether they are economic, social or political (Cloves, 1988, p. 63). Political dance is dance that expresses a political conviction that is guided by ideological content, style, meaning, symbol and imagery. Political dance can also be nationalistic or incorporate radical political views. Moreover, political dance can make a statement about society or suggest the reallocation of goods or the authoritative values of a society.

Throughout time, dance has been used to heighten political awareness and social consciousness. Some African-American choreographers have used dance as a medium of political and social protest. "Strange Fruit," choreographed by Pearl Primus, is a dramatic and highly symbolic protest against lynching, which increased at an alarming rate following World War I. Donald McKayle's "Games" (1951) is a powerful testimonial to games that children play as they come in conflict with law and authority, symbolized by the police. Further, Urban Bush Women has produced a number of politically charged dances. One piece shows the dilemma of a Black woman who in vain attempts to hail a taxi in New York City. This piece invites the question—how does sex, race, class, status and politics come to affect perceptions of power and powerlessness in urban centers? From an African context, the Boot Dance of the gold miners in South Africa is a testament of the struggle these men face on a daily basis under the exploitative apartheid policy. Processes of rhythm, time and assertion of movements are vital to this dance.

During the nationalist period, educated Africans used dance to foster the growth of "traditional" consciousness and to encourage political unity (Hanna, 1977, p. 126).[4] When independence came, Africans revitalized some traditional dances and formed dance companies such as Les Ballet Africaines in Guinea and the National Dance Company of Senegal whose members could be used to increase national identity while serving as cultural ambassadors abroad. Nevertheless, for an African dance company selecting a title such as Les Ballet . . . " may be a misnomer, which is not to say that an African dance cannot be a ballet.[5] In this example, the term ballet robs the dance of its original political content since ballet is primarily associated with the West, the territory of the former colonizers who had just been jettisoned.

A closer examination reveals that nationalistic themes are also prominent in the highlife. Judith L. Hanna writes "whereas in the traditional context, people were concerned only with their local areas, independence has stimulated some Africans to attempt to submerge their differences in favor of the nation, the focal point of the loyalty" (Hanna, 1976, p. 169). The impact and meaning of political dance are immense. Since African dance comes in a variety of styles and has a political function, it would be useful to observe whether dances performed by the National Dance Company of Zimbabwe, for example, could be utilized to diffuse ethnic tensions between the Shona and Ndebele populations in the post-independence era.

African Dance—The International Component

A nationalist vision of dance can coexist within an international framework and can serve to enhance intercultural relations. Two components of intercultural relations are interhuman awareness and cross-cultural communications. Dance should be used to enhance this symbiotic relationship. The dances of Africa are relevant from an interhuman perspective. As we begin to penetrate the superficial boundaries between different cultures, and look below the surface, some basic similarities as well as differences emerge, such as the function of dance in human society. In Africa, each dance has its own music, movement and costumes, but most fundamental of all, each dance has a function and motivation that is understood by members of that community (Warren, 1972, p. 2).

Some longstanding factors which have weakened the strength of this assertion are ethnocentrism and puritanism (Hanna, 1980, p. 33). The early missionaries viewed the dances of Africa as licentious, savage, and heathenistic. Further, research on this subject has been problematic since when European scholars wrote about African art, dance and culture, they studied these subjects from a purely religious and sociological perspective while neglecting the fact that history, even when it is in the form of choreography, is fundamental to a critical study of this magnitude (Laude, 1978, p. 11).

It is essential to approach African dance from an unbiased cultural and artistic perspective to know and understand the function of dance in African society. The practical experiences and intellectual contributions of Africans should be given foremost consideration since they can speak of the roots of this art. Moreover, teaching and research modes should accentuate the connections between the history of the dance and the values of the people to truly serve as adequate resource tools in the expression of a cultural phenomenon.

African dance teaches us priceless lessons about other societies when we make cross-cultural comparisons. For example, the issue of men dancing in Africa has significant cross-cultural overtones. The entire concept of men dancing in traditional African society is seen in a totally different context in comparison with the view of men dancing in most countries of the West. The war dances in particular are signs of virility, strength, and the sexual prowess of men because they are characteristics held in high regard in many African societies (Hanna, 1977, p. 111). By contrast, in Western society men who dance are sometimes labeled as effeminate or homosexuals merely because they dance. Only in more recent times have these prejudices and labels been lessened in part due to the popularity of such famous dancers as Gregory Hines and Mikhail Baryshnikov. These men show grace, agility, and strength in their dancing which the warrior dances have traditionally reinforced.

Dance troupes also figure in this analysis since they are often sent abroad to promote international understanding and cooperation through artistic and cultural exchanges (Hanna, 1983, p. 22). In such exchanges, it is sometimes difficult for an audience to be receptive when they must view a performance and the repetition of a specific set of events that seems foreign to them; this could leave the audience at a loss for an understanding or appreciation of the event (p.22). State departments, public relation offices and dance critics, should consider the broad implication of this occurrence.

This factor is especially pertinent with regard to African dance when we stop to consider that most traditional dances are not performance spectacles designed for the proscenium stage. Rather, they are based on religious, historical and social rites that can last anywhere from three minutes to eight days (Gorer, 1972, p. 22). Moreover, Peter Watrous notes that "while purists might argue that taking the ceremonies and music out of context damages them, the staging of the show, with short segments allotted to each group, gives an overview that would be nearly impossible even if one went to Africa" to see the Bantu who recently performed in the United States (Watrous, 1989, p. Y 12). Though African dances have to be abridged when they are performed on the stage, the integrity and essence of the dances must be maintained. If wise choreographic decisions are not implemented, the resulting cross-cultural misunderstanding only leads to the creation of new ethnocentric ideas or xenophobia since the spectators do not have the opportunity to witness traditional African dances in their original cultural context.

Most problems can be eliminated by keeping an open perspective and bearing in mind that there can be multiple levels of interpretation when any given artistic event is performed outside or even within its given cultural framework. This attitude would tend to yield an infinitely more knowledgeable viewing public. Nevertheless, there is an almost inherent universality to thought-provoking art which is magical and penetrates beyond cultural barriers to leave a deep impression on our sensibilities and outlook on matters such as life, love, or even the birth of a child.

Conclusion

One often hears the phrase that dance is an international language. It is only when dance is performed with some prior knowledge of a cultural heritage that we can truly begin to achieve an international language of dance. Nevertheless, we still face dilemmas with regard to international crises and interhuman relations. Understanding the dance is one crucial way of breaking the cultural barriers which have kept people bounded in the past; moreover, it could provide some valuable clues to interpreting events which surround us. These concerted measures will help to destroy the long standing myth of Africa as the dark continent which has been enhanced by colonialist mentality, policies, and stereotyped images perpetuated by the mass media. The challenge that dance and other art forms places before us is to resist the sometimes inherent tendency to stereotype in order to enable a wider variety of intrinsically distinct modes of dance to coexist in our multicultural world. The concept of multiculturalism lends itself to this approach.

The viewpoint that I have stressed on multiculturalism is not without controversy. For instance, John Blacking writes that the notion of multiculturalism in the arts ignores both the individuality and transcendental universality of the arts, and can lead to fatuous divisions of dance styles which implicitly stress the hegemony of particular traditions . . . " whether they are ballet, modern, African, etc. (Blacking,

1984, p. 18). This is a legitimate issue. Nonetheless, every effort must be utilized to eradicate this barrier. If properly used, tools of cultural expression can be utilized to enhance understanding of self, others and the world community.

In this regard the issue of culture and the arts in Africa takes on great urgency. That Africa is culturally and geographically broken is a given (Watrous, 1989, p. Y 12). But there is strength in diversity. If Africa is truly in a cultural crisis, the return to its cultural roots will help reaffirm Africa's existence. Since dance is dynamic, elements can be transferred into a more formal environment such as the political arena.

Dance and cross-cultural awareness are valid links to spanning bridges in international affairs. Since African dance is best expressed in vital living situations, the dances of Africa should be performed before international audiences. Then we would truly be able to achieve a communion in the act and art of dance which would enable us to comment systematically on the political, economic, and social issues of our times. Finally, it would enable us to make the human to human contact which is so vital to the survival of the human race.

Notes

1. With this statement, I do not mean to imply that modern or classical dance cannot reflect the prevailing sentiments of a community nor be educating or enriching. Moreover, in some instances modern, classical, jazz and tap dance do reflect cultural, political and societal as well as anti-societal views.

2. In 1904 the United States Government Regulations of the Indian Office forbade dancing. The repeal of this act did not occur until 1934. For further explanation refer to *The History of Dance* by Mary Clarke and Clement Crisp.

3. Today Senegal has a population of 4 million of which 86% is Muslim. The Wolof are one of the major ethnic groups in Senegal since they comprise 36% of the population. For further explanation of the m'Deup dance, which was performed in Senegal, see Geoffrey Gorer's "The Function of Dance in Primitive Communities" in *The Function of Dance in Human Society*.

4. Nationalistic activity in Africa increased following the Second World War as political parties and institutions grew increasingly commonplace. Ghana was the first colonized African country to gain independence in 1957. With the declaration of the "non" [no] note, Guinea followed suit in 1958. Guinea had rejected the overture proposed by France to become a member of the French community. Within the next few years, a wave of African countries gained independence in the 1960s, but the former Portuguese African colonies did not gain independence until the 1970s.

Recently, Cuba, Angola and South Africa have agreed to withdraw troops from Namibia which has been termed "the last colony" in Africa. Namibia is an international territory on the Atlantic Coast of Southern Africa that has been administered by South Africa since 1920 as declared by the League of Nations. South Africa has continued to administer the territory in defiance of the U.N.

5. In one sense, a ballet can generally be thought of as a dance that tells a story. In this broad context, an African dance can be thought of as a ballet. In the traditional ballet the music, scenery, costume and dance structure the presentation of the story. On the other hand, ballet can also be defined as classic theatrical dancing. In the text of this paper, I have noted that ballet is associated primarily with the West; however, Russia has a rich ballet history and was influenced by the French and Italian schools.

Works Cited

Acogny, Germaine. *Danse Africaine*. Cote d'Ivoire: Les Nouvelles Editions, 1980.

Blacking, John. "Dance as Cultural System and Human Capability: An Anthropological Perspective." In Janet Adshead (ed.), *Dance—A Multicultural Perspective*. Surrey, England: National Resource Centre for Dance, 1984.

Blassingame, John W. *The Slave Community: Plantation Life in the Ante-bellum South*. New York: Oxford University Press, 1979.

Burros, Marian. "Gullah Cooking: Improvising on Cultures Past." *The New York Times*, 4 May, 1988. P. C 1 & C 6.

Clarke, Mary and Clement Crisp. *The History of Dance*. London: Orbis Publishing Limited, 1981.

Clovis, Allen. "Nation Building . . . Cultural Perspective." *The International Review of African American Art* 8.1 (1988): 62-63.

Council of Europe. European Teachers Seminar on "Teaching About Africa South of the Sahara. *(EECS/EGT 85/15)*. Strasbourg, France, 1984.

Drewal, Margaret Thompson and Gloria Jackson, comps. *Sources on African and African-Related Dance*. New York: American Dance Guild, 1973.

Dunham, Katherine. "Excerpts from the Dances of Haiti: Function." *Journal of Black Studies* 15.4 (1985): 357-379.

—. *The Dances of Haiti*. Los Angeles: Center for Afro-American Studies, University of California, Los Angeles, 1983.

Emery, Lynne Fauley. *Black Dance in the United States from 1619-1970*. Palo Alto, CA: National Book Press, 1972.

Emezi, Herbert O. "A Bibliography of African Music and Dances: The Nigerian Experience, 1930-1980." *A Current Bibliography on African Affairs* 18.2 (1985-86): 117.

Franklin, John Hope. *From Slavery to Freedom: A History of Negro Americans*,

3rd ed. Vintage Books, New York: Random House, 1969.

Gailey, Harry A. "Senegal." *Encyclopedia Britannica*. Vol. 24. Danbury, CT: Grolier Incorporated, (1989): 551-559.

Gorer, Geoffrey. *Africa Dances: A Book About West African Negroes*. London: Faber & Faber, 1938.

—. "The Function of Dance in Primitive Communities." In Franzika Boaz (ed.) *The Function of Dance in Human Society*. New York: Dance Horizons, 1972.

Graham, Ronnie. *Stern's Guide to Contemporary African Music*. London: Zwan, 1986.

Green, Doris. "African Oral Tradition Literacy." *Journal of Black Studies* 15.4 (1985): 405-425.

Hanna, Judith Lynne. *The Performer-Audience Connection: Emotion to Metaphor in Dance and Society*. Austin: University of Texas Press, 1983.

—. "African Dance Research: Past, Present, and Future." *African Journal* 11.1-2 (1980): 33-51.

—. *To Dance is Human: A Theory of Nonverbal Communication*. Austin: University of Texas Press, 1979.

—. "African Dance and the Warrior Tradition." *Journal of Asian and African Studies* 22.1-4 (1977): 111-133.

—. "The Highlife: A West African Urban Dance." In Judy Van Zile (ed.), *Dance in Africa, Asia and the Pacific: Selected Readings*. University of Hawaii at Manoa: MSS Information Corporation, 1976.

—. "The Status of African Dance Study." *Africa* 36 (1966): 303-307.

Hazzard-Gordon, Katrina. "African-American Vernacular Dance: Core Culture and Meaning Operatives." *Journal of Black Studies* 15.4 (1985): 427-445.

Highwater, Jamake. *Dance: Rituals of Experience*. Toronto: Methuen, 1985.

Jahn, Jahnheinz. *Muntu: The New African Culture*. Marjorie Green, trans. New York: Grove Press, 1961.

Kealiinohomoku, Joanne. "A Comparative Study of Dance as a Constellation of Motor Behaviors among African and United States Negroes." New York: CORD, Dance Research VII, 1976.

Laude, Jean. "Introduction." In Michael Huet (ed.), *The Dance, Art and Ritual of Africa*. New York: Pantheon Press, 1978.

Merriam, Alan P. *The Arts and Humanities in African Studies*. Bloomington, IN: African Studies Program, 1972.

Opoku, A. M. and Willis Bell. *African Dance: A Ghanian Profile*. Legon: University of Ghana, 1965.

Pearcey, Eilean. "African Dances: A Review of Festac '77, the Second Black and African Festival of Arts and Culture at Lagos and Kadunna, Nigeria." *Dance and Dancers* 28.12 (1977): 22-25.

Pern, Stephen. *Masked Dances of West Africa: The Dogon*. Amsterdam: Time-Life Books, 1982.

Primus, Pearl. "Dance as a Cultural Expression." In C. Lynn and John Nixon (eds.), *The New World Today in Health, Physical Education, and Recreation*.

Englewood Cliff, N.J.: Prentice-Hall, Inc., 1968.
—. "Primitive African Dance." In Anatole Chujoy (ed.), *The Dance Encyclopedia*. New York: A. S. Barnes & Company, 1949.
—. "Living Dance of Africa." *Dance Magazine*, 1946.
Spencer, Frank. "Dancing in West Africa." *The Dancing Times—A Review of Dancing in Its Many Phases*, 1945.
Stone, Ruth. *African Music and Oral Data: A Catalogue of Field Recordings, 1902-1975*. Bloomington: Indiana University Press, 1976.
Twining, Mary Arnold. "Movement and Dance on the Sea Islands." *Journal of Black Studies* 15.4 (1985): 463-479.
Thompson, Robert F. *African Art in Motion: Icon and Act*. Los Angeles: University of California Press, 1974.
Turenne, Michelle. "Danse Africaine." *Reflex, Magazine de la Danse*, 1985.
Warren, Lee. *The Dances of Africa: An Introduction*. Englewood Cliffs, N.Y.: Prentice-Hall, 1972.
Watrous, Peter. "A Continent of Music: Putting Africa on the Stage." *The New York Times*, (12 May 1989): P. Y. 12.
Welsh Asante, Kariamu. "The Jerusarema Dance of Zimbabwe." *Journal of Black Studies* 15.4 (1985): 381-403.

African Influences
in Brazilian Dance

▲▲▲▲▲▲▲▲▲▲▲▲▲▲▲▲

Myriam Evelyse Mariani

Brazil offers a rich field of study in many aspects of society, especially in relation to the African influences. Brazil has received and absorbed African Blacks from the very beginning of its existence as a nation, and they have become a decisive factor in the development of the country. The Portuguese, as a colonizing people, depended in large measure on the Africans' work; as a consequence, millions of Africans were forcibly transported to the New Land, until slavery was abolished in 1888.

The exploitation of the mines, the creation of an agrarian economy, and the conquest of the interior all depended on the collaboration of the Blacks. Therefore, Africans and their descendants were important elements of the Brazilian population since the sixteenth century, and they have contributed greatly to the economic, artistic and cultural development of the nation. (MAP I)

In sculpture, painting, music and dance, the contribution of this population has been of enormous importance. Music and dance were part of the essence of the African's life. The dance (religious, funeral, hunting, war and love) was a deep rooted institution among the African people from whom the slaves for the Brazilian trade were drawn.

Within the field of dance and related disciplines much emphasis has been placed upon the worth of dance as a cultural tradition. The contribution of dance to the cultural context of a specific society has

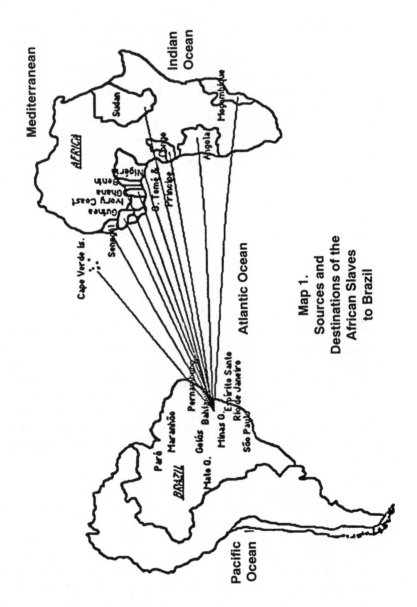

Map 1.
Sources and
Destinations of the
African Slaves
to Brazil

been the subject of much research.

The anthropologist Alan P. Merriam states that: "no work of art should be studied or evaluated in ignorance of its cultural context."[1] For Alan Merriam, "dancing is people communicating with other people; it arises out of the people's thoughts, it is couched in the framework of human culture and society . . . It is, in the broadest sense, human behavior."[2]

However, until recently, few studies have been done on dance in Brazil, especially on the connection of the Samba form, its movement analysis, and its meaning within the cultural context.

Semba is an Angolan word which was adopted in Brazil as Samba during the second half of the nineteenth century. From the senzalas (slave quarters), it spread over the country influencing customs and impregnating them with its sensual rhythm. Acquarone, in his "História da Música Brasileira," comments on the Samba:

"The famous Samba had its origin in the batuque Angola-Congolese. From it came numerous transformations until it was transformed into the Samba of today, so characteristically national."[3]

The Samba was originally a generic term designating the choreography of certain round dances imported from Angola and the Congo. It became not only one of the most characteristic musical forms but also one of the favorite dances of Brazil. Presently, the Samba is the most popular form of dance in Brazil and has reaches its major importance during the annual commemoration of the Carnival, principally in the contest among the Schools of Samba, in Rio de Janeiro. The Schools of Samba are associations which get together, once a year, to portray a theme related to Brazilian folklore and history, through music, song and dance.

Carnival, which combines the people's poetry and fantasy creations with the Schools of Samba, represents an important aspect of Brazilian popular art. Roberto da Matta, a Brazilian anthropologist, in his book "Carnavais, Malandros e Heróis," gives a clear and objective commentary on this social institution:

"The carnival is a time in which routines are transformed into moments of high creativity—a time to be lived intensively throughout songs, dances, laughs, plays, and corporal contacts."[4]

Dance is a vital part of the socio-cultural life. The value of developing studies in this area is in order to understood its origins and relate it to the beliefs, social structures, and life of its people. The knowledge of an ethnic movement vocabulary is more meaningful and further enhanced when accompanied by knowledge of the purposes, occasions, conditions and the social-cultural contexts in which it occurs. This form of art can be looked at as a symbol of human behavior and as a part of a social process which reflects and also influences the behavior. Therefore, it should be considered within the values of the culture in which it originates.

The Brazilian Samba, which is seen during the contests among the Schools of Samba, in Rio de Janeiro, is based upon common experiences and employs a kind of dance activity available to all participants who share the underlying emotion of life on those particular days. The essential dynamics of the Brazilian society are being acted out through the dance and through this form of cultural representation.

In this way, the Samba can be traced from its original form—Semba, which was part of an important aspect of the African slaves' amusement—the dance, as well as a way of preserving the African culture, as a way of understanding the process of change, to the present contests among the Schools of Samba.

The following article presents concise research related to a relevant aspect of the African influence in Brazil: the Samba dance and its significant features such as the legacies, history and the meaning of this form of dance within its cultural context.

Batuque and Samba

The Batuque and the Samba, a legacy of the African slaves who came from Africa to Brazil during the colonization of the country by the Portuguese, are popular dances all over the national territory. They have regional variations, influenced by the African nations because of the influx of slaves. One of the most significant characteristics of these types of dances is the choreography which has a circle formation with a soloist in the center, who is replaced by another dancer after his choreographic exhibition, generally marked by the rhythm of the drums. Alfredo de Sarmento (1880) describes the Black dance thus:

"Form a circle of dancers in the center of an arena, remaining around it the spectators. As soon as the circle is formed, two to three partners jump into the center and the amusement starts. The dance consists of a constant flow of body movement, marked by movement of the feet, head and arms. These movements become quick in accordance with the music which becomes more alive than before and then, one can admire a prodigious shaking/swinging of the hips."[5]

Batuque

The Batuque is one of the oldest dance expressions of Brazil. Alvarenga states that "in Brazil, there was information about it since the XVIII century."[6] Its more probable origin is in similar dances which started in Angola and Congo, from where they were transported to Brazil.

In Brazil, the word Batuque is used as a generic designation for certain types of dances and rhythms accompanied by percussion instruments. According to Cascudo, "the percussion instruments gave baptism to the dance which originated on the African continent, specially by the stamping of the feet, clapping of the hands and the umbigada—an invitation to replace the solo dancer." The Angola-Congolese Batuque had the greatest influence on the Afro-Brazilian rhythms and dances, which were once accompanied by percussion instruments.

The dance, in its most common form, consists of a circle in which musicians and spectators participate, while one or more soloists dance in the center. Violent hip swings and hip movements, foot work, clapping of the hands and snapping of the fingers characterize the dance, which counts as a specific element of the "umbigada" (touching of navels, FIGURE 1) given by the dancers.

In Luanda (Angola) the substitution of the dancers was indicated throughout the "umbigada," which the Africans called "semba." According to Cascudo, "In Angola, there are two forms, the stamping of the foot in front of the person chosen and the umbigad (semba) . . . In Congo, the invitation is made with the stamping of the feet or a quick greeting."[7] It was, in general, through the touching of the belly (navel) on another person that the dancer chose who would substitute for him.

The Batuque may or may not be accompanied by songs, but it is always sustained by a group of percussion instruments which constitute the Batuque. Georg Wilhelm Freireyss describes a trip he took in Minas Gerais in 1814-1815 in which he had the opportunity to watch a Batuque:

"Among the dances, the Brazilian batuque deserves to be mentioned. The dancers form a circle . . . the center dancer moves advances, and touches with the belly another person's belly in the

Fig. 1. Batuque/Umbigida

circle, from the opposite sex. In the beginning, the music compass is slow but it keeps increasing and then, the center dancer is replaced each time he gives the umbigada."[8]

The Batuque can be found not only as a circle dance, but also as a dance of two columns facing each other and consisting exclusively of the act of "umbigada." The dance is performed with a column of males close to the instruments which are laid on the floor and in front there is the column of women. They are separated by a space in which they dance with the action of "umbigada" (touching navel to navel). When the batuqueiro (the male who dances the Batuque) faces his female partner, between one umbigada and another, he starts to sway his body, kneel, spin always within the rhythm of the tambu (fundamental instrument of the Batuque, a kind of drum). These movements are called "jongar." The batuqueiro doesn't keep dancing with the same partner. After three "umbigadas," he changes to another female.

According to the poet Tomás Antonio Gonzaga, the Batuque was not done in society. "Until before 1780, that kind of dance only could be performed in the huts of the common people, the Black women . . . stamping their bare feet on the floor."[9] The Black woman was an indication of inferior social condition. Bare feet were also an indication of inferior social conditions, at that time, it was prohibited for Blacks to wear shoes.

During the nineteenth century, the Batuque of the Blacks began to be persecuted. After 1814 there were some legal texts which prohibited it: "Brincadeira de negro torna-se fato social perigoso" ("Black game became a dangerous social fact").[10]

The Church abominated some dances including the Batuque because it was sensual, and said to be linked to prostitution in the slave quarters. It was considered to be a ritual dance of procreation because of the umbigada action.

Despite their slave condition, the Africans discovered a way of keeping their Batuque. The Catholic church demanded respect for Sundays as a holy day. The Blacks, though, founded the Fraternity of Our Lady of Rosary, as a symbolic solidarity. This was their saint, the black one, godmother and protector, and in this way nobody could impede or stop them.

By the beginning of the nineteenth century, the Batuque became very popular among several social classes, including the White families. Lindley wrote: "The minuet and the popular dances are known and practiced only in the more elevated classes; but this is the national dance, of all the classes. When they lay their formalism aside, they give themselves to the interest and delight which it incites."[11]

According to Henry Koster, he saw a dance of the free slaves, in Pernambuco, by the beginning of the nineteenth century.

> . . . there was a circle with a player, who started to play favorite songs, with repetitions of the refrains, and frequently, one of the verses was improvised. The dance was done in the center of the circle, by a man, which would do sensual movements while choosing a partner, who would move towards the male direction, also with provocative body movements.[12]

Some modifications were made because it was not only the enslaved Blacks who danced it but the free Black people who were increasing in number within the other classes of society. The Batuque became less ostensive with the mixing of customs, forcing the Blacks to use new strategies in the preservation and continuity of their cultural manifestations. The Batuques were changing, incorporating popular commemorations of white origin and adapting to urban life. The African music and dance were suffering a process of transformation, losing certain elements and acquiring others, in function of the social environment. In this way, since the second half of the nineteenth century, the "Modinha," the "Maxixe," the "Lundu" and the "Samba," started to appear. (See Definition of Terms.)

Samba

At the end of the nineteenth century, the popular dances known as Batuques started to be known as the Samba. Several forms of the Samba were born in Brazil as a direct result of the cultural contact between the enslaved Blacks and the free men in the past, and among people of all social conditions in the present. The Samba came with the slaves from Africa (Congo and Angola) to Brazil and, during the centuries, the Africans left a heritage to their descendants in the various forms of Batuque, still recognized, but also mixed with other dances with which they had contact.

The word Samba is probably of Angolan origin, and it is often associated with specific types of body movement. For the groups from Angola, Kusamba means to skip, gambol, expressing overwhelming feelings of joy. The Brazilian term Samba can be linked with another word, semba, found in Kimbandu, Ngangela and other Angolan languages, and meaning pelvic movements that were often qualified as obscene by external observers. Semba also refers to a belly bounce, a dance tradition from the eastern hinterland of Luanda, which lived on in Brazil under the famous name "umbigada." The dance determined the verb sambar, dançar as well as the word sambista, he who sings or dances the Samba. According to Kubik: "Some tests I made with Bahian musician friends in 1975 have confirmed that the Brazilian nasal pronunciation of the term samba constitutes the most likely Portuguese phonetic adaptation of the Angolan word semba."[13]

In this way, the term samba originated from semba, African name for the characteristic "umbigada" (of the Batuque) and it became common during the second half of the nineteenth century.

Some characteristics of these dances of African influence are:
- accompanied by clapping of hands;
- percussion instruments; rhythmically rich music;
- improvisation;
- large circles of men and women;
- when in the center of the circle, the soloist performs movements of great agility and rhythm;
- umbigada (was usually performed).

The general sense of the Batuque, in Africa, was to dance with the sound of the "tambores" (drums) and to pass the chance to dance to another, with the "umbigada." According to Carneiro, three kinds of Batuque/Samba can be identified in Brazil, which were combined with each other and with other popular and social dances, giving birth to a great variety of dances related to it.[14]

Dance of umbigada: (in Luanda region) circle formed by dancers, having at its center a Black male or female who after executing several steps, will give an umbigada (semba) to the chosen person who substitutes for him/her in the center of the circle.

Pair Dance: this kind of Batuque is peculiar to Congo and Angola. Forming a circle, pairs jump to the center of it and start to dance movements of the hips, head, feet and arms.

Circle dance: always is a circle formation. Inside it are the players of percussion instruments. The dance is always the same, varying only by being quicker or slower according to the rhythm.

Besides these kinds of Batuque/Samba, there is also another variation, which is done in lines:

Line dance: some of the kinds of line dances are the Cordao (Pernambuco), Em Fileira (Alagoas), Samba de Lenço (São Paulo), Batuque (SP). In the Samba de Lenço, there are two lines facing each other. One of the dancers goes to the opposite line and waves a handkerchief at the person he/she wants to dance.

The Samba acquired supplementary denomination which refers to certain details of the choreography. Lundu and Baiano are old forms of "umbigada" dance.

Lundu: is an African song and dance of Angolan origin, brought to Brazil by the Bantu. It came under condemnation by church authorities because of its lascivious character and umbigada, the choreographic element on which an invitation to the dance is represented by the touching of navels by the couple. It was the first African dance done by the rich classes of Brazilian society during the eighteenth century and it was danced until the end of the nineteenth century, when it declined in popularity. The dance is described by L.H. Azevedo thus, "In the center of a circle of spectators, a soloist couple develops the dance, which includes stamping of the feet, marked movements of the hips and the umbigada."[15]

The *Baiano* succeeded the Lundu in the northeast. The Baiano is both a dance and music. Not only the umbigada is used but also the snapping of fingers and shaking of handkerchiefs in front of the chosen person as an invitation to the dance. The Samba Baiano received supplementary denominations which come from the details of choreographic execution. The Samba de Chave, in which the text refers to a lost key, the soloist pretends to find it in the center of the circle and is replaced by whoever finds it. One characteristic of the Samba Baiano is that the dance is done in a contest form to see who executes better what the texts ask from the soloists: who finds the key better, who moves the hips better. In time, the Samba started to suffer certain modifications, such as the absence of the umbigada. In the choreographic characteristics of a soloist in the circle, there was a new detail— the soloists danced with the arms up.[16]

Three areas of Batuque's forms[17]:

1.Coco Zone (Ceara, Rio Grande do Norte, Paraiba, Pernambuco, Alagoas).

2.Samba Zone (Maranhão, Bahia, Rio de Janeiro, São Paulo, Minas Gerais).

3.Jongo Zone (Rio, São Paulo, Minas Gerais, Goias).

The variety of the Batuque found in Brazil shows a constancy in form: Dance of Umbigada, Dance in Pairs, Dance in Circle and Dance in Lines. For Carneiro[18] and Cascudo[19] some of the forms of Samba (present and past) can be classified as:

Variety	Umbigada	Kind of dance
Lundu (Para) 18th & 19th cent.	x	UD/CD
Baiano (Northeast) 1908	x	PD
Coco		
Bambelo (Rio G. do Norte)	x	UD
Troca de Parelha (Pernambuco)	x	PD
Cordao (Pernambuco)	-	LD
Roda (Pernambuco)	x	UD/CD
De Pares (Pernambuco)	x	PD
Coco (Ceara/Paraiba)	-	PD
Milindo (Ceara)	-	PD
Solto (Alagoas)	x	PD
Trocado or Troca de Parelha (Al)	-	PD
De Farelha (Alagoas)	-	PD/CD
Em Fileira (Alagoas)	-	LD
De Farelha Trocada or De Visita (Alagoas/1917)	x	PD
Virado (Alagoas)	x	UD/CD
Samba		
Tambor de Crioulo (Maranhao)	x	CD
Samba de Roda (Bahia/Sao Paulo)	x	UD/CD
Bate-bau (Bahia)	x	UD
Samba (Rio/Sao P./Ceara/Par./Per.)	x	UD/CD
Partido Alto (Rio de Janeiro)	x	UD/CD
Samba de Road (Sao Paulo)	-	UD/CD
Samba Rural (Sao Paulo)	-	CD
Samba de Lenço (Sao Paulo)	x	LD/PD
Batuque (Sao Paulo	x	LD
Jongo		
Caxambu (Rio de Jan./Sao Paulo)	-	CD
Jongo (Rio de Janeiro)	x	PD/CD

CD = Circle Dance; LD = Line Dance; PD = Pair Dance
UD = Umbigada Dance; x = Presence of umbigada (simulated or effective); - = Absence of umbigada

The national Samba was danced with the partners together, in a regular rhythm, far from the African model, the old Batuque, which was danced in a circle, in a collective sway, until the soloist was called to the center of the circle. Motional emphasis was on the pelvis, buttocks, especially pelvis thrusts or circular pelvic movements, which are an indicative of a Congo/Angola background.

The Samba is also described in "Encyclopedia of Latin America" as:

"A generic term designating, along with the batuque, the choreography of certain round dances imported from Angola and the Congo. A characteristic element of the folk samba and of all Afro-Brazilian dances is the "umbigada," a sort of invitation to the dance, manifested by the touching of the couple's navels . . . Singing always accompanies the dancing. Mostly in binary rhythm, the Samba presents a highly syncopated accompaniment, exclusively by percussion instruments."[20]

Carnival/Schools of Samba

The School of Samba is a popular association which has as its main goal to participate, as a group, in Carnival, on Sunday and Monday before Ash Wednesday. It is a manifestation of a Brazilian culture, expressed by a group of people, through song and dance, with the description of a plot (enredo), legends and traditions. Some of the main Schools of Samba in Rio de Janeiro are: MANGUEIRA, PORTELA, BEIJA FLOR, ACADEMICOS DO SALGUEIRO, MOCIDADE INDE-PENDENTE DE PADRE MIGUEL, IMPERIO SERRANO, UNIDOS DE VILA ISABEL.

The Samba, of all the Brazilian dances, is the best known. It has several forms and types in the urban and social pictures. In Rio de Janeiro, the Samba existed in its original form as a circle dance, with soloists, among the people of the "morros" (slums). From the "Samba de Morro" was born the "Carioca Urban Samba," which had its appearance in the second decade of the twentieth century. The "Samba de Morro" is a circle dance, with lots of varieties in its rhythm and poor melodies; the "Samba Urbano" is a hall dance, done with partners, with diverse themes such as: love, life in the slums, and historical events.

With the coming of Carnival, the Samba de Morro went to the city, and was presented in the Ranchos, Cordoes and Blocos. The "Cordoes" were initially, masked groups, presenting elements with diverse costumes, following a master, who would give them directions with the use of a whistle. The "ranchos" were a form of more complete "Cordhoes," which included women. The steps and choreography were directed by a Master of Hall. The dances were accompanied by song. They received characteristics from the Pastoris and Ternos (Northeast) such as the form of procession, as well as from the Cucumbis, which were musical processions at Christmas and Epiphany, and also from the Cordoes. The "Blocos" were a mixture of the "Cordao" and "Rancho" with a critical theme.

Life was changing and the new generation was more inclined to favor a different flow of rhythm. The movement was ripe for the Samba to appear and to develop, and it displaced the Choros and the Ranchos. The Carnival marches increased in vivacity, and adapted themselves to the new fashions and tastes. After 1930, an extensive commercialization of music began to flourish. ·

After the Rancho-escolas, the Schools of Samba appeared and, in this way, their formation was born slowly in the 20s. The first School of Samba, DEIXA FALAR, was founded in 1928. After 1930, several "Blocos" adopted the name of School of Samba, but preserved some aspects which were incorporated in the former recreational organization. They maintained a great deal of the old characteristics such as Orchestra, Master of Hall, Flag Bearer, but also penetrated into white urban space. Therefore, the Carnival in Brazil, one of the most interesting phenomena of the Africanization of folklore, started to incorporate a parade with floats (allegoric cars), masks, costumes and dances.

Artur Ramos defined the Carnival in Rio de Janeiro as the "frontier between the Black culture, frontier without precise limits, where the institutions and cultures are joined."[21] Renato de Almeida describes the event: "the dance is done in the streets, each person performs it the way they want, creating steps, in a lasting longing creative capacity."[22] The steps were born with the people and were called "Samba de Rua," because it was born on the streets and squares, during the Carnival.

No other festivity produces so much unity. Blacks, Whites, rich and poor have, during Carnival time, the same objective and they stay together. The groups parade dancing, giving a vision of movement and dynamism, with each participant performing a different gesture than the other, but in relation to the Samba steps. Therefore, there is also an emphasis on innovations and personal interpretation of each gesture, which will become a dance, with moments of high creativity. The participants move the entire body, free form the social routine, and reveal the body through unrestricted gestures: the arms are open and high, demonstrating an expression of freedom and happiness. They say something with the feet when dancing the Samba and singing the Samba-enredo, the Samba music composed for the School's theme of that year.

Roberto da Matta reports: "in the Schools of Samba, there is an individual and collective meeting of people of different classes, positions, ethnicities, professions, neighborhoods and nationalities."[23]

Nowadays, the Escola de Samba represents the spirit of the Brazilian people. It is a festival, a rite, an entertainment, a street opera. The spectacle is an artistic and a folklore manifestation of a new generation. Its origin was once influenced by the Black groups, and their soul was transferred into art, a kind of art which contains the echo of the African laugh, drum sounds and dances, always present within the Brazilians.

Definition of Terms

This section encompasses the definitions of some African influences, places and dances of the Brazilian culture.

Bantus: Speakers of the Bantu language (Angola, Congo, Mozambique).

Batuque: A ritual dance of procreation of Angolan and Congoles origin. Its principal characteristic is the "umbigada" (navel to navel/semba).

Blocos: Carnival groups, scattered bands of revelers preceding or following a few players of percussion instruments (Gardel, 1967:10).

Cambinda cults: Folkloric dance in which the dancers move in a squat position (Ferreira, 1975:262).

Choros: Laments related to the melancholy character of the music. The term Choro is applied to the music performed and also to the performing group; with improvised performances and with Afro-American elements. Great popularity in the sixth and seventh decade of the nineteenth century. In the nineteenth century, the term was applied to various instrumental ensembles—usually flute, clarinet, trombone, cavaquinho (small Brazilian guitar), and some percussion instruments. When a singer participated as a soloist, the music was called seresta; when the improvisation was entirely instrumental, it was called Choro (Appleby, 1983:70-73).

Cordoes: Carnival groups which go out together singing and dancing (Ferreira, 1975:385). They are preceded by a standard bearer (Gardel, 1967:10).

Cucumbis: Musical procession on the occasions of Christmas and Epiphany (Ferreira, 1975:408).

Embigada: Same as umbigada—the act of touching navel to navel.

Jongo: A circle formation dance from Africa, in which the umbigada is performed by a soloist who dances inside the circle which moves counterclockwise.

Marchas carnavalescas: Carnival marches. Genre of popular urban music of which choreography consists of a rhythmic walk in circles (Ferreira, 1975: 893).

Minuet: French dance characterized by the nobility and balance of its movements. Ternary compass (Ferreira, 1975:933).

Modinha: One of the forms of popular music during the nineteenth century. Style and musical language for the mature musical expression of sentiments of nativism and nationalism (Appleby, 1983:60). Sentimental aria about love with two themes: one with the sentimental sequence and the other with the refrain. It is a voice of sorrow, lament and nostalgia; a confession of the sad things in life which hurt in the heart. Usually done in binary compass but also found in ternary (Almeida, 1942:642-64).

Pastoris: Dramatic representation with dances, songs and praises, danced in front of the nativity scene, between Christmas and Epiphany, to Commemorate Jesus' birth (Ferreira, 1975:1053).

Rancho carnavalesco: Group of people who dance on the streets and sing in chorus. They sing the most popular songs of the carnival or the characteristic march of the group, usually carrying allegoric standards (Ferreira, 1975: 1197).

Rancho Recreativo: Institution of the Blacks which replaced the Entrudo (p. 106). A group of people, representing several characters, singing and dancing during the popular commemorations of the Christmas cycle (Ferreira, 1975:1197). Groups of masqueraders which include a band and a chorus specializing in the "marcha rancho," which has a markedly slow cadence (Gardel, 1967:33).

Samba: Song dance of African origin (semba), binary compass and syncopated accompaniment. Also, the song which accompanies this dance (Ferreira, 1975:1276).

Samba carioca: This was born from the samba de morro. It is related to the batuque Angola-Congolese.

Samba-enredo: Samba composed specially to be sung during the contest of the schools of samba in the carnival. The words of this samba and the plot of the spectacle in parade have a common theme which is always a patriotic historical (Ferreira, 1975:1276).

Samba de morro: Hill's samba.

Samba rural: Circle formation with a soloist inside; also done with several lines. The women dance with arms up. The "umbigada" is not present in this dance.

Ternos: Also known as congo or congada. It is danced in Recife since 1674 by the Blacks in honor of Saint Benedict and Our Lady of Rosary. *Umbigada:* In the circle dances brought to Brazil by the Black slaves, it is the bumping of navels by the soloist on the person who will replace him (Ferreira, 1975:1435).

Notes

1. Susane Walther, "A Cross Cultural Approach to Dance Criticism," *Dance Research Collage X-Cord* (New York: Congress on Research in Dance, Inc., 1979): 67.
2. Anne Herman, "Ritual in the Celtic World: The Dance of the Ancient Druids," *Dance Research College X-Cord* (New York: Congress on Research in Dance, Inc., 1979): 209.
3. F. Acquarone, *Historia da Music Popular Brasileira* (Rio de Janeiro: Editora Paulo Azevedo Ltda., 1948): 121.
4. Roberto da Matta, *Carnavais, Malandros e Herois. Para una Sociologia do Sistema Brasileiro* (Rio de Janeiro: Zahar Editora, 1978): 87.
5. Luis da Camara Cascudo, *Dicionario do Folclore* (Rio de Janeiro: Instituto Nacional do Livro/MEC, 1962): 760.
6. Oneida Alvarenga, *Musica Popular Brasilena.* Fondo de Cultura Economica (Mexico: Tierra Firme, 1947): 11.
7. Cascudo 760.
8. Cascudo 105.
9. Jose Ramos Tinharão, *Musica Popular e Indios, Negros e Mesticos* (Rio de Janeiro: Editora Vojes Ltda., 1975): 133.
10. Muniz Sodre, *Samba, O Dono do Corpo. Ensaios* (Rio de Janeiro: Editora Codecri, 1979): 126.
11. Tinhorão: 135.
12. Hildegardes Vianna, "Nascimento e Vida do Samba," *Revista Brasileira de Folclore,* 35, Ano II (Rio de Janeiro: Ministerio da Educacao e Cultura, Departmento de Assuntos Culturais/Campanha de Defesa do Folclore Brasileiro, Janeiro, Abril 1973): 50.
13. Gerhard Kubik, *Angolan Traits in Black Music, Games and Dances of Brazil* (Lisboa: Estudos de Antropologia Cultural, __ 10, 1979): 18.
14. Kubik 18.
15. Edson Carneiro, *Samba de Umbigada* (Rio de Janeiro: Conselho Nacional de Folclore/MEC, 1961): 10-12.
16. David P. Appleby, *The Music of Brazil* (Austin, TX: University of Texas

Press, 1983): 60.
17. Alvarenga 114-116.
18. Caneiro 151.
19. Caneiro 33-35.
20. Cascudo 15, 77.
21. *Encyclopedia of Latin America*, (1974): 546.
22. *Enciclopedia Mirador Internacional. Vol. I* (Enciclopedia Britanica do Brasil Publicacoes Ltda., 1976): 207.
23. Maria Amalia Correa Giffoni, *Dancas Folcloricas Brasileiras e Suas Aplicacoes Educatives* (Sao Paulo: Edicao Meloramentos, 1964): 251.
24. Roberto da Matta, *Ensaios de Antropologia Estrutural. O Carnaval como un Rito de Passagem* (Petropolis: Editora Vojes Ltda., 1977): 61.

Works Cited

Acquarone, F. *Historia da Music Popular Brasileira*. Rio de Janeiro: Editora Paulo Azevedo Ltda., 1948.
Almeida, Renato. *Historia da Cultura Brasileira, Vol. I*. Rio de Janeiro: MEC/CFC & Fename, 1973.
—. *Musica e Danças Folcloricas*. Rio de Janeiro: Cadernos de Folclore, No. 4, MEC, 1968.
Alvarenga, Oneida. *Musica Popular Brasilena*. Fondo de Cultura Economica. Mexico: Tierra Firme, 1947.
Alves, Henrique. *Sua Excia. O Samba*. Sao Paulo: Edições Simbolo. Second Edition, 1976.
Appleby, David P. *The Music of Brazil*. Austin, Texas: University of Texas Press, 1983.
Araujo, Ari & Erika Herd. *Expressões da Cultura Popular. As Escolas de Samba do Rio de Janeiro e o Amigo da Madrugada*. Rio de Janeiro: Editora Vozes/SEEC, 1978.
Arnold, Denis. *The New Oxford Companion to Music*. Oxford: Oxford University Press, 1983.
Bastide, Roger. *Estudos Afro-Brasileiros*. São Paulo: Editora Perspectiva, 1973.
Cabral, Sergio. *As Escolas de Samba*. Rio de Janeiro: Editora Fontana Ltda., 1977.
Carneiro, Edson. *Samba de Umbigada*. Rio de Janeiro: Conselho Nacional de Folclore/MEC, 1961.
Cascudo, Luis da Camara. *Dicionario do Folclore*. Rio de Janeiro: Instituto Nacional do Livro/MEC, 1962.
—. *Folclore do Brasil*. Rio de Janeiro: Editora Fundo de Cultura, 1967.
Debret, Jean Baptiste. *Viagem Pitoresca e Historica do Brasil. Tomo I —Volumes I e II*. Belo Horizonte, M.G.: Livraria Itatiaia Editora Ltda., 1978.
Delpar, Helen (ed.). *Encyclopedia of Latin America*. McGraw-Hill, Inc.,1974.
Dreller, Gerald. Afro-Brazilian—An Expression of Popular Culture in

Selected Examples of Bahian Literature. Unpublished doctoral dissertation, University of Illinois-Urbana/Champaign, January 1974.

Ellmerich, Luis. *Historia da Dança*. (Terceira Edição). São Paulo: Ricordi, 1964.

Enciclopedia Mirador Internacional, Vol. I. Enciclopedia Britanica do Brasil Publicações Ltda., 1976.

Ferreira, Aurelio Buarque de Holanda. *Novo Dicionario da Lingua Portuguesa*. Rio de Janeiro: Editora Nova Fronteira, 1975.

Gardel, D. Luis. *Escolas de Samba*. Rio de Janeiro: Livraria Kosmos Editora, 1967.

Gaffney, Floyd. Evolution and Revolution of Afro-Brazilian Dance. *Journal of Popular Culture*. Vol. 13 (1), 1979/1980.

Giffoni, Maria Amalia Correa. *Danças Folcloricas Brasileiras e Suas Aplicações Educativas*. (Segunda edição). São Paulo: Edição Meloramentos, 1964.

Hazzard-Gordon, Katrina. Afro-American Core Culture Social Dance: An Examination of Four Aspects of Meaning. *Dance Research Journal*, 15, No. 2 (Spring), 1983.

Herman, Anne. Ritual in the Celtic World: The Dance of the Ancient Druids. *Dance Research Collage X-CORD*. New York, 1979.

Herskovits, Melville J. *The Myth of the Negro Past*. New York: Harper and Brothers, 1958.

Johnson, Samuel. *Dictionary of the English Language*. London: Gollanez, 1982.

Kubik, Gerhard. *Angolan Traits in Black Music, Games and Dances of Brazil*. Lisboa: Estudos de Antropologia Cultural #10, 1979.

Limeira, Eudinise de Albuquerque. *Comunicação Gestual*. Rio de Janeiro: Editora Rio, 1977.

Lopes, Ney. *O Samba na Realidade . . . A Vitoria da Ascensão Social do Sambista*. Rio de Janeiro: Codecri, 1981.

Matta, Roberto da. *Carnavais, Malandros e Herois. Para una Sociologia do Sistema Brasileiro*. Rio de Janeiro: Zahar Editora, 1978.

—. *Ensaios de Antropologia Estrutural. O Carnaval como un Rito de Passagem*. (Segunda Edição). Petropolis: Editora Vozes Ltda., 1977.

Mauss, Marcel. *Sociologie et Anthropologie*. Paris, France: Presses Universitaires de France, 1960.

Moraes Filho, Mello. *Festas e Tradições Populares do Brasil*. Belo Horizonte, M.G.: Livraria Itatiaia Editora Ltda., 1979.

Motta, Roberto. *Os Afro-Brasileiros*. Recife: Editora Massangana, 1985.

Nascimento, Abdias. *O Quilombismo*. Petropolis, Rio de Janeiro: Editora Vozes Ltda., 1980.

NBC-American Television Network. A Reportage and Coverture of Brazilian Way of Life. February, 1986.

Nettl, Bruno. *Folk and Traditional Music of Western Continents*. Englewood Cliffs, New Jersey: Prentice-Hall, Inc., 1973.

Pierson, Donald. *Negroes in Brazil. A Study of Race Contact at Bahia*. Carbondale: Southern Illinois Press, 1967.

Ramos, Arthur. *Introdução a Antropologia Brasileira Segundo Volume. As Culturas Europeias e os Contactos Raciais e Culturais.* Rio de Janeiro, 1947.
———. *O Folclore Negro do Brasil.* (Segunda Edição). Rio de Janeiro: Livraria Editora Casa do Estudante do Brasil, 1935.
———. *The Negro in Brazil.* Washington, D.C.: The Associated Publishers, Inc., 1951.
Rangel, Lucio. *Sambistas e Chorões.* Editora Paulo de Azevedo Ltda., abril/maio 1962.
Ribeiro, Jose. *Brasil no Folclore.* Rio de Janeiro: Editora Aurora Ltda., 1970.
Rodrigues, Ana Maria. *Samba Negro. Espoliação Branca.* São Paulo: Editora Hucitec, 1984.
Rugendas, Johann Moritz. *Viagem Pitoresca Atraves do Brasil.* (8a edição. Belo Horizonte, M.G.: Livraria Itatiaia Editora Ltda., 1979.
Siqueira, João B. *Origem do Termo Samba.* São Paulo: Ibrasa. Instituição Brasileira de Difusão Cultural S.A., MEC, 1978.
Skidmore, Thomas E., Simon Collier, and Harold Blakemore. *The Cambridge Encyclopedia of Latin America and the Caribbean.* Cambridge, N.Y.: Cambridge University Press, 1985.
Sodre, Muniz. *Samba. O Dono do Corpo. Ensaios.* Rio de Janeiro: Editora Codecri, 1979.
Tinharão, Jose Ramos. *Musica Popular de Indios, Negros e Mestiços.* Rio de Janeiro: Editora Vozes Ltda., 1975.
Tupy, Dulce. *Carnavais de Guerra e Nacionalismo no Samba.* Rio de Janeiro: ASB Artegrafica e Editora Ltda., 1985.
Verger, Pierre. *Noticias da Bahia—1850.* Bahia: Editora Corrupio, 1981.
Vianna, Hildegardes. Nascimento e Vida do Samba. *Revista Brasileira de Folclore, 35,* Ano II. Rio de Janeiro: Ministerio da Educação e Cultura, Departamento de Assuntos Culturais/Campanha de Defesa do Folclore Brasileiro, Janeiro/Abril 1973.
Walther, Susane. A Cross Cultural Approach to Dance Criticism. *Dance Research Collage X-CORD.* New York: Congress on Research in Dance, Inc., 1979.
Warren, Lee. *The Dance of Africa.* New York: Prentice-Hall, Inc., 1972.
Zebila, Lucky. *La Danse Africaine ou L'Intelligence Du Corps.* Paris: Editions L'Harmattan, 1982.

TRADITION TRANSFORMED

Dancing Under the Lash: Sociocultural Disruption, Continuity, and Synthesis

▲▲▲▲▲▲▲▲▲▲▲▲▲▲▲▲

Katrina Hazzard-Gordon

Though a sizeable body of literature on dance has been generated in the past two decades, none of it has focused on the socio-historical context from which African-American secular social dance has emerged. An assessment of at least some of these circumstances would be a contribution as important as that body of literature focusing on the structural and functional aspects of the dance. The primary purpose of this paper is to make a contribution in that direction by looking at the transformation process from African ceremonial to African-American secular social dance, and a brief examination of the specific contexts in which that transformation occurred.

Life under slavery, repressive though it was, allowed some opportunity for community and cultural development. In the hostile environment in which Africans found themselves it seems indeed miraculous that any African customs were able to persist. But as antagonistic to African culture as slavery was, it could not exercise total control over all areas of bondsmen's lives. This "unregulated sociocultural space" which existed in the slave quarter and which Africans created for themselves, provided them with at least some latitude in which certain aspects of African culture could survive.

In addition to opportunity provided by this unregulated socio-cultural space, at least two other factors seem significant for the survival of African-based traditions: one, that the surviving culture prove functional for the practitioners; two, that it be somehow functional and perceived as relatively non-threatening for the slaveocracy. Once the enslaved Africans left the ship and "settled in," they could begin, with the sociocultural material available to them, to forge a new culture through interaction. As a new African became part of the fabric of slave life, acquaintances and group relationships developed. Though the environment of bondage provided little with which African-Americans could create culture, it could not prevent an African-based cultural tradition in dance and other areas from flourishing as Africans continually sought ways to circumvent restriction.

In the early days of the slave regime, the constant and widespread importation of new slaves from Africa and the West Indies served to shore up some of the African cultural decline that was naturally taking place as a result of the slave experience. Even after the international slave trade was outlawed, pirates and smugglers continued bringing small numbers of Africans to America,[1] and this constant, though dwindling, influx of Africans renewed the vitality of African culture among the enslaved. It is quite possible for instance, that newly imported Africans participating in plantation dance forms did exert a re-Africanizing influence on the dance itself.[2] Undoubtedly, much of the plantation dancing must have seemed at least familiar to the newly imported African or West Indian slave.

The conditions of slavery in North America varied somewhat across time and according to region, and the circumstances under which enslaved Africans reproduced and objectified their lives were also somewhat dissimilar. On some plantations they worked in gangs or groups; on others they worked as individuals with task assignments; the work pattern affected the model of culture that emerged. For example, one could surmise fairly accurately that the work song more than likely achieved a fuller development among Africans sharing a gang labor experience.[3] The type of labor they engaged in had significant impact on their daily routine and consequently their cultural existence. Thus, as slave culture and community emerged, it initially took on a regional rather than a national character. Determined largely by the ethnic composition of enslaved Africans in the region, the work routine, and type of labor, the model of culture was different from one region to the next. So just as one cannot speak of a national American culture emerging early in the colonial period, African-American culture had not yet acquired its national character.

Not all Africans were confined to plantation field labor; some were house servants, urban laborers, or the servants of city dwellers. Thus, the social environment in which they found themselves helped shape their emerging culture. The opportunity and format for dancing among skilled urban artisans appears to have differed from that of field laborers. But, whether they grew rice, tobacco, cane, or cotton, served in a household, or worked as an urban artisan, African Americans' efforts to establish independent culture were strictly limited. Whites, for example, attempted to eliminate Africans' access to drums. Such measures were less than entirely successful, but they created an environment in which African Americans found it extremely difficult to make collective assertions of autonomy by retaining African cultural practices. Bondsmen nevertheless developed models of culture that retained much of the African character across generations spanning more than three hundred years, but many of these models were not immediately recognized by whites as having African origins.

During the enslavement period, in which the African was transformed into the African-American, several significant metamorphoses occurred. First and most important for an understanding of African-American dance culture, is the change in the Africans' understanding of sacred and secular. No such clear-cut distinction in the Western sense existed for most of the Africans who arrived on the New World shores. The social and religious community were one and the same, and political leaders as well as human ancestors mediated between the living community and the world of the deities. Unlike the western God, the African ancestral deities each embodied a wide range of seemingly contradictory attributes. The dichotomy of good and evil religious figures as in the West was unknown to these Africans.

The major deities or (orisha) were capable of performing great feats as well as doing great harm to humans and required appeasement in the form of sacrifices and offerings. Since African deities were indeed capable of a wide range of activities including erotic gesture, North American Protestantism would come to define African religious beliefs and practices as sinful, and to strictly forbid traditional African methods of worship. Though numerous bondsmen converted to Christianity, even among them the African religious traditions remained vital. Among African-Americans generally much of African religious style, fervor, format and predisposition in worship persisted in both sacred and secular vestment.

The process of change from African to African-American was protracted, but a clear demarcation emerged between ritual, or sacred, ceremonial dance and the secular dancing which occurred at festivities and parties. We cannot be sure exactly when this delineation appeared, but the processes responsible for its development began in the middle passage. By the time the first generation of Africans were born on these shores the process was probably well established. Although African bondsmen continued to use dance as worship, a new secularized dance eventually made its appearance. By the early eighteenth century the sacred-secular split was fairly well established with respect to dancing.

Both sacred and secular dancing among bondsmen originated in an African worship system which included a wide range of praise methods, including a "party for the gods," or *bembe* as they came to be known in Cuba.[4] Certain religious ceremonies, as they appeared in parts of West Africa, included drumming, drink, food and dance as well as a general atmosphere of festivity. At least three types of bembe were observed among the Lucumi or Cuban Yoruba: "Bembe Lucumi," "Bembe Lucumi Criollo," and "Suncho." Bembe Lucumi was more generally African than the latter two. Its songs were sung in the Yoruba language, its drum rhythms were strictly traditional and were executed on the sacred two-headed bata drum. Bembe lucumi criollo permitted a loosening of tradition, its songs were in a creolized language and its rites were more communal and simpler. The third type, suncho, appears to have been the true "ocha party" or party for the gods. Suncho, unlike the other types of bembe, did not necessarily observe a religious occasion such as an initiation or holy day; bembe suncho appears to have been purely for enjoyment. In fact, religion seems to have been more of a pretext than a motive for this occasion.[5] Although there is no evidence that the bembe ever established itself as an institution among bondsmen in North America, elements of the bembe or Orisha party were probably retained in the form of "the shouts" held both openly and surreptitiously among North American slaves. African religious elements such as musical style, ecstatic behavior, spirit possession, and holy dancing, were observed to have found expression in these shouts. Frederick Law Olmsted leaves us this account:

> On most of the large rice plantations which I have seen in this vicinity, there is a small chapel, which the Negroes use as their prayer house. The owner of one of these told me that, having furnished the prayer-house with seats having a back rail, his Negroes

petitioned him to remove it because it did not leave them room enough to pray. It was explained to me that it is their custom, in social worship, to work themselves up to a great pitch of excitement, in which they yell and cry aloud, and finally shriek and leap up, clapping their hands and dancing, as it is done at heathen festivals. The back rail they found to seriously impede this exercise.[6]

Apparently, American bondsmen did not confine their African based rituals and practices to purely religious occasions. As one commentator noted:

Tonight I have been to a "shout" which seems to me certainly the remains of some old idol worship. The negroes sing a kind of chorus, three standing apart to lead and clap, and then all the others go shuffling round in a circle following one another with not much regularity, turning round occasionally and bending the knees, and stamping so that the whole floor swings. I never saw anything so savage. They call it a religious ceremony, but it seems more like a regular frolic to me.[7]

During numerous African religious ceremonies, particularly those of the Yoruba, music is performed by a liturgical trio of sacred bata drums, okonkolo, itotele and iya. The "three standing apart to lead and clap" mentioned above appear to be an example of adaptation of a traditional West African pattern to a new sociocultural environment, in which the role of the sacred trio is transferred from drum to voice and handclaps.

Though the ceremonial context and the specific uses of movement of each enslaved ethnic group's dances were different, the basic vocabulary of West African movement was strikingly similar across ethnic delineation. As a result, in the new culture creating environment, inter- ethnic assimilation in dance was probably more easily facilitated than in other aspects of African culture, i.e., language. As it came here in the motor muscle memory of the various West African ethnic groups, the dance shared common characteristics which cut across ethnic distinctions. Such common characteristics included segmentation and delineation of various body parts, including hips, torso, head, arms, hands, and legs the use of multiple meter as polyrhythmic sensitivity, angularity, multiple centers of movement, asymmetry as balance, percussive performance, mimetic performance, improvisation, derision dances and call and response. These aesthetic and technical commonalities continued to act as governing principles as dance moved from its sacred ceremonial context to the numerous secularized uses it acquired under slavery.

Structurally the line and the circle were both surviving commonalities which many of the West African ethnic groups shared. In that there are no surviving sacred African-American line dances, it is safe to assert that secularization of the line formation occurred earlier and more thoroughly. Accelerating that process was the fact that the African religious line dances in the plantation context shared a similar line formation with the numerous secular European reels, in which men and women faced each other in lines. The "madison" and the "birdland" of the 1950's, the "bus stop" of the 1970's and the "soul train" line are clear examples of contemporary secular line formations. The circle, on the other hand, has retained a sacred identity well into the twentieth century as the ring shout formation most prominently observed along the South Carolina and Georgia coasts.[8] Historian, Sterling Stuckey, is certainly correct in asserting the primacy of the circle as a significant variable in inter-ethnic African assimilations.[9]

Unlike French or Spanish slavery carried out in the atmosphere of Catholicism with its pantheon of saints, slavery under North American Protestantism did not provide the elaborate collateral structures for religious syncretization as that which occurred in much of Latin America and the Caribbean. Consequently, the African theological background to many customs and practices including dance would disappear though the practice itself, or a reasonable facsimile, would remain. The customs, divorced from their original religious context, would nevertheless persist, eventually relegated by the practitioners to the realm of the secular, magic or folk custom; African-American motor behavior as secular dance, root work or hoodoo, and folk medicine are clear-cut examples.

Bondsmen performed a wide variety of dances including some that were adopted from their masters. But the majority of dances were distinctly African in character. These dances included wringin' & twistin', which would later form the basis of the twist, the buzzard lope, breakdown, pigeon wing, cake walk, charleston, "set de' flo'," snake hips (which formed the basis for all Afro-American dances requiring sharp popping accents demarcating each line of movement as in "the jerk" and the breaking style known as "pop locking"), and the shout, which unlike the others, retained both a sacred and secular character. Many of the dances included a basic step as well as a series of improvisational embellishments which frequently imitated motions of the work routine. Formerly enslaved African Americans frequently mentioned "pitchin' hay," "corn shuckin'," and "cuttin' wheat" as various embellishments in the cakewalk.[10] Considering the large number of African dances that actually celebrated through imitation, significant environmental factors such as herd size, events in the life cycle, or actual events involving the use of physical labor, it is not surprising that African-American bondsmen would adopt a similar principle in creating new dances.

In the dance known as "set de flo'," the principles of competition and dexterity came into play. Set de flo' took a variety of forms but the most interesting appears to be the form in which a circle was drawn marking off an area in which the competing dancers performed. The musician, usually a fiddler, would call out complicated step routines for the dancers to negotiate without stepping outside or on the drawn circle. Dexterity was often demonstrated by the dancer placing a glass of water on the head and performing as many steps as possible without spilling the water.

In this dance we have the demonstration of a number of African aesthetic and technical principles. The challenge posed by the fiddler-caller is one familiar to West Africans in their dancing. The all important sense of asymmetry as balance, control, and coolness is further demonstrated. Although the dancer may be performing a frantic, fury of complex steps or figures, they never lose the asymmetrical juxtaposition of coolness, equilibrium, and control. This principle can be observed among many West African groups. Shango, or thundergod, devotees sometimes dance with a burning fire in a container balanced on their heads. Among the Egbado Yoruba, gifted dancers have been observed dancing with delicate terra cotta sculptures on their heads while simultaneously demonstrating raw energy in the arms and torso.[11] This principle would later be demonstrated in the footflashing repetitions of tap dancers like Jimmy Mordacai, Bill Robinson and the Nicolas Brothers, as well as in break dancing. Unfortunately, little is known of the secret and well-hidden dances of enslaved Africans, but enough is known of the open, observable activities to state that the nature of dance, particularly the qualities of derision and resistance, have been modified little.

The outlawing of the international slave trade in the first decade of the nineteenth century assured that new Africans would be far more difficult to obtain than previously. Increasingly after 1800, most Africans living in North America had been born there. This factor had dual consequences for the development of African-American culture.

First, it meant that each new generation would be further removed from contact with indigenous Africans or African cultural practices in their original context. Although dwindling importations and illegally smuggled Africans served to shore up some of the natural cultural decline that was taking place, it was not enough to wholly sustain or stave off the effects of slavery on diminishing African culture.

Secondly, unlike the West Indies or parts of Latin America where, because of sheer numbers, Africans actually regrouped into ethnic moieties, Africans in North America found that option an impossibility with respect to sustaining specific cultural traditions. Thus, the conditions necessary to encourage an inter-African assimilation prevailed. Those customs, traits and habits under which ethnic specifics could be subsumed or most comfortably absorbed, while sustaining something of their original character, emerged most vigorously and became the initial outline for the emerging African-American cultural complex. Without implying that all ethnically specific traits vanished, let me state that in the language, religion, dance, music, food preparation style, folklore and herbal medicinal practices which compose the bulk of African-American culture, strong commonalities emerged throughout slave territory whether in Virginia or Mississippi.

This brings us to a third and equally important factor in the emergence of an African-American dance culture, the role of slaves as workers and the effects of a changing technological base on their lifestyles and work rhythms. Both the outlawing of the international slave trade and the increasing use of the cotton gin took place in the first decade of the nineteenth century. With respect to dance movement imitating the work routine, mechanization would dramatically change that relationship. With the development of the cotton gin and increase in cotton production "cotton culture" gave the South a more homogeneous profile than it had previously experienced. "King cotton" opened areas which had primarily grown tobacco, rice or indigo, or which had only experienced minimal cotton production. This homogenization touched the cultural lives of bondsmen in ways that cultural historians have yet to examine. It synchronized bondsmen's work rhythms across previously diverse regions; it affected language by adding to the daily vocabulary, daily routines and yearly schedules; it changed the environmental profile and modified the tools as well as the materials from which the folk culture was created. From Virginia through Texas, Africans experienced, for the first time since landing on these shores, as a result of "king cotton," something which exerted a universal influence on their cultural lives. The dominance of "king cotton" even affected the lives of bondsmen not directly involved in the production of the crop itself.

These three factors: an increasingly stable slave population resulting from the cessation of the slave trade, inter-African assimilation and a technologically based system of widespread cotton production provided the basis for a fairly stable, homogeneous, dominant cultural variant to emerge throughout the South. Though many regional variants remained intact, and new ones developed, it is from this basis that a more complex African-American culture would develop. It is here that we will briefly touch on the dominant themes and ceremonies during which African-American dance styles would develop. They include holiday and weekend dances, corn shucking dances, large urban dances (including congo square, John Canoe, Negro Election Day and Pinksters day.

Almost all plantation masters allowed their enslaved population some form of recreational dancing. But dancing appears to have been the form of recreational activity raising the least and at times the most opposition among slaveholders. On the plantation, the reasons and circumstances for secular dancing varied as the enslaved Africans danced for themselves as celebration, recreation and mourning—and for the entertainment of their masters. Recalling the inducements offered in the middle passage, these rewards were usually money, extra food for one's family, or a pass to another plantation.

Under the slave regime, secular dance developed specific characteristics that enabled it to function as forms of social intercourse and cultural expression, as an assimilation mechanism, and as a medium of political expression. For the African, dance was both a means to camouflage insurrectionary activity as well as other kinds of resistance behavior; for the masters it was a means to pacify the desire of their bondsmen to rebel.

The position of the enslaved African within the system, whether he was field laborer or urban artisan, house slave or freeman living outside the official bondage of his brethren, influenced the specifics of African retention and the particulars of each type of dance format as they arose under slavery. This is not to imply that there were not cultural similarities that cut across the lines separating house servants from field hands; indeed, there were. What is notable, however, is the fashion in which each class used secular dance to meet its needs and objectify its particular pattern of life.

In the process that was North American slavery, there were no formally sanctioned institutional supports for the retention of African religious culture, of which dance is an important part. Slave masters who sought to establish "praise houses" and permitted their bondsmen to "shout" or to engage in secular dancing often met with the exacting disapproval of their peers. But the benefits of allowing dancing more often than not overshadowed the criticisms as one master testifies.

> I would build a house large enough, and use it for a dancehouse for the young, and those who wish to dance, as well as for prayer meetings. and for church on Sunday—making it a rule to be present myself occasionally at both, and my overseer always. I know the rebuke in store about dancing, but I cannot help it. I believe negroes will be better disposed this way than any other.[12]

Masters recognized the usefulness of allowing at least some dancing among their enslaved people.[13] Almost all bondsmen were allowed to celebrate Christmas and some form of dancing was usually allowed as part of this holiday celebration.[14] An article in a southern journal describes the holidays to be celebrated on one southern plantation:

> Holidays—We usually have two, one about the 4th of July and one at Christmas. The one in July is celebrated with a dinner and whiskey. The Christmas holiday is a very different thing. It lasts from four to six days and during the jubilee it is difficult to say who is master. The servants are allowed the largest liberty. They are furnished with whiskey and egg-nog freely, and all the means necessary for good dinners and suppers. They are permitted to invite their friends from neighboring plantations, and to enjoy themselves in any way that suits them. Dancing is their favorite amusement and they go to it, I can assure you with a "perfect rush."[15]

Additional evidence indicates that Christmas festivities were sponsored by a majority of masters and included dancing, drinking, extra food, and visits to other plantations as described by the *Southern Cultivator.*

The allowances given Africans during the Christmas season were by no means uniform. With so much going on masters were hard pressed to keep track of all activity. With three or more days usually available some masters shared the monitoring responsibilities by staggering the dances and parties so that Africans on one plantation could entertain those from neighboring plantations and in turn be entertained.[16] Other masters less sympathetic to the demands of the season forbade their enslaved people to leave the plantation.

> Believing that the strolling about of Negroes for a week at a time, during what are called Christmas Holidays, is productive of much evil, the writer has set his face against the custom. Christmas is observed as a sacred festival. On that day as good a dinner as the plantation will afford is served for the Negroes, and they all sit down to a common table, but the next day we go to work. From considerations both of morality and needful rest and recreation to the negro, I much prefer a week in July, when the crop is laid by, to giving three days at Christmas.[17]

Saturday and Sunday also provided a break in the regular work routine on many plantations. If not all Saturday was spent away from the labors of the field, at least part of Saturday and usually all day Sunday were spent away from the regular tasks. Masters saw Saturday afternoons as a time for slaves to attend to their personal needs such as washing, gardening, or cleaning up the quarters. Saturday off was handled differently by masters. One farmer prescribed half of Saturday off for only the females slaves: "I give all my females half of every Saturday to wash and clean up, my cook washing for young men and boys through the week."[18]

On most plantations all hands stopped work on Saturday at noon. This was, of course, subject to seasonal changes. Hours of work varied according to season and region. Generally masters encouraged and provided for regular weekly dances. They were keenly aware of the morale-maintaining function served by these occasions. A small farmer leaves us this account on the management of Negroes:

> Negroes are gregarious; they dread solitariness, and to be deprived from the little weekly dances and chit-chat. They will work to death rather than be shut-up. I know the advantage though I have no jail, my house being a similar one, yet used for other purposes. I have a fiddle in my quarters and though some of my good brethren in the church would think hard of me, yet I allow dancing; ay I buy the fiddle and encourage it, by giving the boys occasionally a big supper.[19]

Masters who saw clearly the utility in allowing regular dances provided for them to occur weekly. Some masters even purchased slave musicians to provide music. A Mississippi planter tells us:

I must not omit to mention that I have a good fiddler, and keep him well supplied with catgut, and I make it his duty to play for the negroes every Saturday night until 12 o'clock. They are exceedingly punctual in their attendance at the hall, while Charley's fiddle is always accompanied with Ihurod on the triangle, and Sam to "pat."[20]

The relationship between work and secular dance, particularly the holiday and weekend plantation dances appears to be one of relief. Bondsmen accepted dances and other celebrations as an opportunity to relieve the burdens of their existence. Under slavery they made the most of every form of enjoyment permitted them including food, drinking, fellowship with others and, of course, dancing. And they broke the rules. Though drinking except when approved or administered by owners, was forbidden, they enjoyed homemade alcoholic beverages at these frolics, and they distributed them clandestinely when necessary. Apparently some even went as far as to build their own stills.[21]

The musical instruments at American slave dances were fashioned primarily after African instruments and strongly resembled instruments found in their communities elsewhere in the New World. And although African-American musicians did adopt certain European instruments such as the violin, the fiddle so frequently mentioned in descriptions of early slave dances was not the European violin but rather an African gourd fiddle which, like the banjo, bondsmen constructed for their own use from a technique passed down from older Africans. Isaac D. Williams, an ex-slave recalls:

We generally made our own banjos and fiddles, and I had a fiddle that was manufactured out of a gourd, with horse hair strings and a bow made out of the same material. When we made a banjo we would first of all catch what we called a ground hog, known in the north as a woodchuck. After tanning his hide, it would be stretched over a piece of timber fashioned like a cheese box, and you couldn't tell the difference in sound between that homely affair and a handsome store bought one.[22]

Throughout West Africa, among the Mandigo, Bambara, and Fulani people we find the prototype of the gourd fiddle or "susa" as it is known among the Fulani. There it is constructed using a gourd for the body, and horsehair for strings. The bow is bamboo with horsehair. It is played held in the bend of the elbow rather than under the chin.

According to Foday Musa Suso the "susa" is an ancient instrument.[23] In addition to banjo and fiddle, drums, tambourines, gourds, bones, quills, kettles, hand claps, jawbones, hoes, any metal pot or piece, or wooden box was used as accompaniment for dancing. Contrary to popular fiction, these instruments were not adopted as a substitute for the outlawed drum. Each of these instruments have been found actively used in places where playing the drum was well developed such as Cuba and Brazil.

Frederick Douglass once remarked that he believed that slave "holidays were among the most effective means in the hands of slaveholders of keeping down the spirit of insurrection among slaves." . . . "but for those [dances, frolics, holidays] the rigors of bondage would have become too severe for endurance and the slave would have been forced to a dangerous desperation."[24] Douglass is correct in noting the safety-valve effect in permitting slave dancing; many slaveholders certainly saw it that way. A good percentage even violated religious dictates and insisted on providing their enslaved Africans with the opportunity to dance. These occasions were certainly intended as opportunities for them to buy into the contract of their own oppression, but bondsmen, often used dances as opportunities for resistance or even for seizing their freedom. It is clear from the amount of insurrectionary activity that took place during slave holidays and days off that the role of dance in the slave community was not limited to escapist entertainment. No matter how intent slaveholders were to make the African American's cultural response a tool of their own oppression, the bondsmen managed to control enough of their culture to create an environment for strong resistance themes to become evident in both collective and individual dance behavior among both urban and rural bondsmen.

In order for slavery to be an effective system of controlling African labor, restraint of Africans had to be secured through both legal and extralegal sanction. Fear of slave rebellions loomed large in the picture of slavery, especially as the need for labor intensified.

Laws forbidding the use of drums would eventually help shape the profile of black culture in North America and qualitatively change the nature of any event where dancing occurred among Africans. Different instruments had to be substituted, ones that would not be seized and— to satisfy the slaveocracy—could not be used to incite or signal rebellion. In Charleston, South Carolina, one piece of legislation was enacted in 1740, the year following the Stono Rebellion; it was specifically aimed at those occasions on which Africans might gather for dances.[25]

Interplantational dances were a source of worry to the slaveocracy. They usually lasted at least until midnight and attracted Africans from neighboring plantations who sometimes walked as much as fifteen or more miles to partake of the festivities.[26] By bringing together large groups of Africans, slave dancing affairs provided situations in which bondsmen could plot insurrections and exchange information concerning such activities, and they provided a potentially explosive situation in which Africans outnumbered whites.

There is ample evidence that a significant number of slave insurrections were either plotted in part at dances or scheduled to take place on occasions when dances were most likely to occur.[27] This appears to be true throughout slave territory even in the West Indies. One analysis of rebellions in the British Caribbean revealed that 35 percent were either planned for or took place in late December.[28] The high pitch that could easily be attained on those festive occasions could serve as a pretext for touching off a previously planned rebellion.[29] Evidence indicates that the celebration of dance was directly linked with insurrectionary activity giving these occasions a striking resemblance to war dances, or dances in which preparation for battle was the central theme. An armed open rebellion reported to have taken place in South Carolina in 1730 was planned to begin when Africans "should assemble in the neighborhood of the town, under the pretense of a dancing bout."[30]

Throughout slave territory the drum had long been used to signal the call to public gatherings and dances even after its use was forbidden. Such was the case in both Congo Square, New Orleans and in coastal Georgia.[31] Bearing in mind such use for the drum, it is probable that some slaves who joined the Stono uprising were attracted by the sound of the drums and initially thought that they were being informed of a dance:

> They increased every minute by new Negroes coming to them, so that they were above Sixty, some say a hundred, on which they halted in a field and set to dancing, Singing and beating Drums, to draw more Negroes to them.[32]

Plantation affairs whether held on a holiday or a weekend represents one type of affair, and were essential in the development of regional culture. But in the areas immediately surrounding towns such as Charleston, New Orleans, or Mobile something very different from the plantation dance developed. The large public dances that occurred on the edge of town appear to have been characteristic of urban enslaved Africans. Bondsmen from the countryside certainly participated, but urban Africans dominated these affairs. Many plantation owners refused to allow their enslaved people to participate in social activities in town, fearing that contact with urban bondsmen would somehow weaken their control. Most free blacks and enslaved, skilled artisans resided in urban areas; here some hired out their own labor and rented their own shelter.[33] Since, in the urban environment the African often lived away from the watchful eye of his master, a condition that allowed him more freedom of movement than his plantation counterpart, urban Africans were regarded by many plantation owners as lacking sufficient regulation and restraint.[34]

The relative liberty of movement among urban Africans was a continuing source of complaint for the white inhabitants of most urban areas.[35] Though some plantation masters discouraged and in some cases openly forbade their plantation hands to associate with urban slaves, bondsmen nevertheless met at dances held on public property. These large public dances, like the organization of slave worship, provided an arena in which African culture could flourish across lines dictated by the African's position in the labor process and inhibited the diversity of class-bound manifestations in African culture. Only the public urban dances provided the format that brought together plantation laborers, house servants, urban artisans and free African Americans in a celebration of African based dance culture. Unlike plantation dances, where the overseer or the master could control the social interaction of his particular bondsmen by forbidding urban or free African Americans on his property, no such controls existed at these large public dances.

Urban bondsmen even occasionally took the liberty of initiating a dance without proper approval or the required supervision of armed whites; when they did, they presented the authorities with a situation in which crowd control was difficult. These public affairs would attract upwards of two hundred African Americans. The *South Carolina Gazette* gives a description of one such unsanctioned affair:

> The Stranger had once an opportunity of seeing a Country Dance, Rout or Cabal of Negroes, within 5 miles distance of this town, on a Saturday night; and it may not be improper here to give a description of that assembly. It consisted of about 60 people, 5-6th from Town, every one of whom carried something, in the manner just described; as bottled liquors of all sorts, Rum, Tongues, Hams, Beef, Geese, Turkies and Fowl both drest and raw, with many

luxuries of the table as sweetmeats, pickles & (which some did not scruple to acknowledge they obtained by means of false keys, procured from a Negro in Town, who could make any Key whenever the impression of the true one was brought to him in wax) without doubt, were stolen and brought thither, in order to be used on the present occasion or to be concealed and disposed of by such of the gang as might have the best opportunities for this purpose: *Moreover*, they were provided with Music, Cards. Dice & c. . . .
Then they *danced, betted, gamed, swore, quarreled, fought*, and did everything that the *most modern* accomplished gentlemen are *not ashamed of.*[36]

The atmosphere of frolic and confusion provided a situation in which contact with insurrectionists, runaways, and other dissenters could be made.[37] *The South Carolina Gazette* continues:

They also had their private committees; whole deliberations were carried on in too low voice, and with much caution, as not to be overheard by the others much less by the Stranger, who was concealed in a deserted adjacent hut, where the humanity of a well disposed grey headed Negro man had placed him, pitying his *seeming* indigence and distress. The members of this secret council had much the appearance of Doctors in deep and solemn consultation upon life or *death* which indeed might have been the scope of their meditations at the time. No less than 12 fugitive slaves joined this respectable company before midnight, 3 of whom were mounted on good horses; these after delivering a good quality of Mutton, Lamb and Veal, which they brought with them, directly associated with one or other of the private consultations; and went off about an hour before day being supplied with liquor & c and perhaps also received some instructions.[38]

The dance format among both rural and urban Africans provided opportunities for resistance; however, the situation presented by public, urban dances, which occurred outdoors, appears to have provided more opportunities for collective resistance. Those dances appear more closely linked than the rural dances to planned, armed, coordinated insurrection attempts.[39] Antoine Simon LePage du Pratz, a Louisiana resident from 1718 to 1734 observed:

Nothing is more to be dreaded than to see the Negroes assemble together on Sundays, since under pretence of Calinda, or the dance, they sometimes get together to the number of three or four hundred, and make a kind of Sabbath, which it is always prudent to avoid; for it is in those tumultuous meetings that they sell what they have stolen to one another, and commit many crimes. In these likewise they plot their rebellions.[40]

By 1817 in New Orleans the dancing proved troublesome enough for the city to enact legislation restricting the dancing to Sundays before sundown and to one location, Congo Square. Contrary to the interpretations of several historians of slavery, the establishment of Congo Square represents a restricting rather than an encouraging of slave dancing and culture.[41] Nevertheless, both Congo Square and the large public dances of urban Africans encouraged an inter-African mixing which was essential in the emergence of an African-American culture as such.

Congo Square, New Orleans and Charleston, South Carolina were by no means the only locations in which large public slave dances and celebrations were held. In Somerset County, Maryland complaints were lodged with the judicial authority that slaves were:

Drunke on the Lords Day beating their Negro drums by which they call considerable Number of Negroes together in some Certaine places.[42]

Throughout the state of North Carolina particularly in the areas surrounding Wilmington, Fayetteville, Hilton, Edenton, New Bern and Hillsboro, Africans danced publicly and celebrated the John Canoe festival. Harriet Brent Jacobs describes the tradition:

Every child rises early on Christmas morning to see the Johnkannaus. Without them, Christmas would be shorn of its greatest attraction. They consist of companies of slaves from the plantations, generally of the lower class. Two athletic men, in calico wrappers, have a net thrown over them, covered with all manner of bright-colored stripes. Cows tails are fastened to their backs, and their heads are decorated with horns. A box, covered with sheepskin is called the gumbo box. A dozen beat on this, while others strike triangles and jawbones, to which hands of dancers keep time. For a month previous they are composing songs, which are sung on this occasion. These companies, of a hundred each, turn out early in the morning, and are allowed to go around 'till twelve o'clock, begging to contributions. Not a door is left unvisited where there is the least chance of obtaining a penny or a glass of rum. They do not drink while they are out, but carry the rum home in jugs, to have a carousal. These Christmas donations frequently amount to twenty or thirty dollars. It is seldom that any white man or child refused to give them a trifle. If he does, they regale his ears with the following song

Poor massa, so dey say;
Down in de heel, so dey say;
Got no money, so dey say;
Not one shillin, so dey say;
God A mighty bless you, so dey say.[43]

The climax of the John Canoe doorstep entreaty came when the company broke into the "buzzard lope," a dance which was well known among African-Americans in the coastal Carolinas.[44] The performance of this dance leads one to agree with Herskovits that the Ashanti Yankoro or buzzard could indicate a possible origin for this celebration.[45] Whatever the origins there were demonstrable continuities with John Canoe festivals held throughout the West Indies and even with the "Dia de Reyes" celebrations in Cuba.[46]

Pinksters celebrations, familiar to the Dutch and Africans in Dutch settled areas, particularly New York, lasted from three days to a week. Beginning usually on the first Monday of Pentecost, this celebration involved weeks of preparation.

When the long-awaited opening day arrived, slaves from the countryside made their way to the nearest town or city, New York City, Kingston, Albany, Poughkeepsie, to name but a few—to join with the urban colored in the carnival. The Albany festivities topped all others. There the celebration was held at the head of State Street, later the site of the State Capital. Booths were set up to dispense refreshments of all sorts, including liquor, for the ban on strong drinks was temporarily lifted. A master of ceremonies presided, his principal task being to beat on the kettle-drum which provided the music for the singing, dancing, and parading which enlivened the occasion. In New York City dancing contests between local and Long Island slaves were staged in the streets for the entertainment of all, as well as for whatever shillings might be tossed to the contestants. The "jug" and the more difficult "breakdown" were performed to the rhythm of clapping hands and stamping feet.[47]

Like John Canoe himself in North Carolina, or Warrin, King of the Jamaican John Canoe festival or King Zulu of our own Mardi Gras, Pinkster festivities included a "king" or individual on which the attention of both participants and onlookers was focused.[48]

Throughout New England, in Norwich, Hartford, Derby and New Haven, Connecticut, in Newport and Kingston, Rhode Island, Salem, Massachusetts and Portsmouth, New Hampshire, large annual celebrations known as "election day" were celebrated. The festivities included a parade, dining and dancing as well as an election of a "Negro governor."[49] The earliest known "Negro Election Day" is believed to have occurred in Salem, Massachusetts, May 27, 1741.[50] And probably, though not certainly, the last "Negro Governor" was elected in Humphreysville, Connecticut in 1856.[51] Election day as the other festivals in which a "king" or "governor" was chosen demonstrated continuities with black Latin American and West Indian celebrations. Believed by some scholars to be derivative of African political institutions these festivities served a variety of functions.[52]

In their own land they had elected kings or chiefs chosen from among descendants of royal blood, and many practices of a judicial and social nature which bear a strong resemblance to those found among them in America. As time went on these customs were greatly modified, partly by association with different customs, but chiefly through the mere action of time and the failure of fresh arrivals from Africa, until finally the meetings became little more than an opportunity for a good time.

Each delineation within the system of slavery developed particularisms with respect to dance culture. The public dances and festivities of the urban slaves and the corn shucking frolics of the plantation bondsmen are clear examples of such specificity. The dances that emerged during holiday celebrations or among urban enslaved Africans reflect little of the agricultural necessity of the period, but the corn shucking dances provide a good example; these affairs brought together Africans engaged in various aspects of plantation labor.

Corn shucking or corn husking, a fairly common activity on a considerable number of plantations, was frequently accompanied by dances that were marked by an increased atmosphere of competition. The corn shucking itself was conceived of as a competitive event in which work and social activity were combined. The social exchanges prevented the African from viewing this labor-intensive situation as a totally unpleasant task.[53] A *New York Sun* article describes the atmosphere of competition and enjoyment surrounding the corn shucking:

The corn was divided into two piles as big as a house and two captains were appointed. Each chose sides just as the captains in
spelling matches do, and then the fun began.[54]

Competition between shucking teams functioned so as to give the
Africans a feeling of control over the task at hand, to speed up the
actual labor process and to make it more tolerable. The competitive
component of a corn shucking was provided by dividing the laborers
into two or more teams and offering a prize or reward for the team that
finished first. An ex-slave from Georgia recalled:

> In corn shucking time no padderolers would ever bother you. We
> would have a big time at corn shuckings. They would call up the
> crowd and line the men up and give them a drink. I was a corn gen-
> eral—would stand out high above everybody, giving out corn songs
> and throwing down corn to them. There would be two sides of
> them, one side trying to outshuck the other.[55]

The intensity of the social activity, that is, the social life that occurred
around these occasions, seems to have been the most important aspect
of the event, at least to the Africans. Seen in the context of plantation
life, corn shuckings provided them with a format for community participation in the work routine, but more important, shuckings provided a
format for community participation in slave social life and culture.
Africans from neighboring plantations attended these corn shuckings.
Both house and field slaves contributed to the labor and partook of the
accompanying festivities. As much as the mores of slavery allowed, the
corn shuckings were a time when the division of slave labor on the plantation was temporarily disregarded, as were divisions of caste and class.

The cultural format that developed out of the corn shuckings fit
together in a cohesive philosophical outlook. The songs that were sung
were in the call and response pattern and the dance was no less a community form.[56]

David C. Barrow, Jr., left us this account of a dance that accompanied a corn shucking:

> With the cotillion a new and very important office, that of "caller-
> out", though of less importance than the fiddler, is second to no
> other. He not only calls out the figures, but explains them at length
> to the ignorant, sometimes accompanying them through the per-
> formance. He is never at a loss, "genmen to de right" being a suf-

ficient refuge in case of embarrassment, since this always calls forth a full display of the dancers' agility and gives much time.[57]

The dancer and the caller-out interact in a pattern similar to that of call and response in song. The dance style in which a caller evokes the dancers to ever-increasing feats of endurance and virtuosity is well planted in slave dancing by way of its African origins in which the drummer, now the caller-out, and the dancer respond to each other. In certain African cultures it took the form of competition, a test of endurance; in the culture of plantation slavery at the corn shuckings it may have taken the form of the "caller-out" calling out dance steps so rapid and complicated as to tax the dancers' skills. David Barrow adds more insight into the corn shucking "cotillions":

> Endurance is a strong point in the list of accomplishments of the dancer, and other things being equal, that dancer who can hold out the longest is considered the best.[58]

The caller-out functioned to coordinate the dance movements of those involved. Insofar as the participants were from several plantations, each with its own familiar dances, the caller-out represents the establishment of a community consensus concerning the dance; dancers from various plantations could participate. The caller-out made community participation more possible by eliminating or at least raising plantation particularisms in dance to the level of an accepted community cultural standard.

The corn shucking apparently was a gala event for everyone concerned; however, it was not without its strains of resistance to the conditions of bondage. The dances as well as the songs often turned to satire. It seems that whenever they could, slaves used culture as an instrument of criticism, ridicule, and resistance.

Their dances acted to deconstruct the imposing and powerful presence of whites. In this respect dance was an ever safer tool for self-assertion, ridicule and criticism than song.[59] If the songs of the slaves in which they voiced their disapproval of slavery were not understood by whites, the dance was even less understood and therefore a much safer form of self-assertion. The practice of deriding whites through the use of dance probably had its origin in the African dances of derision practiced by many of the West African ethnic groups. To the observing whites it may have appeared to be merely comic imitation for entertainment or fun.[60] This dance ritual of deconstruction allowed slaves to assert themselves and to keep the spirit of resistance alive on a personal level. Authority was made to look small and insignificant; and disregard for the power of the slaveocracy was openly displayed.[61] The context of enjoyment as well as the lowered defenses provided a situation of maximum camouflage. Ostensibly the affair was one of enjoyment, not of protest, but for African Americans, whose options to strike back were limited according to their bondage, the ritual of deconstruction was satisfying and sustained "derision" as an African trait.

African Americans were able to assert their personalities as the looseness of the occasion and the lowering of norms of conduct between whites and blacks provided opportunities in which the entire slave community could lodge a complaint or levy a judgement that might otherwise result in police action. At these occasions a culture of resistance could meet with community comment and participation. Dance and appropriate songs that ridiculed whites could and did emerge on a community level.

This discussion of slave dances and their various functions, social control, individual release, community fellowship and consolidation, cultural institution building and resistance does not complete the picture however. There were other activities quite different from those outlined here in which status differentiation within the slave community and interracial concubinage figured significantly. The dancing as well as other behaviors in these institutions were governed by a set of aesthetic and technical principles further removed from their African origins than the dance activities already discussed. Such was the case with "slave balls."

From this outline African-American dance as a national phenomenon begins to take shape. Though not discussed here nascent cultural institutions related to the reorganization of black labor, would also play an important role in promoting the institutional context from which African-American dance would develop. The three essential macro-sociological factors described earlier and the numerous occasions, festivals and uses of dance provide the socio-historic background to some of contemporary America's most vibrant folk cultural and entertainment forms.

Notes

1.   William E. B. DuBois, *The Suppression of the African Slave Trade to the United States of America; 1638-1879* (New York: Dover Publications, 1970): 109-118; see also Philip D. Curtin, *The Atlantic Slave Trade: A Census*

(Madison, Wisconsin: University of Wisconsin Press, 1969): 72-74; Mannix and Crowley, 191-262.

2. Dena J. Epstein, *Sinful Tunes and Spirituals* (Urbana, Ill.: University of Illinois Press, 1977): 188.

3. LeRoi Jones, *Blues People: Negro Music in White America* (New York: Morrow, 1963):18. See also Eileen Southern, *The Music of Black Americans: A History* (New York: W. W. Norton. 1971): 179; Janheinz Jahn, *Mutu* (New York: Grove Press, 1961): 223; Miles Fischer, *Negro Slave Songs in the United States* (Secaucus. N.J.: Citadel Press): 21, 120, 156.

4. Fernando Ortiz, *Los Instrumentos De La Musica Afrocubana*, vol. III (Publicaciones de la Direccion de Cultura Del Ministerio De Educacion, Habana, 1952): 367-378.

5. *Ibid.* 376.

6. Frederick Law Olmsted, *A Journey in the Seaboard Slave States* (New York, Mason Brothers, 1856): 449.

7. Rupert Sargent Holland, ed., *Letters and Diary of Laura M. Towne, Written from the Sea Islands of South Carolina, 1862-1884* (Cambridge: Riverside Press, 1912): 20.

8. Lydia Parrish, *Slave Songs of the Georgia Sea Islands*. See also Stearns and Stearns *Jazz Dance*.

9. Sterling Stuckey, *Slave Culture* (New York: Oxford University Press, 1987).

10. Edward R. Turner, *The Negro in Virginia* (New York: Hastings House Publishers, 1940): 90.

11. Robert Farris Thompson, "An Aesthetic of the Cool: West African Dance," *African Forum* 2.2 (Fall 1966): 13.

12. "Management of Negroes," *DeBow's Review* 11 (July-December 1851): 372.

13. Alice Bauer and Raymond Bauer, "Day to Day Resistance to Slavery," *Journal of Negro History* 10 (October 1942): 389.

14. Epstein, *Sinful Tunes and Spirituals* 41.

15. Foby, "Management of Servants," *Southern Cultivator* 11 (August 1853): 227-28.

16. Eugene Genovese, *Roll, Jordan, Roll* (New York: Random House, 1976):574.

17. "Management of Negroes," *DeBow's Review* 19 (July-December 1855): 362.

18. "Management of Negroes," *DeBow's Review* 11 (July-December 1851): 371.

19. *Ibid.*

20. "Management of Negroes upon Southern Estates," *DeBow's Review* 11 (July-December 1851): 372.

21. George Rawick, *American Slave* supplement 2, 4.3, Texas Narratives, 970.

22. Isaac D. Williams, *Sunshine and Shadow of Slave Life: Reminiscences as Told by Isaac D. Williams to "Tege."* East Saginaw, Michigan: Evening News

Printing and Binding House, (1885): 62.

23. Interview with Foday Musa Suso, Mandingo griot, musician and kora master. Providence, Rhode Island, October 29, 1986.

24. Frederick Douglass, *Life and Times of Frederick Douglass* (London: Collier-Macmillan Ltd., 1961): 147.

25. And for that as it is absolutely necessary to the safety of this province that all due care be taken to restrain the wanderings and meetings of negroes and other slaves, at all times, and more especially on Saturday nights, Sundays and other holidays, and their using and carrying wooden swords, and other mischievous and dangerous weapons, or use or keeping of drums, horns, or other loud instruments, which may call together or give sign or notice to one another of their wicked designs and purpose; and that all masters, overseers and others may be enjoined, diligently and carefully to prevent the same, *Be it enacted* by the authority aforesaid, That it shall be lawful for all masters, overseers and other persons whomsoever, to apprehend and take up any negro other slave that shall be found out of the plantation of his or their master or owner, at any time. Especially on Saturday nights, Sundays or other holidays, not being on lawful business, and with a letter from their master, or a ticket, or not having a white person with them; and the said negro or other slave or slaves, met or found out of the plantation of his or their master or mistress, though with a letter or ticket, if he or they be armed with such offensive weapons aforesaid, him or them to disarm, take up whip: And whatsoever master, owner, or overseer shall permit or suffer his or their negro or other slave or slaves, at any time hereafter, to heat drums, blow horns, or use any other loud instruments, or whosoever shall suffer and countenance any public meeting or feasting of strange negroes, or slaves in their plantations, shall forfeit ten pounds, current money, for every such offense, upon conviction or proof as aforesaid; provided, an information or other suit be commenced within one month after forfeiture thereof for the same. *Statutes at Large for the State of South Carolina VII*, 410.

26. Rawick, "South Carolina Narratives," 2, part 1, 327.

27. In late June 1835, several rumors circulated in Madison County, Mississippi, that a slave revolt was to commence; there were two possibilities. One set of rumors confirmed Christmas Day 1835 as the appointed time. Edwin A. Miles, "The Mississippi Slave Insurrection Scare of 1835," *Journal of Negro History* 42 (1957): 49. Whites became aroused, seized and tortured several suspected bondsmen. Under torture, several slaves admitted that a revolt had been planned for July 4th, a holiday, "at which time it was felt that the slaves could assemble without suspicion." *Ibid.*, 50. Prompted by the discovery of a plot in early 1709 in Surry, James City, and Isle of Wright counties, Virginia, H.R. McIlwaine, ed., *Executive Journals of the Councils of Colonial Virginia* (May 1, 1705-October 23, 1721): 234-235-236. See also Herbert Aptheker, *American Negro Slave*

Revolts (New York: International Publishers, 1969): 169. Lt. Governor Jenings of Virginia issued a proclamation "to prevent negro slaves assembling together." Cecil Headlam, *Calendar of State Papers, Colonial Series, America and West Indies:* 1710-1711, 25 (London: 1860): 238. Despite the proclamation, another well-developed plot was discovered in April 1709, again in Surry and James City counties. Governor Jening's letter to the Council of Trade and Plantations dated April 24, 1710, illustrated the significance of holiday dances to the slave community:

> There hath of late been very happily discovered an intended insurrection of the negroes, which was to have been put into execution in Surry and James City Countys on Easter Day; but the Chief conspirators having been seasonably apprehended, their design is broke. *Headlam.*

28. Robert Dirks, *Natural History* 84, no. 10 (December 1975) p. 88.
29. An account of such a gathering is given in a letter written from Charleston South Carolina, dated October 22, 1720.

> I shall give an account of a bloody tragedy which was to have been executed here last Saturday night (the 15th) by the Negroes, who had conspired to rise and destroy us and had almost bro't it to pass: but it pleased God to appear for us, and confound their Councils. For some of them propos'd that the Negroes of every Plantation should destroy their own Masters; but others were for rising in a Body, and giving the blow at once on surprise; and thus they differ's. They soon made a great Body at the back of the Town, and had a great Dance, and expected the Country Negroes to come & join them; and had not an overruling Providence discovered their Intrigues, we had been all in blood. For take the whole Province, we have about 28 thousand Negroes, to 3 thousand Whites. The Chief of them, with some others, is apprehended and in irons, in order to a tryal; and we are in Hopes to find out the whole affair. *Boston Weekly Newsletter*, October 15-22, 1730.

30. One, that the negroes in each family in the dead of night, were to murder all their masters and the white men of every family, in the neighborhood in which there were no Negroes. *There was so much distrust and want of confidence,* however, among them that they resolved to adopt the other proposition, which was, they should assemble in the neighborhood of the town, under the pretense of a "Dancing Bout" and when proper preparations were made, to rush into the heart of the city, take possession of all arms and ammunition they could find, and murder all the white men, and then turn their forces to the different plantations. Edwin C. Holland, *A Refutation of the Calumnies Circulated Against the Southern and Eastern States* (Charleston: A.E. Miller, 1822): 59, in Cornell University Rare Book Collection.

31. George W. Cable, "The Dance in Place Congo," *Century Magazine* 31 (April 1886): 517. For a more recent example of the drum used to call or signal a meeting or dance see Georgia Writers Project W.P.A., *Drums and Shadows* (Athens: University of Georgia Press, 1940): 174.

32. General Oglethorpe to the accountant, Mr. Harman Verelst, October 9, 1739, in Candler, comp. *Colonial Record* (Georgia), 22, part 2 (Atlanta. Ga.: Franklin Printing and Publishing Co., 1904-1918): 235. See also Epstein, 40, 44.

33. Richard C. Wade, *Slavery in the Cities* (New York: Oxford University Press, 1964): 48-54, 55-59. See also August Meier and Elliott M. Rudwick, *From Plantation to Ghetto* (New York: Hill and Wang, 1966): 66.

34. Farley Reynolds, "The Urbanization of Negroes in the United States," *Journal of Social History* 1 (Spring 1968): 246. See also Marion deB. Kilson, "Towards Freedom: An Analysis of Slave Revolts in the United States," *Phylon* 25 (Summer 1964): 176.

35. A letter to the *South Carolina Gazette* in 1772 reveals what was probably a typical occurrence of the time regarding the control of urban slaves:

> Whoever may please to talk or ride, from this town, only so far as where the road divides near the Quarter-House, from about 3 hours before sun setting on Saturday afternoon, till 11 o'clock at night, and from about two hours before sun-rising till an hour after it sets on Sunday, will not be long at a loss to answer the question: For tho' he will find the numbers passing and repassing between these periods never to be less than *four hundred,* but often exceeding seven yet he will rarely meet with more than 40 or 50 tickets or letters in the hands of the *Country Negroes* and never more than 4 or 5 such [licenses] among those that belong to the Town, who generally make four-fifths of these strollers. *South Carolina Gazette,* September 17, 1772.

36. *Ibid.*

37. For a more complete description of runaways in cities, see Wade, 209-225

38. *South Carolina Gazette,* September 17, 1772.

39. LePage duPratz, *History of Louisiana* (Baton Rouge: Louisiana State University Press, 1975): 380, 384, 387.

40. *Ibid.*

41. For a discussion which views Congo Square as a means to encourage slave dancing see John Blassingame, *The Slave Community* (revised and enlarged edition). New York: Oxford University Press, (1979): 36.

42. Russell R. Menard, "The Maryland Slave Population, 1658 to 1730: A Demographic Profile of Blacks in Four Counties," *William and Mary Quarterly,* 3rd ser. 32 (Jan. 1975): 29-54.

43. Harriet Brent Jacobs, *Incidents in The Life of a Slave Girl.* Boston, (1861): 179-181.

44. Ira DE A. Reid, "The John Canoe Festival," *Phylon* 3.4 350. See also Dougald Mac Millan, "John Kuners," *Journal of American Folklore* 39 (Jan.-Mar., 1926): 53-57. See also Frederic G. Cassidy, "Hipsaw" and "John Canoe," *American Speech* 41 (Feb. 1966): 45-51: See also "Slave's Holiday," *Natural History* 84.10 (Dec. 1975):82-90.
45. Reid, *op. cit.* 356.
46. For descriptions of "Dia de Reyes" see Fernanto Ortiz, *Los Bailes Y El Teatro De Los Negros En El Folklore De Cuba*, Habana: Ediciones Cardenas Y Cia, 1951 see also, Ortiz, "La fiesta Afrocubano del 'Dia de Reyes'." Extracto de los Archivas del folklore cubano. Vol. I, El siglo XVIi, 1925. For a description of John Canoe dancing and festivities in Jamaica see Margaret Shedd, "Carib Dance Patterns," *Theatre Arts Monthly* 17.1 (Jan. 1933): 65-77.
47. Edwin Olson, "Social Aspects of Slave Life in New York," *Journal of Negro History* 26 (Jan. 1941): 66-77.
48. George Rogers Howell, *Bicentennial History of Albany. History of the County of Albany, N.Y.*, from 1609 to 1886 (New York: W. W. Munsell, 1886): 725.
49. Herbert S. Aimes, "African Institutions in America," *Journal of American Folklore* 18 (1905): 15.
50. Joseph P. Reidy, "Negro Election Day & Black Community Life in New England, 1750-1860," *Marxist Perspectives* (Fall, 1978): 102.
51. Orville H. Platt, "Negro Governors," *Papers of the New Haven Colonial Historical Society* 6 (1900):335.
52. *Op. cit.*, Aimes, 16.
53. Genovese 38.
54. "Corn Shuckin' Down South," *New York Sun*, November 11, 1895, 4. See also George Wiley M.D., *Southern Plantation Stories and Sketches* (Freeport, N.Y.: Books for Libraries Press, 1971): 41-52.
55. Fisk University, *Unwritten History of Slavery* (Nashville: Social Science Institute, 1945): 50.
56. William Cullen Bryant, "Southern Negro Life," *DeBow's Review 9* (1850): 325-27.
57. David C. Barrow, "A Georgia Corn-Shucking," *Century Magazine* 24 (May-October 1882): 878.
58. *Ibid.*
59. Bertram Doyle, *The Etiquette of Race Relations in the South* (Port Washington, N.Y.: Kennikat Press, 1968): 22-23.
60. Rudi Blesh and Harriet Janis, *They All Played Ragtime* (New York: Alfred A. Knopf, 1950): 96.
61. *South Carolina Gazette*, September 17, 1772.

Works Cited

Aimes, Herbert S. "African Institutions in America," *Journal of American Folklore*, 18, 1905.

Aptheker, Herbert. *American Negro Slave Results*. New York: International
    Publishers, 1969.

Barrow, David C. "A Georgia Corn Shucking," *Century Magazine* 24 (May-
    October 1882).

Bauer, Alice and Raymond Bauer. "Day to Day Resistance to Slavery,"
    Journal of Negro History 10 (October 1942).

Blassingame, John. *The Slave Community*. New York: Oxford University Press,
    1979.

Bryant, William Cullen. "Southern Negro Life," *DeBow's Review* 9, 1850.

Cable, George W. "The Dance in Place Congo," *Century Magazine* 31 (April
    1886).

Candler, Comp. *Colonial Record* (Georgia) XXII pt. 2. Atlanta: Franklin
    Printing and Publishing Co., 1904.

Cassidy, Frederic G. "Hipsaw" and "John Canoe," *American Speech* 41 (Feb.
    1966).

"Corn Shuckin' Down South," *New York Sun*, Nov. 11, 1895.

Curtin, Philip D. *The Atlantic Slave Trade: A Census*. Madison, Wisconsin:
    University of Wisconsin Press, 1969.

DeBow's Review 10 (July-December 1851).

DeBow's Review 11 (July-Dec. 1851).

DeBow's Review 19 (July-December 1855).

Douglass, Frederick. *Life and Times of Frederick Douglass*. London: Collier-
    Macmillan Ltd., 1961.

Doyle, Bertram. *The Etiquette of Race Relations in the South*. Port Washington,
    N.Y.: Kennikat Press, 1968.

DuBois, William E. B. *The Suppression of the African Slave Trade to the United
    States of America, 1638-1879*. New York: Dover Publications, 1970.

du Pratz, LePage and Antoine Simon, *History of Louisiana*. Baton Rouge:
    Louisiana State University Press, 1975.

Epstein, Dena. *Sinful Tunes and Spirituals*. Urbana, Ill.: University of Illinois
    Press, 1977.

Fischer, Miles. *Negro Slave Songs in the United States*. Secaucus, New Jersey:
    Citadel Press, 1978.

Fisk University. *Unwritten History of Slavery*. Nashville: Social Science
    Institute, 1945.

Genovese, Eugene. *Roll Jordan Roll*. New York: Random House, 1967.

George Writers Project, W.P.A. *Drums and Shadows*. Athens: University of
    Georgia Press, 1940.

Headlam, Cecil. *Calendar of State Papers, Colonial Series, America and West
    Indies*, 1710-1711, 25. London: 1860.

Holland, Edwin C. *A Refutation of the Calumnies Circulated Against the Southern
    and Eastern States*. Charleston: A.E. Miller, 1822.

Holland, Rupert Sargent, ed., *Letters and Diary of Laura M. Towne, Written from
    the Sea Islands of South Carolina*, 1862-1884. Cambridge: Riverside Press,
    1912.

Howell, George Rogers. *Bicentennial History of Albany, History of the County of Albany, N.Y., from 1609-1886.* New York: W. W. Munsell, 1886.

Jacobs, Harriet Brent. *Incidents in the Life of a Slave Girl.* Boston: 1861.

Jahn, Janheinz. *Muntu.* New York: Grove Press, 1961.

Jones, LeRoi. *Blues People: Negro Music in White America.* New York: Morrow, 1963.

Kilson, Marion deB. "Towards Freedom: An Analysis of Slave Revolts in the United States," *Phylon* (Summer 1964).

MacMillan, Dougald. "John Kuners," *Journal of American Folklore* 39 (Jan.-Mar. 1926).

Mannix, Daniel P. and Malcolm Cowley. *Black Cargoes.* New York: Viking Press, 1962.

McIlwaine, H. R. (ed). *Executive Journals of the Council of Colonial Virginia,* vol. III, May 1705-Oct. 1721. Richmond, Virginia: Virginia State Library, 1928.

Meier, August and Elliot M. Rudwick. *From Plantation to Ghetto.* New York: Hill and Wang, 1966.

Menard, Russell R. "The Maryland Slave Population, 1658 to 1730: A Demographic Profile of Blacks in Four Counties," *William and Mary Quarterly* 3rd ser. 32 (January 1975).

Miles, Edwin A. *The Mississippi Slave Insurrection Scare of 1835, Journal of Negro History* 42, 1957.

Olmsted, Frederick Law. *A Journey in the Seaboard Slave States.* New York: Mason Brothers, 1856.

Olson, Edwin. "Social Aspects of Slave Life in New York," *Journal of Negro History* 26 (Jan. 1941).

Ortiz, Fernando. *Los Instrumentos De La Musica Afrocubana.* Publicaciones de la Direccion de Cultura Del Ministerio De Educacion: Habana, 1952.

—. *Los Bailes Y El Teatro De Los Negros En El Folklore De Cuba.* Habana: Ediciones Cardenas Y Cia, 1951.

—. "La Fiesta Afrocubans del Dia de Reyes," *Extracto de los Archivas del Folklore Cubano.* Vol. I, El siglo XVII, 1925.

Peck, John Mason. *Forty Years of Pioneer Life,* Edited by Rufus Babcock. Philadelphia: American Baptist Publication Society, c. 1864.

Platt, Orville H. "Negro Governors," *Papers of the New Haven Colonial Historical Society,* 6, (1900).

Poupeye, Camille. "Danses dramatique en theatres exotiques." Brussels: *Les Cahiers du Journal des Poetes,* 1941.

Rawick, George. *American Slave,* "South Carolina Narratives," Part 3, vol. 3. Westport, Connecticut: Greenwood Press, 1972.

Reid, Ira De A. "The John Canoe Festival," *Phylon,* 3.4.

Reidy, Joseph P. "Negro Election Day & Black Community Life in New England, 1750-1860," *Marxist Perspectives* (Fall, 1978).

Reynolds, Farley. "The Urbanization of Negroes in the United States," *Journal of Social History* 1 (Spring 1968).

Shedd, Margaret. "Carib Dance Patterns," *Theatre Arts Monthly* 17.1 (Jan. 1933).

South Carolina Gazette, September 17, 1772.

Southern, Eileen. *The Music of Black Americans: A History*. New York: W. W. Norton, 1971.

Statutes at Large for the State of South Carolina VII.

Stuckey, Sterling. *Slave Culture*. New York: Oxford University Press.

Thompson, Robert Farris. "An Aesthetic of the Cool: West African Dance," *African Forum* 2.2 (Fall 1966).

Turner, Edward R. *The Negro in Virginia*. New York: Hastings House Publishers, 1940.

Wade, Richard C. *Slavery in the Cities*. New York: Oxford University Press, 1964.

Wiley, George. M.D. *Southern Plantation Stories and Sketches*. Freeport, N.Y.: Books for Libraries Press, 1971.

Williams, Isaac D. *Sunshine and Shadow of Slave Life: Reminiscences as Told by Isaac D. Williams to "Tige."* East Saginaw, Michigan: Evening News Printing and Binding House, 1885.

Dianne McIntyre: A Twentieth Century African-American Griot

▲▲▲▲▲▲▲▲▲▲▲▲▲▲▲▲▲

Cynthia S'thembile West

Many dance scholars have noted the African influence in the contemporary dance theater of African-Americans, but no one has ever looked at modern dance in comparison to the form and structure of African music. Dianne McIntyre's modern dance stories are linked to Africa in this way.

"The drum is talking to the dancer and the dancer is talking back to the drum in the body," says twentieth-century griot, or storyteller Dianne McIntyre. Like the ancient African griots who told their stories through the events that occurred over days, weeks, months, years, decades, and centuries, McIntyre's dances chronicle African-American history in the African way. For McIntyre "dance is music moving" like the sound of the drum in the dancer's body.

Dianne McIntyre's dances, like African stories, are functional dramas. Of her own work McIntyre says,

> I want the dance to have some kind of meaning, some kind of impact on myself, the dancers, and the people who experience it, so that it has some function. I know the dances in Africa are so connected to the people in terms of their society, their daily life. In that same way I want the dance to have a close connection with what people's lives are about. Because of that the themes I select often deal with our history and whatever we feel from the inside in our daily lives.

Photo © Johan Elbers

Dianne McIntyre and Olu Dara

Deborah Jowitt of the Village Voice has said that, "Almost all of McIntyre's dances are dramatic, but few of them deal with literal drama. We deduce events and climates from her dances by the way they affect the dancers' speed, stability, energy, space." But to manipulate these aspects, McIntyre's stories use African elements, namely: call and response, a torso inclined slightly forward with bent knees, flat-footed shuffles, sweeping curves, complex rhythmic runs, circles, and shouts. These African characteristics give McIntyre's dances dynamic vitality, so that the stories inspire, and comment on life. Her dances place us on a cliff overlooking the landscape that is African-American life. Through her eyes we too become surveyors of that landscape, the dance takes us to that other level, if only for a moment.

Just as Africa is evident in the stance and walk of peoples of African ancestry, Africa is the core component of Dianne McIntyre's work. Africa is also apparent in the complex rhythmic expressions of African-Americans: instrumental sounds, hand clapping, dance steps, and song patterns. Combining the rhythmic density of the Jazz musicians, the rhythmic separation of upper and lower halves of the body with improvisation, McIntyre emphasizes and uses the infinitely diverse components of Africa's musical form. The effect of this variable holistic structure is vital, powerful, and transformative. This is the special quality that makes Dianne McIntyre's stories, dance derived from African roots, different and special.

Born in Cleveland, Ohio, July 18, 1946, Dianne came to New York in 1970, after graduating from Ohio State University and teaching for a year in Wisconsin. She performed with Gus Solomons Jr. before forming her own company, *Sounds in Motion*. Dance Visions Inc. in 1972. The company name tersely reflects her attitude about the function of the dance. "I think of the dancer as a musical instrument, so that the dancer becomes a part of the band." No one instrument, or dancer is dominant over another. This quality make McIntyre's dances African. "The famed unity of the arts in African performance suggests a sensible approach in which one medium is never absolutely emphasized over others."[1]

McIntyre spent years studying and listening to the language of Jazz musicians.

I tried to teach myself to move the way they sounded, and thereby expanding my vocabulary from that traditional modern dance that I had been taught. So that musicality was what I then thought of transferring to other dancers . .. I heard a great sense of speed.

There are certain things they (Jazz musicians) do in runs that are intricate and very very fast. I hadn't seen parallel things in movement. That type of thing, those intricate rhythms with the speed and the center of the body with the drums, was done in African music and dance, but I did not see that in modern (dance), or transferred to other parts of the body in a modern type movement.

Dianne then decided to work with dancers in the same way that musicians worked with each other. Working with the dancers as instruments, movement became another voice in the band.

In preparing for choreography, one of Dianne's priorities was to learn the social dances of the 20's and 30's. "One of the things that keeps us really connected as a people are the dances that we do socially over time," McIntyre asserts. Over the years African-Americans have continued to communicate with each other through social dances. Not only do social dances show the temperament of the times, but they also define the attitudes of those who danced them. The kind of non-verbal exchanges African-Americans have in social dances tell how we feel about each other, and indicate our "joy and exhilaration" dancing together. "That kind of community feeling in the dance can say a lot of things we don't have to say verbally," exclaims McIntyre. For Dianne, the mess-around, and the shim-sham-shimmie, African-American social dances, reflect what we know about ourselves from ancient times, even though we may not know the specifics of certain stories. They contain the material from which she builds. "I couldn't do what I do in a freer way unless I knew that stuff," concludes McIntyre.

Dianne's voice has been colored and shaded by many experiences. Although she had no intentions of creating a ballet when she went to Haiti in 1974, a very special dance, *Union*, came out of that Haitian experience. *Union* celebrated Africa as it swelled with hot equatorial rhythms. The rhythms sliced the dancers' bodies, while plaintiff riffs from Ahmed Abdullah's trumpet, Babafumi Akunyan's conga, and Charli Persip's drums pierced space and Langston Hughes' praise poems. Gwendolyn Nelson's scat-like vocals ran circles around the runs of the dancers, which paralleled the runs in the music. The dancers' arms thrust toward the earth like straight-edged spades attached to rapidly revolving wheels. Torsos tilted forcefully forward as if on the edge of the world. In *Union* each plod is a step that builds to a run, and becomes an act of defiance, growing in speed and intensity, emphasizing every element as vital and important.

For me, *Union* is like a high-spirited church meeting. Take out even one element of the drama, and church no longer has vitality, life, or energy. Poet-writer Ntozake Shange has said, "the company is literally flying, cutting the air, as the lights fade. The music goes on. Our lives depend on our coming together. While we breathe, there can be no bows. There is no rest." So like the church meetings where we come together as an African people, *Union* saves us. On the one hand *Union* escalates in fury and ancestral presence, while on the other hand *Union* melts and slows momentarily to allow the dancers, African people, time to pause, to take a breath, to recover, to commune. *Union* functions as an African ritual.

Union is an African dance of life, alive with the ever changing dynamics of call and response, shouts, bent-knee stances, and improvisation. The ballet thrives on the unique and dynamic interaction of these components. The structure of the story challenges the dancers to put themselves in the spaces of the runs, which may be as brief as the splitsecond of a sixteenth note. Often McIntyre's choreography dares them to create their own rhythms which may be parallel to, or against the melody. McIntyre's dancers are inside the beat. "Most dancers in Africa step inside rhythms. This necessitates phrasing every note and step with consummate vitality."[2] In fact the Akan say "the ideal dancer never seeks applause while dancing, but spontaneously incites enthusiasm through total commitment to his footwork and kinetic flair."[3]

Although Dianne McIntyre's dances contain African elements, hers are not the only dance works to exhibit African traits. Dance historian and critic Zita Allen says that McIntyre "shares a spiritual kinship" with Alvin Alley. Like the works of Alley, McIntyre's dances take a visual journey through particular periods and events in African-American history. She, like her colleague, fuses symbols with movement and music to portray the experiences and sensibilities of African-Americans.

Alvin Alley's classic, *Revelations*, tells literal stories about African enslavement in the U.S., while McIntyre's, *Union*, conjures up emotional memories of the same period. *Union* and *Revelations* are similar. Both explore the dynamic tension between extremes of emotion, although McIntyre does this within the framework of the African music tradition. Each of the dancemakers, however, uses African elements: call and response, the Negro spirituals, vital energy, and speed to tell stories of Africans in America.

Dianne McIntyre's stories are linked to relationships between African-Americans, the communities to which they belong, and their ancestors. In her stories, African-Americans assert their voices through the dancers, and respond to the conditions of their lives on their own terms, just as the slaves asserted their will and determination at the praise-meetings in the slave quarters of the plantation South.

McIntyre says her dances parallel African dance because "I think about the dance as a divine offering. It is not a dance for the sake of some kind of artistic merit, or success, or entertainment." A McIntyre dance is a praise-meeting or church session. Historically, praise sessions were always dance sessions. Through paying homage to the forces that created life and themselves, the African slaves reinforced their beliefs, and healed themselves not only physically, but psychologically as well.

> In contrast to most white churches, a meeting in the quarters was the scene of perpetual motion and constant singing. Swaying the body, patting the foot, clapping hands, and shouts have always been a part of the African tradition. After the praise-meeting is over, there usually follows the very singular and impressive performance of the "shout" or religious dance of the negroes. Three or four, standing still, clapping their hands and beating time with their feet, commence singing in unison one of the peculiar shout melodies, while the others walk round in a ring, in single file, joining also in the song. Soon those in the ring leave off their singing, and others keeping it up the while with increased vigor, and strike into the shout step, observing most accurate time with the music. This step is something halfway between a shuffle and a dance, as difficult for an uninitiated person to describe as to imitate. At the end of each stanza of the song the dancers stop short with a slight stamp on the last note, and then, putting the other foot forward, proceed through the next verse. ... the shout is a simple outburst and manifestation of religious fervor.[4]

Through these important religious events African people transformed themselves, and lifted their spirits. This transformation occurs today through African-American dance forms.

Circle of Soul, McIntyre's most recent dance story, is an example of how the ring shout is manifest in contemporary African-American theater. The circular physical-structure of the piece, as well as the dynamic ongoing energy, kinesis, and repetition make *Circle of Soul* African. In the opening landscape the dancers stand making a circle on the fringes of the stage with the musicians in the center. The dancers move steadily. One movement connected to another and another and another, linked in time and rhythm, moving continuously, always wedded, and always redefining the circle, relates directly to the shouts that overran southern U.S. slave plantations.

Circle of Soul is a twentieth century ritual developed from an African griot perspective. The story evolves out of the language created by the dancers and the instrumentalists. Just as an African dancer and drummer parallel each other, the dancers and musicians match each other in this work, as in all of Dianne McIntyre's dance stories. Despite *Circle of Soul's* non-literal thematic approach, a story unfolds through the insinuation of gesture, trap drums, trumpet, and blues-songrhythm. The dancers cavort, and sashay in blue-night-green pants and tops, like people gettin' down on a Friday night. Contrasting material flares over the backs of their pants like small loincloths, and wafts gently as they carve concentric circles around the instrumentalists while they got-down. "Get-down sequences are virtuosic. Getting down encloses a dual expression of salutation and devotion."[5]

The dancers as soloists or group performers play the dozens, tease, romp, support, and pull each other with innuendoes that demonstrate emotional states. Their voices respond to, question, and comment on the music's insistent delta-deep-downbeat. Olu Dara's trumpet, harmonica, and blues-chant vocals drive the dancers, who in turn drive the musicians. The musicians moan and slide sensually as they parallel each other. The steady wail of down-home blues slowly and steadily drives the dancers faster and faster, hurling them into the belly of the sound as it emanates from centerstage.

This centrifugal pull happens partly because Olu Dara's music has a very strong rhythmic base that McIntyre says, "takes us back to (our) social dances." In Olu's music the dancers had to drop into the rhythm. They also had to drop, according to Dianne, "certain kinds of technical ideas of what real dance might be to them, and get to the bottom of it, so that the depth of the dance is not colored by something that technically puts a veil over it."

Unlike Cecil Taylor's compositions, which McIntyre says are like beautiful firecrackers, Olu Dara's music "stays rooted in a rhythm." "If there was a rule in it," McIntyre stresses, "that (rule) would be that you may go off the rhythmic base in terms of improvisation, but you always come back and establish it because it would be sacrilegious not to honor that rhythm." The weightiness the dancers feel and the viewer sees in *Circle of Soul* emphasizes that rhythm. "So," McIntyre states, "in a way, working with Olu, the body becomes a kind of drum in itself."

While emphasizing the percussive instrument that the body can be, Olu's compositions also have "great sensuality." "Because it does come out of the blues, often that connection between men and women is inherent in his music," say McIntyre. This is what McIntyre believes makes Olu's music allied to music in different parts of Africa. Even though the beats are harder to hear in Cecil Taylor's compositions initially, they too, like Olu's scores, parallel Africa.

Olu Dara and McIntyre have collaborated on other works. They are familiar with individual nuances of style and point of view. Even though Olu scats and pulls notes to a groan, slurs over time signatures, and jumps barlines in a musical hopscotch of bluesy suggestion, the score covers the dancers like a luxurious patchwork quilt of grandmother dreams for bold, insouciant children. *Circle of Soul* is a ritual of community, a celebration of African life, a divine offering to the gods. "Received traditions of standing and sitting and other modes of phrasing the body transform the person into art, make his body a metaphor of ethics and aliveness and ultimately, relate him to the gods."[6]

Everything Africans do in the traditional sense is somehow connected to the gods or deities. Whether they are Yoruba or Akan, human life is intricately intertwined with the will of the deities, and the insight gained from communicating with them through the dance.

Although McIntyre's twentieth century dance stories are not exact recreations of specific events and deeds, they have firm roots in the traditions of African music. When the lead drummer in a djembe orchestra plays a run that is embellished by another djembe drummer, both voices are necessary and vital to the orchestration. So too, when the two-headed songba drum voice enters the arena, that drummer acknowledges the importance of maintaining and enlarging the orchestral sound. Djembe and songbas may repeatedly, at least to the Western ear, exchange roles as lead or embellisher, but they do so with equal responsibility and mutual respect. This is the unspoken creed in African music as in Dianne McIntyre's dance stories.

This African formula has been transferred in the traditions of African-American Jazz musicians. They have a sympathetic way of moving together while they improvise. Working together consistently over time makes their bonding stronger. In the same way McIntyre has always wanted her dancers to develop a particular closeness dancing with one another. According to Dianne, the dancer "could be the soloist on top of the music being a certain kind of base, or they could be rhythmically playing with each other. They could be call and response with each other. I have in mind for the dancer to be another voice in the band or orchestra in the (same) way that the musicians are with each other. So therefore, it would be like the music in Africa, or like the way African dancers work with their music." Like the rat....ta....ta, rat....ta ....ta... of the djembe orchestra, McIntyre's stories slice the space, and make room for definite visions, and the hope of dreams fulfilled. Every time a note slides or slinks, skips or jabs the space in one of her dances, some aspect of Africa is paralleled. The run of a dancer across the stage parallels a run of a musician's instrument. As dance historian and critic Zita Allen points out, "movement mirrors music mirroring movement in a kind of ricocheting reflexivity of the two major elements of Dianne's choreography." McIntyre's dance stories show the richness of the African musical form.

McIntyre's concept has always been that the music and the dance are parallel. For her, "the music has not been the accompaniment." "Neither is dominant over the other," she reiterates frequently. In fact, she smiles, "it must be something in my African genetic background. I can't say exactly why I made that kind of decision. I always thought on it was right for the dance and the music to be on parallel planes."

McIntyre's 1982 non-literal story *Eye of the Crocodile* was a musical ritual, using sound and movement as a springboard for a story of changing moods and cycles. Cecil Taylor and his Segments Ensemble trod along with the dancers on a journey of sight, sound, and emotion. With the consistency of melting ice cream, the dancers melted with the steady stream of notes from the ensemble. Together like twentieth century African warriors, they bopped over concrete streets and flew over skyscrapers, taking musical routes through Harlem, Brownsville, Chicago, Atlanta, St. Louis, Kansas City, meccas of African-American Jazz music.

Cecil Taylor, who McIntyre says has the fastest fingers in the world on the piano, has consistently been in the advance guard of Jazz music. Early in his career Taylor had vowed "to make energies and techniques of the European composers useful, to blend them with the traditional music of the American Negro, and thus create a new energy." By the time Cecil worked with Dianne on *Shadows* in 1979, and on *Eye of the Crocodile* in 1982, he had perfected a style that he had explored during the so-called "Free Jazz" period of the '60's. Simply expressed, Taylor explored the concept of energy as a function of time, and the reciprocal effect of energy and movement: "energy creates movement or is created by movement." The Jazz formula, "theme, improvisations, theme," had no validity for Taylor. "Just as the transitions between solo and collective improvisations were blurred, it was by no means always clear where the composed parts stopped and the improvisation began."[8]

McIntyre's dancers had to be able to hear what Cecil was doing in the creation of *Eye of the Crocodile*. "It took longer for the newer people," she says.

> They had to hear that these were individual compositions. Your ear had to be tuned to the subtleties of the differences of the compositions. What I was doing in the music was what I felt from what I heard Cecil doing. It wasn't an intellectual way of putting down something. It was a feeling, and then at the same time Cecil would compose what he saw us doing. So the work with Cecil was totally cyclical. It was all coming at the same time: fast and furious.

Cecil's music had always inspired Dianne to dance.

Black, silver, and gold costumes shimmered in diffused amber light as clusters of dancers oozed in McIntyre's provocative opening for *Eye of the Crocodile*. Blunt angles and wide rectangular positions overtook the swelling roundness of the opening clusters. The dancers enveloped each other in part three, and like nerve impulses moving rapidly over synapses, the dance intensified. Frenetic impulses were caught, and passed from dander to dander like sound in djembe orchestration. The duet for McIntyre and another dancer was both frantic and contained, and ended with McIntyre wrapping her arms around the other's neck, encasing it like a snake.

Eye of the Crocodile crescendoed in section four. Soft fluid advances changed to pulsing skitters rapidly crisscrossing the space. This African voyage, demonstrating oneness through speed, direction, attitude, and position, came to an end as the dancers slowed, and the quick pace of Cecil's piano keys came to a halt.

Just like the halt of Cecil Taylor's fingers at the piano, McIntyre's stories, like the memories of good stories, linger. They are songs whose melodies and harmonies stimulate the senses through rhythm and improvisation. Just as the drumming and rhythmic orchestration of the African dancer's body take ritual to new levels of physical and psychological awareness, Dianne McIntyre's stories transform. Like the steady pulse of marching songs, the dances always insist as they plow forward, relentless in their demand for physical accuracy and skill just like African dance. The dancers are challenged by the speed of McIntyre's modern dance vocabulary: broad outflung gestures, flapping the arms, and off-centered balances. In addition to the extreme physical demands of the choreography, the dancers are also challenged to create their own melodies within the structure set by McIntyre and the musicians. McIntyre's dancers meet that challenge. They have the uncanny ability to create improvisational riffs with split-second precision. They are wizards of the complementary phrase. Like African dancers, they are perfect improvisors of mood and sound. These unique performers give McIntyre's stories their memorable, mesmerizing effect.

Perhaps one of the most enchanting dance stories of McIntyre's sixteen year career as head of a New York dance company was *Take-off From a Forced Landing*. The remarkable exploits of Dianne's mother, Dorothy Arline Layne McIntyre, one of the first Black women pilots (1940), form the backbone of the story. The work evolves metaphorically around piloting. Parallels are drawn between the skill and imagination required to pilot an airplane, and those skills necessary to pilot events in life. Using a collage of dance, music, a commissioned score by Jazz composer/cornetist Butch Morris, and dialogue, Dianne McIntyre tells how her mother taught her to "fly" in her own way. New York critic Deborah Jowitt had this to say about *Take-off From a Forced Landing*, "Dianne McIntyre constructs parallels between the dreams, ambitions, and setbacks of her own mother, a pioneering, black female pilot, and the aspirations of that woman's three children."

Although highs and lows are woven into the fabric of the story, composer/conductor Butch Morris' intriguing score keeps the fantasy alive. Morris has the ability to make any music he touches dramatic. McIntyre calls his music "the intrigue music, high adventure, drama, and fantasy." Butch can take even music that has a strong rhythmic or blues base and give it those same adventurous, dramatic skips and loops of the score for *Take-off From a Forced Landing*.

Take-off From a Forced Landing parallels African and African-American folk tale characters, specifically Anansi the spider (West African) and Brer Rabbit. In these stories the smaller creature usually overcomes the bigger, stronger adversary. Consistently the spider and the rabbit show that intelligence and resourcefulness are winning combinations. This same winning recipe makes McIntyre's dance fantasy, *Take-off From a Forced Landing* universally significant.

The title, *Take-off From a Forced Landing* implies that a way must be found to resume flight once momentum toward a personal goal is stopped, blocked, or detoured. Despite the difficulties of becoming a Black female pilot in the '40's, Dorothy Arline Layne McIntyre successfully reached her goal. Her courage and persistence are examples that other African-Americans can follow, especially children. Dorothy's actions are metaphors for resourcefulness and ingenuity just like the Anansi and Brer Rabbit tales. And like the African tales, this dance fantasy demonstrates how we/African-Americans, as our African forebears, value family ties, children, and knowledge. In *Take-off From a Forced Landing*, Sounds in Motion Dance Company has a broad strip from which to "take-off" again and again. Here McIntyre's characters, like her mother, make their own choices.

Knowing how to "take-off" physically and psychologically at just the right moment is embodied in McIntyre's dance stories, and in African dance. Her jumps contain a torque, a suspension commonly seen in African dance, that freezes the dancer in midair. This requires rugged physical stamina, skill, nerve, guts, and knowing exactly when to "take-off." Precision and timing are crucial elements which heighten the drama and rivet attention. McIntyre's signature is defined by suspended buoyancy, swaggered sliding walks, hands flung out forcefully with each finger carving its own world in the space, and sustained balances that float on stage. Although the dancers repeatedly execute the same moves in many of her dances, none of the dances lose their vibrancy, nor do any two dancers look alike. The improvisatory structure of the story allows room for individual freedom and creativity. Each dancer has their own unique "take-off."

The dance stories of twentieth century griot Dianne McIntyre represent Africa in America. McIntyre's stories not only demonstrate the powerful African presence in American theater, but they also show that Africa is responsible for much of her mindset and performance style. Using African and modern dance vocabulary, literal and non-literal themes in the context of traditional African music, McIntyre has created a griot style which is narrative, informative, and exciting. Although Sounds in Motion Dance Company officially disbanded in August of 1988, Dianne McIntyre continues her work as a choreographer creating stories of African people.

"Explorations in the dance that I have made over time have helped satisfy that part in me that my work is fictional. And I think of the work also as an offering back to the ancestors from whence all of this energy came, and also to God for just making it possible. And this is the same thing that is in the tradition of the African dance, and the music. It's all an offering," concludes McIntyre.

Looking at the qualities that make dance an offering in the African tradition is the next issue to consider in an analysis of Dianne McIntyre's dance stories.

Notes

1. Robert F. Thompson, *African Art in Motion: Icon and Act* (California: University of California Press, 1974), xii.
2. Thompson 7.
3. Thompson 1.
4. John W. Blassingame, *The Slave Community: Plantation Life in the Antebellum South* (New York: Oxford University Press, 1972), 65.
5. Thompson 14.
6. Thompson xiv.
7. Joachim E. Berendt, *The Story of Jazz* (New Jersey: Prentice-Hall Inc., 1978), 122.
8. Berendt 123.
9. Personal interview with Diane McIntyre, Artistic Director of Sounds in Motion, New York, New York, 7 November 1988.

Works Cited

Asante, Molefi and Kariamu Welsh Asante (eds.). *African Culture: the Rhythms of Unity.* Connecticut: Greenwood Press, 1985.

Berendt, Joachim E. *The Story of Jazz.* New Jersey: Prentice-Hall Inc., 1978.

Blassingame, John W. *The Slave Community; Plantation Life in the Ante-bellum South.* New York: Oxford University Press, 1972.

Clark, Leon E. (ed.). *Through African Eyes: Culture in Change.* New York: Praeger Publishers, 1970.

Nketia, J. H. Kwabena. *African Gods and Music.* Ghana: Institute of African Studies, 1970.

Nketia, J. H. Kwabena. *Ghana: Music, Dance, and Drama: A Review of the Performing Arts of Ghana.* n.p. 1965.

Opoku, A. M. *The Ghana Dance Ensemble.* Ghana: Pierian Press, n.d.

Personal interview with Dianne McIntyre, Artistic Director of Sounds in Motion, New York, NY, 7 November 1988.

Thompson, Robert F. *African Art in Motion; Icon and Act.* California: University of California Press, 1974.

Tap Dance: Manifestation of the African Aesthetic

▲▲▲▲▲▲▲▲▲▲▲▲▲▲▲▲

Cheryl Willis

Many Americans immediately recall the name of Fred Astaire when tap dance is mentioned. However, there is a long line of history that stretches beyond the movie images. The ancestry of this unique art form, which originated in the United States, has been the subject of much debate. Many cultures have claimed the creation of tap dance, since the foot dances of Native Americans, English, Irish, and Africans have been in evidence from the earliest history of this country. The degree to which these dance forms have influenced each other is also a subject of contention. This research, however, will focus on the dance form that evolved from the foot dances of African-Americans, which became known as hoofin', rhythm dance, and jazz tap. Throughout this study this dance form will be referred to as tap dance.

Research for this study has included the works of Richard Farris Thompson, Kariamu Welsh-Asante, Zora Neale Hurston, Marshal and Jean Stearns, Ashenafi Kebede, Alain Locke, John F. Szwed and Roger Abrahams. The primary sources of films and interviews with tap dancers were also used.

This research rests on the following assumption: the deep structure within a culture is found in the retention of characteristics of behavior that are not effected by time and geography; surface structure is effected by time and geography.[1]

In their article "After the Myth: Studying Afro-American Cultural

Patterns in the Plantation Literature," Szwed and Abrahams discuss the encouragement of noninstitutional dimensions of culture during plantation slavery, such as work practices, ways of playing, and systems of magic and curing. In the United States practices associated with political, economic, and social units from the African society were discouraged. Therefore, Szwed and Abrahams refer to the divesting of the African society as "desocietalization" and not a deculturation.[2] The deep structure of a culture is inherent within a society and functions beneath the level of consciousness. Although the surface structure of the African society was denied, the philosophical principles and psychological attitudes (the deep structure) persisted.[3] In studies which detail slavery from the Middle Passage to slave life in the New World, it is apparent that shared practices, beliefs, and behavioral patterns of Africans (the deep structure of the culture) were and are maintained. However, the surface structure of African culture was left behind and, in many cases, was forbidden in the New World; for example, African style sculpture, drums, and clothing.

It is the intention of this research to analyze tap dance as an expression of the deep structure passed on from African culture. The major characteristics of tap dance, which will be considered for analysis within the African aesthetic, are attitude, musicality, and style. Attitude refers to the intention of the dancer as reflected in the movement and creativity of the dance. Musicality treats not only the music which accompanies the dance, but also the music that the dance creates. Style indicates the movement and shape of the body during the performance of the dance.

Attitude

According to Laban's theories of movement, "attitude toward" or "control over" a movement is not necessarily a conscious act that the mover decides to do. However, the attitude which produces the "movement quality is an aspect of behavior and can be considered a product of learning, metabolism, perception of the environment, whatever your particular bias is about what produces differences in behavior."[4]

Attitude is a complex issue when discussing African art due to the comprehensive philosophy of the culture. African culture is wholistic in the sense that all aspects of life are integrated. Life is a system that connects the mind-body-spirit, one relying on and affecting the other.

Philosophy, theology, politics, social theory, land law, medicine, psychology, birth and burial, all find themselves logically concatenated in a system so tight that to subtract one item from the whole is to paralyse the structure of the whole.[5]

Ideas relating to balance and "vital aliveness" are common threads that will be seen throughout this research.[6]

In Thompson's ten canons of fine form in African art, "vital aliveness" possesses qualities of intensity, strong expression, speed, drive, and flexibility. "Vital aliveness" has no age barrier; yet, it connects life with death and man with the spirit.[7]

Balance or personal equilibrium controls "vital aliveness" which gives the quality Thompson refers to as the "Cool." "In Africa coolness is an all-embracing positive attribute which combines notions of composure, silence, vitality, healing, and social purification."[8] Thompson refers to the "Cool" philosophy as an all-important mediating process which is governed by "a strong intellectual attitude, affecting incredibly diverse provinces of artistic happening, yet leavened with humor and a sense of play."[9] The "Cool" has a paradoxical nature: control yet uncertainty, imitative yet original, high intensity yet laid back, serious yet playful, hot yet cool.

Visible and smooth are characteristics directly from Thompson's canon of "Coolness" found in African art. In dance, visibility indicates clarity of movement which is fully in view. ". . . visibility is an embodiment of the resolving power of the cool, i.e., moderation of force in discovery of the mean between that which is faint and that which is conspicuous."[10] Although there are exceptions, in general, African society values openness. It is thought that those who have things to hide generate dissention. The concept of visibility is balanced and more profound than dance movement. According to Thompson the criterion of clarity is important to understand the significance of art.

Compare the Yoruba proverb: if the secret is beat upon the drum, that secret will be revealed in dance.' Nothing should or can remain unrevealed in viable society. This is also a basic premise among the Ndembu of Central Africa, where it is believed that what is clearly seen can be accepted as valid ground for knowledge.[11]

Zora Neale Hurston in *The Sanctified Church* directly relates the concept of openness in African-American culture in her explanation of the absence of privacy. According to Hurston, "It is said that Negroes keep nothing secret, that they have no reserve. This ought not to seem strange when one considers that we are an outdoor people accustomed to communal life."[12] Hurston's statement substantiates the concept of deep structure as it has been maintained in the aspect of openness within the African-American culture.

In the African aesthetic "smoothness is thus identified with a unified aesthetic impact; seams do not show, the whole is moving towards a generous conclusion based on total giving of the self to the music and to society."[13] Therefore, the attitude is a generous giving of a visual whole—a total picture.

In tap dance the attitude of African-Americans is expressed in concepts of visible and smooth. The idea of visibility is apparent in how tap dancers conceptualize the dance. Jimmy Slyde, who recently appeared in the Broadway musical "Black and Blue," described himself as a visual dancer. He approaches tap dance as having a picture in mind that he wants to portray.[14] Chuck Green, formerly of the tap team "Chuck and Chuckles" also acknowledges the visual aspect of the dance. In reference to choreography Green says, "Make the personality intelligent, viewable, where it can be seen, enjoyed. And make someone watching it think it's that they're doing it themselves; their imagination is a reality."[15]

"He [Teddy Hale] was just spectacular," said Gregory Hines, who starred in movies such as "Cotton Club," "White Nights," and "Tap." "I couldn't believe my eyes. I mean, he was just so smooth."[16] Smooth, the characteristic of total giving, was the attitude in a tribute to Sammy Davis, Jr. A film clip was shown of Davis saying the following:

> You can't please everybody, you know, but you please the majority. And don't ever let them say, "Gee, I didn't like the performance." That doesn't mean that everybody is not going to like what you're doing; but at least they'll be able to say, "He performed for me, man; he gave his all!"[17]

Another quality which is essential to the aesthetic of the "Cool" is that of balance. It is found in African culture and Thompson refers to it as mid-point mimesis. "Beauty is the mean."[18] Moderation is the standard: neither too tall nor too short; neither too fast nor too slow; Neither too peripheral nor too self contained; neither too much nor too little. This midpoint mimesis is also found in tap dancer as Chuck Green says, "You have to know how much dancin' to do. You can't just do all you want to do. You got to do what's needed to do."[19]

In African culture personal balance or equilibrium (midpoint mimesis) is developed through contrasts. The balance of contrasts in the African aesthetic produces the "Cool." The demand for one to be flexible and open to change is stressed for "to dwell at one level is to lose the precious power of balance inherent in human capability."[20]

As the African adapts to change, flexibility and vitally alive attitudes are evident "... showing the necessity of persons of caprice and humor within the shaping of human viability. We must accept composure and control, but not at the price of humor—the gift of refusal to suffer."[21]

This aspect of the African aesthetic is evident in tap dance as it is serious yet playful. In the film "Tapdancin'" the balance of intricate rhythms are balanced by jokes, slapstick, or facial gestures. One example of this is Ralph Brown who performs a complex rhythm pattern, but before he finishes the audience bursts into applause. He says, "No, no, no," meaning that the applause was too soon. Then he pauses to think and responds, "What am I saying? Yeah, yeah, yeah," leading the audience in laughter and applause.[22] Another example is in a performance of swinging jazz rhythms by Jimmy Slyde. His sliding movement knocks him off balance; but as he gains control his facial gesture reveals a comic surprise which saves the movement and recaptures the "Cool."[23]

The attitude of the tap dancer is the balance and aliveness referred to by Thompson as the "Cool" and which is inherent in the African philosophy. Later in this article further explanation and examples of attitude will be discussed as it relates to musicality and style.

Musicality

"Rhythm is what it's all about. You've go to have rhythm," said Ralph Brown of the Copesetics.[24] This rhythmic expression in a percussive mode is the first characteristic of musicality. Tap dance is percussive rhythms and the floor is the instrument which is played by the feet. Attaching metal plates to the heels and toes of the shoes, tap dancers as drummers play musical phrases, which consists of motifs, riffs, licks, flams and rolls. It is not only the feet that display this percussive style, but the hands clap and slap other body parts. The voice also maintains a percussive manner as it sings out rhythmical sounds as "ugh," "ah-ah," "umh." Langston Hughes described Bill "Bojangles" Robinson's percussive dance as a "symphonic composition of sounds ... What the ear hears is the priceless African heritages."[26] Ralph Brown views the rhythm of tap dance as a code or a message.[27] Chuck Green sees tap dance as "saying something," or as "telling a story."[28]

When discussing this percussive dance of African-Americans,

one must examine its roots. Thompson designated West Africa as a percussive culture. Instruments are played with a percussive bias and the dance which is also percussive consists of stamping, clapping, taps, and rattles.[29] Vocalizing in the form of vocables,[30] ululation,[31] and calls[32] are prevalent throughout Africa. Thompson describes West African dances as "talking dances" with the expression of the conversation in percussive concepts. As the drums communicate on a verbal basis, the dancers also speak out in bodily rhythms of particular gestures and steps.[33]

It is important here to note that swing is the second characteristic of musicality. Swing must be analyzed to establish tap dance as an offshoot of African dance in the diaspora.

Marshall and Jean Stearns base their book, *Jazz Dance: The Story of American Vernacular Dance*, on "American dancing that is performed to and with the rhythms of jazz—that is, dancing that swings."[34] In tap dance, as in jazz music, the rhythm is based on a swing feel. "Syncopation often takes the form of accenting notes that occur just before or just after the beat."[35] It may be thought of as off-beat accenting or the occurrence of stress where it is least expected. Yet, there is no exact musical notation for where this accent occurs. It is more of a feeling, which is known as the "swing feel."

Jimmy Slyde states, "Swing is from inside. You must have that within, I believe. But to the dance there's balance involved, movement involved, and still you must swing."[36]

This musical concept of swing has been documented by Thompson as an inherent characteristic in African dance and music. As with the African attitude, music also has an equilibrium, a balance of accent, pitch, melody, strength, force, buoyancy and drive.[37] This balance in music and dance is enlivened by deliberate off-beat phrasing of the accents and suspending and preserving of the beat which gives the swing feel to African music and dance.[38]

Thompson confirms that "most dancers in Africa step inside rhythms . . . " To step inside rhythms necessitates a strong and balanced rhythm of the dancer.[39] The dancer does not dance on the beat of the music but establishes a rhythm that balances the music. The concept of stepping inside of rhythms gives evidence to the polyrhythmic aspect of African music and dance. In African music several rhythms happen simultaneously and these rhythms happen simultaneously and these rhythms can employ different meters. Welsh-Asante stresses the ability of African dancers "to stand back from the rhythms of the scene and find an additional rhythm which complement and mediates those other rhythms."[40]

According to Thompson, West African musicians "play 'apart' in the sense that each is often intent upon the production of his own contribution to a polymetric whole."[41] There is a rhythmic structure upon which members (usually the master drummer) may deviate or improvise. This playing apart gives one the space in which to maintain a private or traditional meter and to express one's own full corporeal involvement in what one is doing.[42]

Tap dance, comparable to jazz music,[43] and African music and dance, employs improvisation. It is that which keeps the dance vital and fresh. In the film "About Tap" Gregory Hines told the story about trying to learn the steps of Teddy Hale. He explains that he watched Hale perform three times in one day and each time the performance was different. It was then that Hines realized that Teddy Hale's dance was built on improvisation.[44]

Polyrhythms and "apart playing" are evident in jazz and in tap dance. Baby Lawrence, who called himself a jazz tap percussionist, demonstrates polyrhythms in the film "The Story of the Legendary Baby Lawrence." He and drummer perform four and eight bar breaks against one another's sound. In discussing his concept for tap dance rhythms, which are polymetric, Baby Lawrence explains how he breaks down musical bars and changes the rhythms thereby performing thirty-two rhythms or more in sixteen bars.[45]

Polyrhythms in tap dance can also be observed in the relation of dancer to musician, the dancer steps inside the rhythms of the musicians. In pointing out this relationship, Jimmy Slyde explains that it's a "willingness to receive what the musicians are playing and their willingness to receive what you're dancing. Therefore, you have to have a good rapport; and the more you swing the more you'll find out you have something in common."[46]

Thompson cites an example of a Dan dancer from the northeast of Liberia to demonstrate the dancer/musician relationship:

> He enters the dancing ring in the village square first to salute the master drummer, "to get his motion," i.e., to settle the basic rhythm. He then begins a toe-dragging sequence, kept simple, because the drummer is studying his motion. Slowly he develops his dance; he must keep the drummer active with counter-challenges of percussive footwork.[47]

This example of the Dan dancer, brings to mind the story which

Tommy Sutton told in reference to the development of "time steps," which are part of the basic steps found in tap dance. Sutton explained that during vaudeville the dancer, after discussing his music with the conductor, would enter the stage. As the music started the dancer would do a "time step" to establish the tempo in which he would dance. The conductor would watch the dancer, pick up his signals, and lead the orchestra accordingly.[48]

The time step, based on six measures of a repeated rhythmical phrase and two measures of a break in rhythm, is an example of asymmetrical balance found in both African and African-American expression. Hurston discusses the paradoxical presence of asymmetry in the dancing of African-Americans as containing rhythm and the lack of symmetry. She states:

> There is always rhythm, but it is the rhythm of segments. Each unit has a rhythm of its own, but when the whole is assembled it is lacking in symmetry. But easily workable to a Negro who is accustomed to the break in going from one part to another, so that he adjusts himself to the new tempo.[49]

The musicality of tap dance, which is percussive, polyrhythmic, swinging, and dependent on the interrelationship of the dancer and musician, is a direct outgrowth of the African aesthetic.

Style

The final aspect for discussion that links tap dance to its African roots is style. Style encompasses many of the characteristics that have previously been discussed in the aspects of attitude and musicality. However, style, especially in tap dance, in unique as it emphasizes the individuality of each dancer.

Tap dancer has a unique angular style that is quite similar to the body posture of West African dance. The knees are bent in a supple manner; the arms and fingers are also angular. In tap dance the body is erect with a slight tilt in the hip sockets. Tap dance, which is flat-footed, was elevated to the toes by Bill "Bojangles" Robinson, but was brought back to its heels (the dropping of the heels) by John Bubbles.[50]

Hurston states that angularity is a striking manifestation of African sculpture and doctrine, and that this phenomenon is obvious in "Negro dancing." Every posture is angular.[51] Thompson, in describing the angular posture in African sculpture and dance, substantiates Hurston's theory: "straight line of the back through the neck and head, set over buoyant knees and stable feet. The implication of flexible potency at the hips and knees is striking."[52] And again he states: "The Luba dancer . . . must manifest his suppleness with bent knees, bent elbows, and suave oscillations to the music."[53]

"West Africans cultivate divinity through richly stabilized traditions of personal balance. Presentation of the self through stability is sometimes phrases as 'straightness'."[54] This straightness can be seen in the body posture. "However, the convention would doubtless soon wax boring, were it not honored so magnificently in the breach by kicks, spins, and leaps of certain of the men's dances in Africa."[55] Thompson points out that the preference for asymmetrical posture or stylized instability has continued in dancing of the United States.[56] Hurston ascertains these same qualities and parallels the concepts of straightness to angularity and stylized instability to asymmetry. Hurston explains that through a lack of symmetry in dance, abrupt and unexpected changes occur and in music frequent changes of key and time are evidenced.[57]

In tap dance this personal balance is a part of the structure and control which leaves the dancer open to the risks and the stylized instability of the movement. In explaining his choreography in which slides are used, Jimmy Slyde says, "You can't just meter out slides and say well I'm going to do a slide that's a foot long, cuz it may be a little slippery and you may go three feet. It's not a certainty that you're going to end where you want to . . . "[58]

In African dance the style is vitally alive. The use of the body in a percussive force demands attention to style. "The dancer must impart equal life, equal autonomy, to every dancing portion of his frame."[59]

Although tap dance centers on the feet, the body is a vital part of the dance. In discussing style Chuck Green said, "So you give the body a port de bras which you call a balance, a poise, posture, then you use the tap."[60]

Slyde, referring to the aesthetic of aliveness, describes his dance, "I like to move a lot. Sometimes they call it a blur. Cuz you move too fast you get out of focus, so you have to catch up with yourself. That's where the slides come in."[61]

Vital aliveness is demonstrated through flexibility and suppleness which are prized characteristics in African culture. The supple posture symbolizes the willingness to respond to change. In many West African societies the highest compliment is "to say that a person dances as if she or he had no bones."[62]

In the earlier part of this century tap dance demonstrated a more physical athletic suppleness. Dancers, such as the Nicholas Brothers and the Berry Brothers, performed series of turns, leaps, flips and flying splits into the rhythms of the foot work.[63] Although little acrobatic work is employed by jazz tap dancers today, the flexibility and suppleness which produces a quick response to change in movement is still very much a part of the posture that produces the dance. Subtle shifts of weight allow for the feet to move quickly and the body to change direction. The dancers must be able to move on one foot as does Pegleg Bates[64] or two feet while executing clear, exact rhythmic phrases.

In many societies in Africa the angular posture is evident in the use of "get-down" sequences found in the dance: crouching body positions which have an intense change in vigor and move in close proximity to the earth.[65] Thompson relates "get-down" and improvisation in his observation of dancers in Surinam. He explains that they mark time "until they decide that the psychological moment to improvise has come. Then they crouch, bursting into choreographic flames, showing off marvels of footwork and muscular expression."[66] This display in West Africa and Surinam, which lasts for two or three seconds, is termed the "aesthetic parsimony"[67] of the call-and-response form of dance, assuring, in the overlapping, that everyone who wants to dance can have his turn at getting down. Thompson correlates getting down with solo dancing as an important part of the dance which is performed with vigor and intensity.[68]

Edwina Evelyn, formerly of the tap dance team "Salt & Pepper," compared "get down" to the part of the dance where the dancer is featured in solo. This section of the dance was usually improvised. Evelyn said that many dancers who were soloists improvised the whole dance. In a humorous tone she continued to describe that these dancers usually danced past the musical exit cues because they were just getting warmed up.[69]

It is no secret that tap dancers "steal" steps from each other; however, in a discussion with any of the tap dance masters the philosophy of "take it and make it your own" prevails. Gregory Hines claims that he tried to imitate Teddy Hale, but the older tap dancers told him,

> You can't hope to be a great artist like he is by copying him. You have to take all the steps that you're stealing from him and that we're feeding you and assimilate it; have it come out in your own way . . . Each man, each great dancer has their own unique style and it separates them.[70]

At the 1990 African Dance Conference, Dr. Bernice Reagon addressed the issue of African artistic expression in dance. Imitation in dance is part of the African aesthetic;[71] however, as long as the dance is in the imitative stage it is a premature expression. She stated that the maturity of a movement is measured by the degree that it changes to express the uniqueness of the dancer, the degree that the dancer takes a movement and makes it his/her own. Only by making one's own statement does dance mature.[72] Therefore, creativity, imitative yet original, is highly valued by African and African-American cultures.

With these examples of angularity and asymmetry, balance and stylized instability, flexibility and straightness, "get down" and improvisation, "vital aliveness" and control, one can see similarities in style of tap dance and African aesthetic principles.

Thompson's first canon of fine form of African art is ephebism, the stronger power that comes from youth. Although ephebism means youthfulness, it does not disregard the elderly. In traditional Africa, ephebism is the cherishing of newness and youthfulness in artistic expression. Thompson gives the following example:

> People in Africa, regardless of their actual age, return to strong, youthful patterning whenever they move within the streams of energy which flow from drums or other sources of percussion. They obey the implications of vitality within the music and its speed and drive.[73]

Ephebism is manifested in tap dancers who are stealing the spotlight of today. Men, such as Chuck Green, Jimmy Slyde, Harold Nicholas, Eddie Brown, LaVaughn Robinson, Buster Brown, and Bunny Briggs, are in their sixties and seventies. These men are bringing strong and youthful streams of energy into the dance and using this vitality to keep the tradition alive.

This analysis of attitude, musicality, and style of the African aesthetic with the tap dance tradition of African-Americans, is a starting point for further research into the study of tap dance. Although much has been borrowed or stolen from the aesthetic values of this culture, little has been done to acknowledge and document the aesthetic of African-Americans as an expression of American art, especially in the area of tap dance. Investigation into the deep structure of African-American culture and its expression establishes the connection with its rich African heritage.

Notes

1. "African Aesthetic" lecture class by Kariamu Welsh-Asante, Philadelphia: Temple University, 1989.
2. John F. Szwed and Roger D. Abrahams, "After the Myth: Studying Afro-American Cultural Patterns in the Plantation Literature," *African Folklore in the New World*, edited by David J. Crowley (Austin: University of Texas Press, 1977): 66.
3. *Ibid.* 69.
4. Cecily Dell, *A Primer for Movement Description: Using Effort-Shape and Supplementary Concepts* (New York: Dance Notation Bureau Press, 1977): 12.
5. Jan-Heinz Jahn, *Muntu: The New African Culture* (New York: Grove Press, 1961): 96.
6. Robert Farris Thompson, *African Art in Motion: Icon and Art* (Los Angeles: University of California Press, 1974).
7. *Ibid.* 7-10.
8. *Ibid.* 43.
9. *Ibid.*
10. *Ibid.* 44.
11. *Ibid.*
12. Zora Neale Hurston, *The Sanctified Church* (Berkeley: Turtle Island, 1981): 60.
13. Thompson 44.
14. *About Tap.* A film produced and directed by George Nierenberg. New York City: GTM Productions, 1985.
15. *Ibid.*
16. *Ibid.*
17. *Nightline.* WPVI-TV. Philadelphia: American Broadcasting Company, May 15, 1990.
18. Thompson 26.
19. *Tapdancin'.* Produced by Christian Blackwood. New York City: The Blackwood Film Release, 1980.
20. Thompson 11.
21. Thompson 24.
22. *Tapdancin'.*
23. *About Tap.*
24. *Tapdancin'.*
25. Lynne Fauley Emery, Black Dance From 1619 to Today (Princeton: Princeton Book Company, 1988): 233.
26. bid.
27. *Tapdancin'.*
28. *About Tap.*
29. Richard Farris Thompson, "An Aesthetic of the Cool: West African Dance," *African Forum* 2.2 (Fall 1966): 88-90.

30. Vocables are linguistically meaningless syllables. Ashenafi Kebede, *Roots of Black Music: The Vocal, Instrumental, and Dance Heritage of Africa and Black America* (Englewood Cliffs: Prentice-Hall, Inc., 1982): 3.
31. Ululation is a shrill, high sound, is often produced by women in oriental Africa, to demonstrate pleasure over a performance or activity. Kebede 6.
32. Calls, sometimes known as hollers and whoopin', are primarily used to communicate messages. Kebede 130.
33. Thompson, *African Art in Motion* 89.
34. Marshall and Jean Stearns, *Jazz Dance: The Story of American Vernacular Dance* (New York: Schirmer Books, 1968): xiv.
35. Mark C. Gridley, *Jazz Styles: History and Analysis* (Englewood Cliffs: Prentice Hall, 1988): 7.
36. *About Tap.*
37. Thompson, *African Art in Motion* 7.
38. *Ibid.*
39. *Ibid.*
40. Kariamu Welsh-Asante, "Commonalities in African Dance: An Aesthetic Foundation," *African Culture: The Rhythms of Unity*, edited by Molefi Kete Asante and Kariamu Welsh Asante (Westport, CT: Greenwood Press, 1985): 74.
41. Thompson, *An Aesthetic of the Cool* 93.
42. *Ibid.*
43. Polyrhythms and polymeters are exhibited in jazz music, particularly in the collective improvisation of early Dixieland music. However, there is debate on the origin of polyrhythms since European folk and concert music employed polyrhythmic phrasing in America before jazz originated. Some researchers believe that there was a fusion of cultural influences; because the polyrhythms in jazz, which are derived from ragtime and have roots in the African-American banjo tradition, have an African ancestry. Some scholars believe jazz musicians' preference for polyrhythmic construction, sometimes the actual rhythms themselves, reflect a tradition retained from African preferences, specifically a preference for rhythmic contrast. Gridley 49.
44. *About Tap.*
45. *The Story of Legendary Baby Lawrence.* Film produced and directed by Bill Hancock. Baltimore: H-D Productions, 1981.
46. *About Tap.*
47. Thompson, *African Art in Motion* 2.
48. Workshop for the Promotion for the Foundation of Dance Education held in Chicago, 1980.
49. Hurston 26.
50. Description of Jazz Tap by Dorothy Bradley in *The Story of Legendary Baby Lawrence.*
51. Hurston 26.
52. Thompson 10.
53. *Ibid.* 9.

54. *Ibid.* 24.
55. *Ibid.* 26.
56. Thompson 24.
57. Hurston 54-55.
58. *About Tap.*
59. Thompson 9.
60. *About Tap.*
61. *About Tap.*
62. Thompson 9.
63. Stearns 276-280.
64. In 1914? at the age of twelve Pegleg Bates lost his leg in a car accident in South Carolina. His uncle made him a crude wooden leg and after a few years Pegleg began to take up dancing. By 1928 he appeared in "Blackbirds" and was then considered "The Number One Dancer in the Country." His popularity continued through the forties at the Cotton Club and Apollo Theater. Pegleg Bates still performs today (1990) in the Catskill Mountains. Bruce Kellner, ed., *The Harlem Renaissance: A Historical Dictionary for the ERA* (New York: Methuen, 1984): 27.
65. Thompson 13.
66. Thompson 14.
67. Aesthetic parsimony is another example of mid-point mimesis. *Ibid.*
68. Thompson 14.
69. A conversation in February, 1990, with Edwina Evelyn who performed between 1940-1954 in the tap team "Salt and Pepper."
70. *About Tap.*
71. The idea of the originality of African-Americans is described by Zora Neale Hurston as a modification of ideas. ". . . The Negro is a very original being. While he lives and moves in the midst of a white civilisation, everything that he touches is reinterpreted for his own use." Hurston continues her description mentioning that African-Americans have modified language, food preparation, the practice of medicine and religion. Hurston 58.
72. African Dance Conference held in Washington, DC, February, 1990.
73. Thompson 7.

Works Cited

Asante, Molefi Kete and Kariamu Welsh Asante, eds. *African Culture: The Rhythms of Unity.* Westport, CT: Greenwood Press, 1985.

Blackwood, Christian (producer). *Tapdancin'.* New York City: The Blackwood Film Release, 1980.

Dell, Cecily. *A Primer for Movement Description: Using Effort-Shape and Supplementary Concepts.* New York: Dance Notation Bureau Press, 1977.

Emery, Lynn Fauley. *Black Dance From 1619 to Today.* Princeton: Princeton

Book Company, 1988.

Gridley, Mark C. *Jazz Styles: History and Analysis*. Englewood Cliffs: Prentice Hall, 1988.

Hancock, Bill (producer). *The Story of Legendary Baby Lawrence*. Baltimore: H-D Productions, 1981.

Hurston, Zora Neale. *The Sanctified Church*. Berkeley: Turtle Island, 1981.

Kebede, Ashenafi. *Roots of Black Music: The Vocal, Instrumental, and Dance Heritage of Africa and Black America*. Englewood Cliffs: Prentice-Hall, Inc., 1982.

Keller, Bruce, ed. *The Harlem Renaissance: A Historical Dictionary for the ERA*. New York: Methuen, 1984.

Nierenberg, George (producer). *About Tap*. New York: A George Nierenberg Film, 1985.

Stearns, Marshall and Jean. *Jazz Dance: The Story of American Vernacular Dance*. New York: Schirmer Books, 1968.

Thompson, Robert Farris. *African Art in Motion: Icon and Act*. Los Angeles: University of California, 1974.

TRADITION
CONTEXTUALIZED

TRADITIONAL AFRICAN DANCE IN CONTEXT

▲ ▲ ▲ ▲ ▲ ▲ ▲ ▲ ▲ ▲ ▲ ▲ ▲ ▲ ▲ ▲

Felix Begho

I

The rich variety of dances in different societies of African culture has long generated interest in the subject of dance categorization. Welsh-Asante and Ellfeldt are two of the scholars who have devoted thought to this subject.[1] Welsh-Asante has particularly advanced the idea that African dance must be seen Afrocentrically.

A few years ago, Nigerian civil servants of the Ministry of Information were assigned the onerous task of formulating categories of African dances in readiness for the 2nd World Black Festival of Arts and Culture (FESTAC) in 1977. This represented the first attempt on the continent to bring some classification to African dance.

Whereas the wisdom of this action cannot be questioned, the result of the actions as presented in *Festival News*[2] are questionable. Besides omissions arising from a lack of detailed analysis, some of the categories suggested by the civil servants appear misinformed.

The Traditional Dance Scene

The traditional dance scene, the embodiment of old values, is represented in the adjoining diagram.

Masquerade Dances

The masquerade group of dances constitutes not only the focal point of divergence but also the locus-focus of convergence—indeed, the

THE TRADITIONAL AFRICAN DANCE SCENE

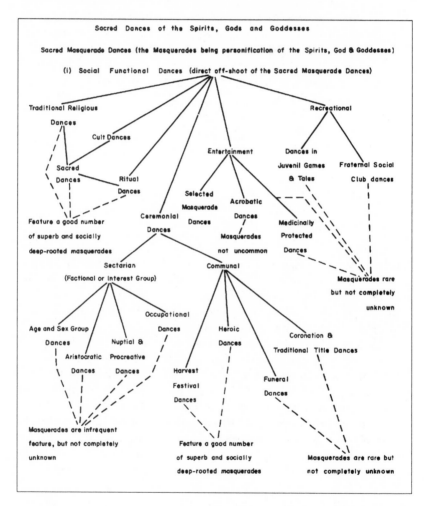

Figure 1

root-source of traditional African dance culture. The high respect accorded masquerades in African communities, the secrecy and taboos surrounding them, and the rituals embodied in their performances more than justify this implication.

Stories of the Yoruba creation myth are only a sample of the known oral tradition which asserts that the gods invented, perfected, and introduced the arts of dance, music, and singing to the world. We, *enia* (human beings) who found ourselves living in aiye (the world) with the gods who descended from *orun* (the heavens) and were the virtual rulers of *aiye* (the world), had to learn these arts from the gods. Little wonder, then, that Africa has numerous dances as specifically of or for the gods. In time, these gods were depicted in masks, and their bearers mimicked the dances of the gods. As a direct result of these god-dances, other dances were evolved for various purposes as need arose—suggesting that society moved from the time of the gods on earth, and innovations and adaptations were made to suit changed circumstances. But the gods were not and have not been forgotten. Their spirits live on in the ancient masks; and many more masks have been created since their time to represent less-than-god heroes and ancestors who are revered as near-god figures.

The practice of mask representation in the serious religious context is under attack throughout the continent. Yet, aside from traditional community sanctions demanding periodic ritual masquerades, youngsters of every generation find most of these masks and their dances fascinating enough to make them form or join masquerade clubs or societies. Herein lies the secret of the buoyancy of the masquerade dances as the towering heights from which things fell apart, but to which they are eternally linked. Almost without exception, the various categories of traditional African dances are permeated by mask-representation of the gods, heroes, and ancestors.

Sacred Dances

Three subcategories constituting the sacred dances of Africa brings one nearer the "time of the gods on earth." Comprising this amalgam are the following:

Traditional Religious Dances

The dances that are relevant in the commemorative worship and invocation of the gods as well as the near-god heroes and ancestors are here referred to as traditional religious dances. Ritualistic sacrifices are made to the concerned god-heads at the shrines dedicated to them, and the dances remembered as (or supposed to be) directly originating from them are performed by devotees as climax to their worship. The music, songs, and, sometimes, incantations for such ceremonies are communally recognized as sacred, and used only in connection with the invocation of the god-heads.

Under this subcategory, also, comes the remarkable ecstatic dance of the possessed priest or initiate who is capable of soaring to spiritual heights. The African thinking is that the priest is endowed with supernatural power imposed on him by forces beyond his control. At such moments, he dances and speaks as the godhead.

Cult Dances

Cult-dances are those dances performed only by the initiates of those secret societies that once utilized the more or less sacred arts of music, dance, and chants (or incantations) in the execution of their self-appointed duty as the conscience of the community and its protective "secret police" organization or government. These dances form an integral part of the societies' sacred ceremonies.

Depending on the force and influence of the cult in the community, its music, dance, song, and entire mode of ceremony may be communally recognized as sacred, or feared as such. In any case, to the initiates of the cult, the entire mode of ceremony (including dance, music, and chants) is something to revere and keep secret from non-initiates.

Ritual Dances

The residual traditional dances which neither belong to the Traditional Religious nor Cult group as explained above, but nevertheless call for ritualistic observances during performances are here termed ritual dances. This implies that some dances which may be grouped under the categories *Ceremonial* (whether Sectarian or Communal) and *Entertainment* are also ritual dances.

In perhaps an unconscious attempt at over-simplification, the entire complex amalgam of sacred dances is often termed ritual. This occurs because some observers base their opinions on the presence of the elements of ritualistic observances in connection with a dance, and not necessarily *during* the *actual performance* of the dance. However, a close examination of African dances readily reveals that ritualistic observances that are not integral to a dance are attendant on a good number of ceremonial and entertainment dances. Indeed, the only category that could be regarded as free from any hint of ritualistic observance is the category of strictly recreational dances.

What distinguishes the category *Ritual Dances* from other categories is that of the *place* and *time* of the ritualistic observances as the dance unfolds. Where the sum total or part of the ritualistic observance does not form an integral part of the entire dance-happening, the term "ritual" would appear, in this writer's opinion, misapplied. Such ritualistic observances are no more than circumstantial necessities indispensable only to the performers, and not to the community at large.

Ceremonial Dances

Perhaps the single largest category of traditional African dances is the group termed ceremonial. Two main subdivisions—sectarian and communal—are discernible, and under them come various subcategories. The distinction between the two subdivisions is founded on the assumption that the former deals with those dances which are expressive of the *ethos* and *pathos* of an allied group within a community at some particular eventful moment or occasion in the group's collective life. The latter is all-embracing, dealing with those dances which are expressive of the *ethos* and *pathos* of the community as a whole at some particular eventful moment in the collective life of the entire community. The various subcategories under each subdivision are as follows:

Ceremonial-Sectarian

Under this subdivision, Age and Sex group, Aristocratic, Nuptial, and Procreative, as well as Occupational dances of all sorts can be distinguished.

(a) Age and Sex Group: The life-cycle from birth to death, in traditional African societies, is stratified into developmental stages according to age and sex. The growth from one developmental stage to the other marks one step up on the ladder of social recognition—i.e., one becomes regarded as a sufficiently matured man or woman to be entrusted other family or communal responsibilities. The occasions of such "graduations" usually afford the graduands opportunity for celebration with music and dance. It is the customary dances by these "graduands" on the occasion of their graduation from the one social stage to the other in their life-cycle that are here considered under Age and Sex groups dances. Dances relevant to circumcision and menstrual rites belong to this subcategory, as do the dances of the aged ones, whether male or female.

(b) Aristocratic: Age, wealth, and power, other than birth, single one out for invitation by the royal head to accept offers of chieftaincy, title and to become a member of the hierarchy of the nation's aristocracy. Such dances as are peculiar to and are restricted to the titled ones on the occasion of their title-taking and other ceremonial occasions. These are referred to here as aristocratic dances, otherwise called chieftaincy dances, and include the dances peculiar to the royal head on various occasions.

(c) Nuptial and Procreative: This subcategory paints another shade of the life cycle celebration mentioned under Age and Sex group. Here, it is not the graduation to the age of marriage or motherhood that is being celebrated, but the accomplishment of winning a partner and bearing children. The customary hilarious dances of such occasions are identified here as Nuptial and Procreative dances.

(d) Occupational: Guilds of craftsmen and other professionals are organized according to the traditions of African society. Bound together by their work experience, members of these guilds frequently give vent to their alliance through dances conceived mostly from their common work experience. Thus, there are special dances for blacksmiths, hunters, and some other traditional professional guilds. These are the dances the guild-members resort to in the expression of their guilds' character on eventful occasions in the guild's particular life.

Ceremonial-Communal

Under this subdivision are the categories Harvest Festival, Heroic, Funeral, and Coronation and Traditional Title dances.

(a) Harvest Festival: The prologue and epilogue of harvest seasons in Africa (that of yam in Nigeria, for example) are noted for dance festivities featuring various types of masquerade and non-masquerade dances, most of which entail animal sacrifices and food offerings to earth and water gods. The prologue marks the traditional cleansing of the community in preparation for the eating of new harvest crops, whereas the epilogue signifies the traditional ushering in of a new planting season and, therefore, an appeasement to the gods to permit yet another rich harvest. The sum total of dance theaters observable during these festivities reveals, almost exclusively, the characteristics of a dance-play within a dance-play. More often than not, masquerades are featured, and the main dance-play of the actor-masquerade-dancers is circumscribed by the supporting dance-play of the singing chorus-dancers. The dances of the masquerades, who are the personifications of the gods, stand distinct from those of the chorus, and belong to the

class of the sacred dances already discussed. Thus, it is the dances of the chorus that are here termed Harvest Festival dances. The overlapping of these two categories—sacred and harvest festival—is noteworthy; for it reaffirms an earlier argument that masquerades are so much a feature of other non-masquerade dances that they (masquerades) must be regarded as the fundamental traditional African dance culture.

(b) Heroic: These are dances of war and victory. The former is intended to dispel fear in the combatants, and activate them physically and psychologically for action. The latter, it would appear, seeks to re-enact the ferocity of renowned warriors in a war-front, either as a kind of imitative rite to ensure victory through telepathy or empathy, or as a kind of jubilation for achievements won through prowess in war. Worthy of note here are: the usual awesome smearing of the warrior's body with charcoal; costumes composed of materials from powerful and quick-footed animals such as the leopard and monkey, as well as wise and prophetic birds like the eagle and parrot; the presence of supposedly protective amulets all over the warrior-dancer's body; and the use of weaponry by the dancer. In the Islamic communities of Africa, the warrior's outfit, acquired through the influence of Islamic religion, may be observed among the warrior dancers, especially the calvaries of the influential royal houses.

(c) Funeral: Funeral dances refer to those dances performed by the community only as part of the funeral ceremony for deceased ones who were sufficiently old before they died, and are deserving of obsequies. The elaborateness of the ceremony and dance usually depends not only upon age, but also upon the social status of the late person. The funeral rites attendant upon the death of an ordinary community elder do not compare with those of a high-ranking chief. By the same token, the death of a traditional ruler (a king) entails far more elaborate ceremonies than the death of a high-ranking chief.

The traditional dirges and the dances performed to them are part of the community's last respect to the deceased. Where a king is concerned, special funeral drums announce to the community the passing away of an important personality, and the community reacts accordingly. Where a renowned hunter or warrior is concerned, it is not uncommon in some parts of Africa that the funeral dirge and dance seek to recapitulate the heroic deeds of the late hero. However, sorrow is combined with restrained joy in the dances used to pay the community's last respect to the departed person.

(d) Coronation and Traditional Title: These dances are those which are customarily reserved by the community for performance only on the

occasions of coronation and conferment of chieftaincy title. They represent a communal effort in dance to hail the new king or chief, and demonstrate the community's good-will and loyalty.

Entertainment

Three subcategories—Selected Masquerade, Acrobatic, and Medicinally Protected Dances—can be distinguished here.

Selected Masquerade

The traditional dance scene is able to perpetuate itself, it appears, by developing dance lovers who do not share the socio-religious beliefs of the genuine traditional masquerade cults, but who are nevertheless sufficiently interested in masquerade dancing to organize themselves into avant-garde masquerade dance clubs or societies to carry on, with modifications, the tradition of masquerade dancing. These modernist societies have a different outlook from the older cults. The beauty of the masquerades and their elegant dancing are the sole cause for the devotion of these forms. Thus, these uncommitted masquerade lovers engage in a satisfying hobby while providing delightful entertainment for their onlookers.

Acrobatic

By acrobatic dances are not here meant the isolated instances of acrobatism in the process of the unfolding of the dances under the categories already discussed. Rather, it here means the gymnastic dance feats of such acrobats who have formed themselves into clubs or societies in order to develop and popularize acrobatic dancing through periodic acrobatic dance displays.

Medicinally Protected

The reference here is to those dance plays where the chief actor/dancer is believed to use not simply the force of the accompanying rhythm to achieve his intended feats, but in essence the force of some supernatural powers that go under various names such as *juju, charm, talisman*, etc. The animal masquerade dancers of some Yoruba areas come to mind here. In a bid to stun their audience, they change from the one animal to the other—animals such as boas and leopards. Despite their mere bravado entertainment function, however, Medicinally Protected dances are known to be preceded by some form of ritualistic observances. The artists concerned often feel that their special techniques and achievements expose them to the envy and victimization of false friends and enemies among their audience. As a precautionary measure, therefore, amulets may be worn by them; and they may invoke the gods and ancestors through ritualistic observances, to protect them against the diabolic activities of such false friends and enemies.

Recreational

Two subcategories can be distinguished here—dances in Juvenile Games and Tales, and Fraternal Social Club dances.

Dances in Juvenile Games and Tales

This refers to those dances indulged in by youths (often more sexually integrated than segregated) as some kind of pastime, and the impetus for which are juvenile moonlight games and tales with accompanying songs.

Fraternal Social Club Dances

One method by which traditional African dances have survived the vicissitudes of time is through education in the traditional dance art under the auspices of Fraternal Social Clubs. These clubs, then as now, are virtually Dance Societies. Membership is often sought by those who want the pleasure of dancing recreationally. It is those dances invented, learned, and perfected in such clubs that are here called Fraternal Social Club dances.

The implication here is that a certain amount of creative skill is encouraged. New dances, other than the previously existing ones that were known to and taught by the dance-masters of these societies, are created. A newly invented dance by any one society is a matter of "top secret" to that society for as long as it is possible to keep the secret from other clubs that in turn have their own "top secrets." This way, the seeds of rivalry that lead to open competition are sown, and at the ensuing competitive dance exhibitions, the "top secrets" of all sides come to the open. Thenceforth, imitative reproductions of one another's "top secrets" become the common practice, and in time these new dances pass into the mainstream of commonly known dances to become part of the repertoire of heritage dances.

It would mean, then, that until the clubs succeed in inventing "top-secret dances," one cannot speak of the dances they practice as being Fraternal Social Club dances.

171

II

The traditional dance scene depicts the tenacity of old values in changed circumstances. The contemporary dance scene however denotes the spectrum of emergent dance forms in the cultural clash of colonial and post-colonial society and is precipitated by an elitist indigenous group—the "educated elite."[3]

Four broad categories are distinguished under the contemporary dance scene as charted in the adjoining page. One of these, the entertainment category, is visibly dominant, having nine subcategories. This dominance of the entertainment category certainly speaks of the emphasis, in contemporary Africa, on secularity, as opposed to the religiosity of more pristine times—indeed, modernism as opposed to traditionalism. The four categories are discussed as follows.

Contemporary Religious Dances

The most significant innovation in the area of religious dancing that contemporary Africa has witnessed exists in the free African churches known under the generic name, *Aladura*, in Nigeria. The name includes the Cherubim and Seraphim, Celestial Church of Christ, and Christ Apostolic Church, among others.

Prior to the appearance of the Aladura churches on the scene of religious worship in Africa and, in fact, a long time after the new churches had gained ground, the orthodox Christian churches of European origin, as well as the Muslim movements of Arabic origin, did not accept dance as an integral part of their religious worship. Today, acceptance has not quite come either—certainly not in the sense of the dance ecstasies in the Aladura churches. However, there is ample evidence that the Aladura style is finding sympathizers even among the hierarchy of the orthodox churches and Muslim movements.

The organ is no longer the only music instrument found in a good number of orthodox churches. Various types of African music-instruments (drums, bells, etc.) have now come to accompany, if not supersede, the organ. With this innovation, the music of the orthodox churches has become more dance-able. The playing and singing choir at harvest thanksgiving and marriage services virtually dance, and so stimulate the less inhibited in the congregation to follow suit. However, the ecstatic spontaneity which grips the entire congregation of an Aladura church and sends all dancing until some dance themselves into trance and begin to see "visions" is yet lacking in the orthodox churches.

The Muslim movements remain a long way from that ecstasy—much longer than the orthodox churches. Nevertheless, it is not uncommon today to find Alhajas, assembled to worship, clap and sway from side to side in dancing fashion as they chant melodious verses from the Koran, and, it is visibly a much more restrained revolution in the mosques than in the orthodox churches. But the traditional inhibition imposed by religious conservatism has been broken, and one can well forecast now that some day Hausa trumpets will blare, and dundun drums will echo from the mosques. The music and dances that are features of the end of Ramadan festivities in Northern Nigeria can well be regarded as harbingers of things to come in the mosques.

Meanwhile, it is the Aladura churches that are pioneers of the practice of dance as an integral part of religious worship in contemporary Africa. That, of course, is not to say that the traditional religious dances associated with the worship of deities and ancestors are nonexistent in contemporary Africa. They are there; but these are the creations of a past era, the relics of which African and foreign researchers are studying.

Cultural Revival Dance Shows

Throughout the emergent new states of Africa, the nostalgia for a classical past, the humiliation felt as a result of prolonged and compelled dissociation from indigenous cultural heritage, and the desire to prove to the former colonial masters that Africa, before the advent of European adventurers was culturally rich, have generated an officially sustained "mania" for cultural revival. By means of competitive states and National Festivals of Art, the national governments of many African states seek to revive, conserve, and propagate traditional African Arts and Culture.

Competitive "Traditional Dance Festivals" constitute, perhaps, the most significant aspect of these often all-embracing arts festivals. It is these competitive dance performances staged at the rather annual official festivals of traditional arts that are referred to here as Cultural Revival Dance Shows.

A serious reflection on these Cultural Revival Dance Shows readily reveals to one that they are self-defeating of the proclaimed official objective to revive, preserve, and promote traditional African dance heritage. Judged by the organizational methods of the very extensive 1974 States and National Festival of Traditional Dances in Nigeria, the concern for official pageantry, more than good art, often makes itself felt at such shows. In quick succession, allowing only about five minutes performance for each group, one dance group after another is called upon to do its bit on a rectangular stage mounted somewhere near the center of a stadium, far removed from the non-participating audience seated around the stadium. This setting is foreign to the traditional setting in which the traditional dancers need audience participation in order to perform. The dancers' helplessness is even further emphasized by the official encroachment compelling a merger of supposedly similar dances—dances which do not bear the same name, and whose overall movements, underlying music, and costume are not necessarily identical.

Surely, with these interferences, it cannot be said that the occasions for these Cultural Revival Dance Shows are occasions for witnessing truly authentic traditional African dances at their best. As Welsh-Asante has argued, African dance finds its source in the richly textured culture of its history.[4]

Entertainment Dances

The overwhelming preponderance of subcategories of Entertainment Dance is a sharp contrast to the dominance of subcategories of Sacred and Ceremonial Dances in Figure 1, which shows the Traditional Dance Scene. The subcategories in Figure 2 are as follows:

A. Metropolitan Neo-Traditional Dances

The increasing detachment of the present generation from the hitherto binding traditional social customs has not left dance unaffected. It has led to the adaptation of a very good number of traditional dances that once served more serious uses for entertainment purposes with or without remunerative motive. This is the response of dance artists to a society which is in fact changing from clusters of small agrarian communities to extended commercial and industrial towns and cities. The white collar city worker, even when he remembers the dances of his people in his village of origin, no longer executes or participates in the execution of these dances as his way of life. He will rather sit back and watch the "illiterate villagers" do what he now considers fun. This way, he gets the satisfaction of relaxation from the ever busy city-life he leads.

The foregoing was the situation which, until the late-1960's in Nigeria, led to the migration of groups of young talented dance artists from the villages to the boisterous cities to provide traditional dance entertainment in exchange for a little cash to live on. Talented as these dancers were, they came with nothing new, nothing different from the

THE CONTEMPORARY AFRICAN DANCE SCENE

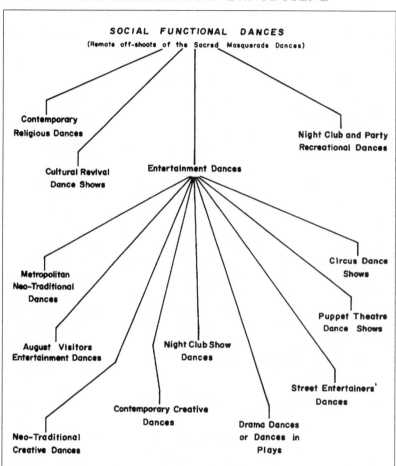

SOCIAL FUNCTIONAL DANCES
(Remote off-shoots of the Sacred Masquerade Dances)

Contemporary Religious Dances

Cultural Revival Dance Shows

Entertainment Dances

Night Club and Party Recreational Dances

Metropolitan Neo-Traditional Dances

Circus Dance Shows

Puppet Theatre Dance Shows

August Visitors Entertainment Dances

Night Club Show Dances

Street Entertainers' Dances

Neo-Traditional Creative Dances

Contemporary Creative Dances

Drama Dances or Dances in Plays

Fig. 2

original versions at home. In fact, they did not consciously aim at inject-
ing innovations into the original versions. Their aim was simply the
reproduction of the original versions in an environment quite different
from where these were normally performed, making, of course, such
concession in the length of the dance as the situation demanded. For
as long as there were enough people to constitute an audience, and
token gifts of money were being showered on the performers, where

gate fees were not formally collected, the show went on until the performers were too tired to dance and the audience was not forthcoming with further gifts. It is these dances which are uprooted from their customary social context in time, place, and motivation, and brought to the city that are termed "Metropolitan Neo-Traditional Dances."

B. August Visitor's Entertainment Dances

The new current of cultural revival attendant on political emancipation from colonialism, whatever its negative aspect, has no doubt had the desired effect of arousing in the African public—whether in the villages or cities—the consciousness to cherish, preserve, and propagate traditional African cultural heritage through active participation.

It is a consciousness which in effect spells death for the activities of the Metropolitan Neo-Traditional Dance entertainers discussed under A. The former patronizers of these entertainers, the white-collar city workers, are now amongst those who are taking the initiative to form Cultural Clubs or societies of "immigrants" in states other than those of their own origin.

As organs for preserving and propagating their distinctive heritage of music, dance, song, folklore, etc., these new cultural clubs command the respect and support of their host communities. Thus, either by invitation or their own initiative, these clubs, now and again, organize special dances to welcome visitors (whether or not of the ethnic group of the club members) to the communities in which the clubs are based.

In essence, the dances presented to these visitors fall under the subcategory "Metropolitan Neo-Traditional Dance." However, the practice is growing whereby the same dances are often presented whenever the occasion of welcoming visitors arises. Over time, therefore, these particular dances are likely to be regarded as dances specifically for welcoming visitors. This is the rationale for considering them as a special subcategory of Entertainment dances.

C. Neo-Traditional Creative Dances

Theater groups that are wholly and solely committed to dance have yet to become a feature of contemporary Africa. Nevertheless, a number of groups exist that are experimenting with the idea of a "modern" traditional dance theater. The choreographers in such groups usually draw on their knowledge of the wealth of traditional dances to present, in new dance forms, stories constructed by them from familiar folklore or contemporary themes.

Insofar as the activities of these experimentalists consist in assembling known movements from various traditional dances and employing these movements to express life images with which contemporary Africans and foreigners who know them are quite familiar, they (the experimentalists) must be considered as creative dance artists working in neo-traditional style. They differ from the already discussed Metropolitan Neo-Traditional dancers in that they do not seek authentic reproduction of any specific traditional dance, but are concerned with creating something new from old forms. Hence the term "neo-traditional creative dances" to describe their creations is appropriate.

D. Contemporary Creative Dance

This term refers to that category of dances, the style, form, and content of which reveal the choreographers' reliance chiefly on improvisational movements to comment on contemporary issues, to relate folklore themes to contemporary situations, or to exhibit the mere beauty of movement. In this regard, Ellfeldt noted:

> Contemporary is, of course, a general term, but it may be taken to mean an approach to dance limited only by the movement capability and sensitivity of the performer, and the imagination, courage, and craft of the choreographer. Preformed patterns such as steps, routines, or combinations are not used. Rather significant movement sequences are drawn out of human experience and the very act of moving. Form develops from the manipulation of these movements according to the dictates of the choreographer. While basic content may come from ancient as well as current sources, it is expressed primarily by the movement selected—colored by the character of the choreographer and performer, and unhampered by conventional ways of moving.[5]

In contemporary Africa, contemporary creative dance as here explained, barely exists, unless as corporate part of the works of a few playwrights. Wole Soyinka's imaginations of "the dance of the dead" (described in his A Dance of the Forest)[6] and "the motor car dance" (described in his The Lion and the Jewel)[7] are rare examples of an issue that this writer discusses elsewhere.[8] Except for such rare examples, the great majority of dance activities in contemporary African theater (including the university-based theater companies) fall under the subcategory Neo-Traditional Creative Dance. The salient difference, then, between "modern or contemporary creative dance" and "neo-traditional creative dance" lies in this: the former is a tendency toward avant-guardism, whereas the latter leans toward conformism.

E. The Night Club Show Dances

Reference here is, in the first place, to those dances in night spots by lightly-clad girls who are backed by a dance orchestra, the leader of which is virtually the manager of the girls. It also encompasses those orchestra-backed acrobatic or gymnastic displays by jugglers and acrobats.

The function of these entertainers is to give dazzling performances to keep customers in place and drinking until they drink or nearly drink their pockets out, to make good profit for the club management.

In Nigeria, Fela and Sunny Ade girls come to mind in this connection. To the catchy rhythm of Fela's band, the teenage but physically matured, topless girls do their breathless show-dance until they are virtually bathing in their sweat. So energetically trying is their dance that one may consider it a reckless dissipation of energy. However, the endurance and total surrender of the teenage girls somehow tend to lend their dance the air of ecstatic religious possession, notwithstanding their near-nakedness and rigorous hip movements that seem to suggest sensuality. This is probably the reason why their band leader, Fela, is popularly known as the "chief priest," and his permanent show spot, "the shrine."

Sunny Ade girls, unlike Fela girls who are topless and shaking from head to toe in seemingly undisciplined manner, have their breasts tightly held in beautifully designed mini blouses that reveal their bellies. Their calmer but unmistakably sensual dance is a graceful one. The impression one gets is not that of ecstatic religious possession, but of a tantalizing manipulation of the hips and shoulders according to the dictates of Sunny's guitar and the accompanying talking drums.

F. Drama Dances (or Dances in Plays)

This group should be clearly distinguished from the dances referred to as Dance Dramas. A dance-drama presupposes a libretto or an understood plot translated into or superimposed upon suitable music, which is then used for a dance composition based on the libretto or understood plot. The resultant dance composition is a harmonious whole: an independent piece of art-work narrating in movement pictures the essential contents of the libretto or understood plot.

The Drama Dance, on the other hand, is a dance in a dramatized play. Without the play, it cannot hold. It is not by itself an independent piece of art work. It has meaning only within the context of the play. But this meaning does not necessarily imply that it advances the plot of the play of which it is part. Where it does not, it is a mere *divertissement*. Its function within the play, then, is simply to hold the scene and sustain interest until the players are ready to enter to begin or continue the play itself. The organized dances at the beginning and midway of Nigeria's Chief Ogunde's and Baba Sala's plays are only divertissements.

In some cases, the dances are intended to advance the plot of the play. This is perhaps the intention of a good number of Nigerian academic playwright/directors who are attached to the universities. In general, the dance in Wole Soyinka's plays make good pointers in this direction. But some dance movements in Ola Rotimi's and Wale Ogunyemi's plays also make good examples. However, the late Duro Ladipo's Oba Koso remains, perhaps, the most ingenious blend of music, dance, and speech on the contemporary Nigerian theater stage.

G. Street Entertainers' Dances

Understood here are the music and dance gimmicks of professional vagabond entertainers, the majority of whom are snake-charmers and magicians of some sort (namely, the itinerant, dagger-bearing entertainers, who make show of their immunity to daggers).

Although magical tricks are primarily the specialization of these entertainers, they use music and dance more often than not to excite and elevate themselves to the desired level of ecstasy, and to attract and arrest the attention of their passers-by audience. Spectacle is the aim of the dancers here; for if it is the mere wriggling of the waist these entertainers intend, they do it assuming very grotesque postures, and with enviable perfection.

H. Puppet Theater Dance Shows

The Tivs of Plateau State in Central Nigeria have a highly developed puppet theater called *Kwagh-Hir*. Specializing in the dramatization of ludicrous folk tales and topical issues (e.g., public execution of armed robbers), the *Kwagh-Hir* is essentially an action theater provided with music background. However, dances are featured now and again, especially in scenes involving animal characters.

During their dance, these animal characters can, and often do, alter their shapes and heights with spectacular flourish to heighten the unfolding drama that is supported by the peripheral dances of accompanying musicians and puppet attendants. It is these dances which form part of the *Kwagh-Hir's* and similar puppet theaters' dramatizations that are here termed "puppet theater dance shows."

I. Circus Dance Shows

In the jumble of "the old" and "the new" in which the ritual or ceremonial demands of the past are played down in order to meet the increasing demand for mere entertainment at festivals and other occasions, it is difficult not to consider such hair-raising shows as the *Utturekpe* (the spider) from Uyo Division in the Cross River State in Nigeria, and *Periangala* and *Owu-Ugo* of the River State's division of Okrika and Ikwerre, respectively, as elements of contemporary African circus in its infancy. Like the eagle in the myth of Owu-Ugo and the monkey in the myth of *Periangala*, masquerades are sent performing atop long posts. In *Utturekpe*, masquerades balanced on motorcycles are sent by means of ropes into the sky and on to the top of long masts. This is done either to special rhythms or to the music that is played for some supporting masquerades and dancers dancing at the base of the masts. These supporting dances add color and contrast to the show of the climbers. It is these supportive dances and those performed by the climbers, when they do dance, that are referred to here as "Circus Dance Shows." The Rivers and Cross River States are not alone in this. In Bendel State, a number of Urhobo Ikenike (stilt dancers') clubs put up similar hair-raising shows. Stilt dancers are known in many African countries.

Night Club and Party Recreational Dances

Reference here is to the dances resulting from the impromptu kinetic response to music of the popular kind by persons who are solely concerned with the fun of a night-out of dancing. Unconscious abandon characterizes the dancing of these fun-seekers.

Little wonder, then, that there usually are as many different dances as there are individuals on the dance floor. The movements of any two people forming a couple need not rhyme. Each couple of the lot is as different from the others as there are individuals. An observer may, therefore, get the impression of movement "confusion," notwithstanding the interest that any one movement or groups of movements may arouse.

To be sure, it is the improvisational genius of some fans and, sometimes, the popular musicians themselves to credit for a good number of *vogue* dances that have now receded into oblivion. For example, the once popular "High-Life" dance in West Africa, while it cannot be said to be really extinct, has nevertheless been superceded by a number of other popular dances deriving their names, as did High-Life dance, from their accompanying music. *Juju, Apala, Sakara, Rara, Akwete, Ekassa, Apola, Odu, Afro-Beat, Fuji, Syncro, Lulu, Boogie, Bump, Reggae, Soul,* and *Rock* are only some of these.

The audience of the popular recreational dance scene can be classified into the locally (or nationally) oriented, and the internationally oriented, according to the foregoing list of vogue dances. Those who show undisguised preference for the *Boogie, Lulu, Bump, Soul,* and *Rock* are invariably the schooled, pleasure-seeking, foreign-fashion-conscious youngsters. The predominantly foreign-oriented education they acquire at school tends to lead them toward other African musical traditions. Thus, it is the international pop music scene, inspired by diasporan African beats, to which they look for innovations to emulate.

In the Yoruba-speaking areas of Nigeria, for example, the locally oriented audience feel more comfortable with *Apala, Sakara,* and *Rara* hits—all three being in text and sound well anchored in Yoruba cultural heritage. The schooling of this audience is much more of home-training than formal European-type education. There is also the question of a generation gap; for this audience is more of the older generation than the internationally oriented audience. In other parts of Africa, where the text and sound of hits are anchored in the ethnic heritage, the same phenomenon is noticeable.

Appearing as compromise between the two extremes—the internationally and locally oriented audience—are *Fuji, Akwete, Ekassa, Odu, Afro-Beat,* and *Syncro.* There is a deliberate attempt on the part of the exponents of these types of African popular music to adapt purely local themes for the international popular music market by employing comparatively Western-type popular music orchestration. The combined elements of "the indigenous" and "the international" account for the very large following. A good number from the audience of both extremes can and do find a common meeting ground in the sound of the African international pop music. *Juju* hit, too, should be discussed because the authentic Juju sound, as produced by I. K. Dairo in the 1950's, has since been commercialized. Sunny Ade's as well as Prince Adekunle's brand of juju music signals the new trends in the commercialization of this Yoruba popular music form.

This chapter has concentrated on types of African dance as

expressed in the context of Nigerian culture. However, the implications for other African societies on the continent and in the diaspora are exceedingly fruitful. When one turns attention to the dance of the African in the United States, Cuba, Panama, Brazil, Haiti, Jamaica, and Colombia, one sees precisely the same expressive roots as I have explored from the Nigerian and more particular, Yoruba, example.

Notes

1. See Kariamu Welsh-Asante, "Commonalities in African Dance," in M.K. Asante and K. Welsh-Asante (eds.), *African Culture: The Rhythms of Unity*. Trenton: Africa World Press, 1990. Also see Lois Ellfeldt, *A Primer for Choreographers*. Los Angeles: National Press Books (1967): 4.

2. Federal Nigeria Ministry of Information, *Festival Week* 1.1 (October 12, 1974): 3-4.

3. E. A. Ayandele, *The Educated Elite in the Nigerian Society*. Ibadan: Ibadan University Press, 1974.

4. Welsh-Asante, *op. cit.*

5. Ellfeldt, *op. cit.*, p. 17.

6. Wole Soyinka, *A Dance of the Forest*. Ibadan: Oxford University Press, 1964.

7. Wole Soyinka, *The Lion and the Jewel*. Ibadan: Oxford University Press, 1964.

8. Felix O. Begho, "Dance in Contemporary Nigerian Theater: A Critical Appraisal," *Nigerian Journal of the Humanities* 1.2 (1979)

In Contest: The Dynamics Of African Religious Dances

▲▲▲▲▲▲▲▲▲▲▲▲▲▲▲▲▲

Omofolabo Soyinka Ajayi

Every culture has its means of reaching the divine, means which have been found compatible with the society's concept of the sacred. There may be many different ways even within a single culture to communicate with the sacred being, but invariably, one form supersedes all others in significance and effectiveness. Such a preferred device is usually considered by the people as an exceptional system of communication and appreciated at the same time as a distinctive artistic form. By the same token, there are some communication means and or, artistic expressions that are expressly forbidden in religious worships. For reasons which may be moral, economic even political, or based on some mythological considerations, the tabooed forms have been found inadequate or inappropriate for religious sentiments.

As a system of strongly held views, religion with its concept of the sacred, often engender intolerance of other religious views and practices especially at first contact when little is known about the other. One would expect such "natural" prejudices to give way to some sort of understanding if not total acceptance with time, but when the initial ignorance is fraught with cultural arrogance and a quest for economic and political power, the level of intolerance is boundless; it promotes a kind of contest for validity and eventually, supremacy which culminates in the attempt to wipe out the religion of the other.

Such was the case with Africa when confronted with new religious forms, notably Christianity and Islam that made little or no attempt to find out the rational of existing religious practices.

1. Dance in African Religions

Dance is undoubtedly a vital means of communicating with the sacred in African religious practices; it is an expressive form fully integrated within the worship system. Already a favored art form among the numerous cultures of Africa, it is not surprising that it holds a preeminent position among methods of communicating with the divine. No religious worship was considered complete in the past without at least one dance performance by the devotees. Although this still holds true today wherever ancient African religions manage to survive, and even where the new religious forms have been effectively "Africanised", the survival of sacred dances in Africa has been extremely difficult. Contact with Christianity and Islam, and the ensuing contest for supremacy over African indigenous religions, almost wiped dance out as a means of divine communication. Coming with their own cultural bias against accepting dance as a form of religious worship, no attempt was made by the new religions to understand why dance was such an important means of sacred expression in African societies; rather every effort was made to destroy it.

The vital role of dance in religious worships in Africa today and in the past, is due largely to three main factors: 1) The cultural concept of the sacred, 2) intrinsic qualities of dance, and 3) the people's attitude towards the body.

1.1 The Sacred as Culture Specific. The concept of the sacred arises out of a universal human need to understand the foundation and function of the universe, and in particular the relationship of human beings with cosmic totality. However, cultural differences emerge as each group of people concretizes its perceptions of the universe in myths which ultimately are based on their specific environment and actual relationship with the land. Such myths become "creation stories" that determine who the Creator is, who or what and how they are created, the nature, form and the realms of the spiritual and the earthly. In determining the relationship between the Creator and the created, further differences emanate as some cultures see a corresponding relationship between the organization of the universe and the emerging human society, while others see no relatedness whatsoever. In the consequent conception of the sacred, the former group is able to visualize a multiplicity of sacred forces functioning as assistants to the Supreme Creator, whereas the latter cannot conceptualize such a possibility. Thus monotheistic religions such as Judaism, Christianity and Islam limit the sacred only to the Creator Deity, while polytheism revel in an abundance of minor deities around the Creator. Fundamental differences like these ultimately affect and determine the constituents of the sacred and how they should be approached and revered. Thus what constitutes the sacred in one culture may be total abhorrence in another.

Africans generally have a holistic concept of the universe. The cosmos is a single unifying entity which embraces the human society (i.e. both culture and nature), and the transcendental powers in a continuous cycle of interaction and regeneration.[1] In a cyclical motion, the earth connects with the sky through the rains, the sun and the rivers, all of which are generative forces nourishing the human society enveloped within the circle. Above in the cyclical continuum, are the transcendental powers, mediators between the Creator Deity and its people, spiritual forces intervening, influencing and affecting the human culture on earth. It is from this embracing totality that the Africans derive their concept of the sacred.

Implicit in this understanding is the belief that everything created by the Creator Deity or Supreme Being must have some of its sacred nature and creative force imprinted on it. This is a fundamental aspect of polytheism. Every creature of the Supreme Being becomes a symbol of the power of creation, the life force of its being. Consequently, the cosmic powers are seen as the Creator manifesting itself in concrete and visible terms to the physical world below, and in the physical world, nature and human beings become symbols of the Supreme, some kind of "god on earth" carrying its presence with them wherever they are found. A perception such as this creates a constant flux and an interchangeability within the subsidiary sacred order where nature assumes cosmic propensities and cosmic forces become personified in cultural heroes and heroines, who are deified and emerge as anthropomorphic deities. It is a situation where the sacred permeates both the religious world of the intangible, infinite spirituality and the more concrete, easily perceptible cultural space.

1.2 The Nature of Dance. Dance is both a sign and a vehicle of communication. It is able to express an action, an idea and, it is at the same time the action and the idea it expresses. For example, a person dancing can be a *sign* of happiness, at the same time this *sign* is a *vehicle* to communicate and express a state of mind. Since a sign derives its meaning from its nature, and a tool assumes its significance from what it is used for,[2] the use of dance in sacred rituals has both intrinsic and cultural imports. As a sign, dance is a multi-communication channel, transmitting information not only through time and space but also kinetically, visually and through other human sensorial perceptions. This enables it to serve as an important vehicle for other means of communication. For example, through its movement patterns, dance kinetically conveys verbal information; music gets visually interpreted and in particular, many African plastic art forms attain their full significance specifically through dance motions.[3] Its versatility as a multi-channel sign system makes dance a communication power house able to give information at many levels simultaneously.

In religious worship where devotees variously seek link with the divine in order to give praise and thanks, ask for general or specific blessings, appease, atone, acknowledge and celebrate the being of the divine in their lives, there is a need for an economic and composite communication sign. Dance with its multi-medium channel of communication, seems to be the quintessential choice for such a multitude of purpose. It is a maximization of facilities for the most effective results, carrying a myriad of messages via many channels simultaneously. Such quality is of course not unique to African dances, what is significant in the African experience and in other cultures that use dance extensively in sacred rites, is the people's attitude to the body—the primary tool of the dance.

1.3 Cultural Body Attitude. As mentioned above, human beings as one of God's creatures have associative sacred attributes in African cultures. Consequently, it is not considered incongruous to use the body in the glorification of god and other divine manifestations. It is a useful tool for both God and man. The secular and cultural dimensions of the body only serve to establish, confirm and enhance the circular (as opposed to the linear) relationship between the Creator, nature and culture. Thus there is no ambiguity in the people's concept between the sacred and the secular body; each is distinct and yet complement each other in the greater glorification of God. Neither does any conflict occur when the same body used in secular concerns is later used in sacred rituals. At the appropriate time, dance is either social, secular, entertainment, or religious, sacred and pious.

The conflicting and ambiguous relationship between the mortification and purification of the flesh which often beset monotheistic religions generally is missing in polytheistic cultures that have built in an extended understanding of the sacred. It presupposes the inclusion of the human society as an active and legitimate participant in the concept of the sacred. By initially recognizing the distinct but related concept of the Creator and its creations, it appears that a safety valve has been created between a possible confusion of the sacred and the secular. This is why the use of the body in dance, a form more readily associated with the secular and the mundane, finds such a prominent and respectable place in the sacred rituals of African peoples.

2. Dance as Worship

The semiosis of a sacred dance becomes fully relevant only within both the contextual and conceptual meaning of the sacred itself. A close affinity evidently exists between the nature and concept of dance and the subject(s) of sacred rites. Essentially, both are intangible and evanescent but able to reach deep down to the profundity of human perceptions and emotions. In addition, both are made "real" through actual experience and/or through some concrete symbolic representations. As indicated earlier, through movement patterns, dance gives form to ideas *in culture* while the sacred is a conceptual thought made manifest as *nature on earth*. There is thus, at a certain level of perception, a relatedness of form which enables dance to serve as a solid bridge, i.e., as an instrument with which to cross over to the ethereal infinite, and also to function as a sign for the devotees' conception of the sacred. The anchor point of communication is that area of liminality where the ephemeral nature of dance fuses with transcendental powers. This is the high point of worship. It is perhaps for this reason—the ability to cross over to the beyond and establish a communication between god and man, that some cultures regard dance as a sacred art in itself.

The aim of worship is in effect to achieve communion with a powerful but intangible force, essentially therefore, worship is a journey from one stage, the earthly/physical, to another, the spiritual/ ethereal. It is a process of making known or, at least making comprehensible the unknown primordial existence that separates man from God. The worship process corresponds closely to Van Genep's classification of "rite of passage" or "transitional rite" into three phases: preliminal, liminal and postliminal (13). Worship then, is a journey from the known preliminal state of earthliness to the unknown liminal state of spiritual non-physicality and back to a spiritually enriched earthliness.

In religious practices, dance serves as an effective route for the journey bridging the liminal, and uniting the spiritual with the earthly. It becomes a significant form of worship, and together with the other means of sacred communication recognized within the culture, it is able to effectively fulfill the multi-faceted functions of religion. Dance serves to bridge the chasm between this world and the other, between the deity and its worshippers. It becomes the anchor point between a high point of human creative perception and the sacred, which Turner describes as the "unformed void or infinite space held to have existed prior to the ordered universe" (202). It creates the liminal state, the high point of the worship where the devotees cross the human threshold to the spiritual realm; it is a meet point of the sacred and secular, between the creator and the created, the desires of a people and their desired goal. To reach this high point of worship, three stages of sacred dances can be identified: i) Invocational, ii) Transcendental, iii) Celebration, each corresponding respectively to the three stages of the "transitional rite" of worship.[4]

2.1 Invocational Dancing. Performed by all assembled devotees to music and drumming, an invocational dance takes place at the *pre-liminary* stages of the worship. It serves to: 1) call the presence of god into their midst, 2) get the devotees in the appropriate worshipful mood, divest their secular aspect and get them ready to enter communion with god, and 3) praise god for his mercies. It is very rare for an invocational dance to begin the service, usually it has been preceded by other forms of sacred actions like prayers, divination, sacrifice and/or chanting. Coming after other acts of invocation, dance functions as a reinforcer helping to heighten the level of perception already achieved and to move the service upwards spiritually.

The pace of the invocational dance is usually slow and does not involve any distinctive style, it is more of an individual personal expression of purging the self of secular earthly preoccupations. Gestures are usually directed heavenward, to the altar or to a sacred icon in praise and invocation of the deity. Moving together sedately, the devotees revel in the commonality fostered by the presence of so many bodies united in purpose and spirit. The kinetic cadence coupled with the rhythmic unity of so many bodies, is able to generate the purification of body and soul and sanctify the worshippers for the more delicate liminal stage that lies ahead. In instances where the performance of officiating persons is emphasized even at this preliminary stage, their performances may take on some of the attributive features of the deity being invoked, although they will not be as pronounced as in the next stage which will be discussed more fully below.

2.2 Transcendental Dance. This is the "dance of the heavens". It is used as i) a tool of reaching the sacred, this will be called 'progression dance' and, ii) a "possession dance" which is a sign that communication has been attained with the deity. The transcendental dance can be performed by any of the devotees, but quite often, a religious body may find it expedient to have an individual or a group of people specially anointed to be the dance medium between the two worlds. Such mediums are given special titles, among the Yoruba people of Nigeria for example, they are generally referred to either as *iyawo, ele-gun* or *esin orisa* (wife, mount or horse of the deity). They are believed to be specially chosen by the deity itself either from birth or later in life through frequent and often unprovoked5 possession by the spirit of the deity.

The progression dance is a process towards possession, it functions in the same way as a tool is used to achieve a purpose. The performance of the first level of the transcendental dance is a willing, conscious action on the part of the medium. A progression dance features and recalls specific and powerful characteristics of the deity being invoked and it is accompanied by distinctive music used just for that deity. By performing the "progression dance", the medium has surrendered himself or herself to be taken over by the spirit of the deity. This stage may be speeded up by sacrifice (visual), words such as prayers or incantations (verbal and aural), and sometimes by the use of drugs (smell/taste). These are signs already built into the semiotic system of the religious dogma and whose signifying powers trigger appropriate meaning in the initiated and willing individual. The expected and inevitable response is heightened memories of the deity—possession.

The possession dance is an indication that the chasm between this world and the other has been bridged. It is an "altered state of consciousness" where the deity now takes over the control of the body of the medium; as the Yoruba say, orisa gun un—the deity has 'mounted' it (the medium). The transition to possession dance can either be very subtle, marked only by some changes in the dance pattern or it can be distinctly noticeable. The medium may give a shout, seize one of the sacred icons or, fall down in a brief trance before going on to the possession dance proper. Certain physical changes which are characteristic of the deity may also be observed in the dancer. Whether subtle or not, the change is always acknowledged by the other worshippers; they may fall into a total silence or take up the shout in chanted praises, the drums also change rhythm to suit the new dance steps. Sometimes the state of possession is accentuated by the addition of some other sacred paraphernalia on the medium.

During possession, the full personality of the deity including habits, emotional dispositions and the social mores he or she symbolizes are danced out and the distinctive physical features of the deity are manifested in the dancer. These are taken as conclusive evidence that it is indeed the spirit of the deity working through the medium. Like the deity, the medium becomes imbued with superhuman qualities and is able to see visions or perform extraordinary feats usually described as "magic". Occasionally some anti-social behaviors are committed by or on behalf of the medium however, these are considered part of the characteristics of the deity and therefore condoned. During possession, which in some cases may last from anywhere between five minutes to seven days, the medium is usually impervious to normal human emotions and sensations especially pain, hunger and thirst.

Although prophesying or seeing visions are later to play a significant role in African forms of Christianity, it should be pointed out that it was not always a common feature of possession, especially in West Africa. In the polytheistic religious practices of East and Southern Africa, where it was used to solve specific social problems, prophesying was more frequent. In West Africa, however, its functions seemed to have been replaced by the divination systems, the possession dance was enough indication that the service had found favor with the deity and that the worshippers were still in favor. If there was no possession when it was considered crucial, for example during the annual celebration of the deity, and in times of social crisis, or when something unpleasant happened during the liminal stage, the service would be suspended for further consultation with the divination system to find out what reparations needed to be made. However, this rarely occurred, for it was believed that consultation with the divination system at the invocational state of the worship would have foreseen this and necessary reparations would have already been made.

The liminal stage, as Turner pointed out is more of a process than a state and it entails getting out of, as well as getting into (202). The process of bringing out the mediums from their transcendental state into the cultural world can either be a gradual or shock therapy. The gradual process involves a systematic elimination of the various acts or objects used to promote the possession. The shock tactics goes abruptly to the opposite physical and mental state of the medium, for example, cold water may be poured on the medium to counter both the heat of the dance and of the spiritual encounter, the vision darkened where the emphasis had been on brilliance, or the rhythm of the music changed suddenly. Again all these are determined by the codification system in the religion and culture. Below is given an example of transcendental dance.

Sango's Transcendental Dance. The two dances that mark the liminal journey during the worship of Sango, the Yoruba deity of thunder and lightning and of justice, are known as *lanku* and *gbamu*, performed only by the *elegun Sango*, the specially consecrated Sango's mediums. When the *elegun* starts missing his or her steps during *lanku* dance, it is known that Sango has mounted his horse, this may also be accompanied by bulging eyes (a characteristic of Sango who once lived as a king).[6] As soon as the officiating priests and priestesses notice the changes, the *elegun* is led away to be costumed in the special possession attire and given the *ose Sango* (double axed wand) and/or sere (rattle wand), both insignias of the deity. Now with exceedingly bulging eyes in a rigidly transfixed face, the medium is brought back to the space of worship to begin *gbamu*, the dance of possession. The music changes to the appropriate beat.

Gbamu is a dance which recreates the very temperamental personality of Sango through an erratic use of space, a fast paced rhythm and jerky angular body movements. The elegun recalls the cosmic manifestation of Sango as the deity of thunder and lightning by pointing the dance wand to the sky and bringing it down to earth in sharp diagonal movement.[7] This is a significant motion which in Yoruba cosmogony symbolically unites the cosmic halves—the earth and the heavens. At the cultural level, it invokes Sango's judicial qualities and his ability to punish social criminals by throwing thunderbolts on them. Paradoxically, the anti-social act of "appropriation" is committed in the name of the *elegun Sango* by his or her attendants. Once accompanied by the possessed one, they are free to take anything that appeals to them in the market; in any case the people usually give the "gifts" readily.[8] The *elegun Sango* may remain in this state for several days without food, surviving only on *orogbo* (bitter kolanut) a form of stimulant. One of the supernatural acts performed during possession is to dance carrying a pot of live embers pierced at the bottom. Palm oil, believed by the Yoruba to have strong healing and soothing properties, is applied to the body of the *elegun* to facilitate a gradual return journey from the liminal.

2.3 Celebrative Dance. This dance wraps up the service and it is again performed by all devotees. It is a means of giving thanks and praise for a successful completion of the worship and particularly of surviving the crucial liminal stage. When possession is expected, there is the added tension of waiting for the sign from the deity and the weighty responsibility of receiving the deity in their midst. Usually the dance reverts to the free individual style, although a few devotees may perform some stylized movements. Mediums, priests and priestesses are, however, expected to perform dances associated with the deity.

3. The New Religions and Effects on Dance

Starting around the tenth century, with the introduction of Islam, and of Christianity a few centuries later, Africa became "colonized" by two monotheistic religions. It was "colonization" because both soon brought in their wake, cultural, economic and political occupation of the continent by the harbingers of the religions. Islam and Christianity are monotheistic religions whose concept of the divine and (consequently) forms of worship are very differently structured from the African prototype. Their spread into Africa conflicted very strongly with existing beliefs not so much from Africa's polytheism, which in any case would usually welcome more religious expressions, but from the new ones which neither acknowledged nor tolerated the existence of another deity, be it major or minor.

It therefore became expedient for the new religions to wage a war of attrition against existing religions not only for survival reasons, but more for an undisputed monopoly of their own notion of the sacred. The Christian missionaries were perhaps the most relentless and unsparing in this respect. There was to be no meeting ground nor were they in the least prepared to find a balancing medium between the indigenous and their own form of religion. Hence there were vigorous campaigns against the various forms of indigenous worships and systematic destruction of other expressions of polytheism. New African Christian converts were coerced into bringing their sacred objects to be publicly destroyed in a bon-fire at the parish as part of the effort to cause an effective break both physically and psychologically with the past. Even in social life anything suspected to be remotely connected with indigenous form of religion (and there were many), was very harshly denounced and condemned as savage, barbaric, unholy and immoral. It was necessary to create a vacuum so the new religious expression could thrive unchallenged.

In these various acts of aggression against the indigenous religions, the primacy of dance in the dogma naturally became very threatened. First, dance did not have any place in the worship form of either Christianity or Islam. Rather, verbal expression dominated the dogma of these religions and spreading the "Word" which had been preserved in writing was and is still crucial to their survival. Secondly, as an integral part of the worship and a vital manifestation of the essence of the deity in African religious practices, dance became highly suspect as perpetuating the religion, and was singularly selected for unrelieving and often indiscriminate attack. Although, unlike the various sacred icons, dance cannot be physically and therefore effectively symbolically destroyed, it was nonetheless subjected to the most sustained insidious attacks. Given its crucial role in the religion, a successful campaign against it hit the nerve center of the religion to ensure a quick end.

It comes as no surprise that African dances were variously distorted, misinterpreted and mercilessly ridiculed. For example, one European, a Mr. Hunter, in a short description that accompanies the photograph of a masked dancer from the Calabar area in Nigeria says:

> With fantastic dances he parades the streets making extraordinary gestures and contortions, high kicking and the like without rhyme or reason. The whole object of this dance is to conciliate the Jujus or Devils . . . The Niger bush native does not pray to his gods to help him but to devil so that he may not be harmed. The Juju dancers primarily object . . . is one of collecting alms. (427)

One immediately asks for Hunter's source of information. Was it the natives who told him they prayed to devils or his own presumptuous arrogance, blissful ethnocentricism and complexities of ignorance? The calculated attempt to denigrate the dance seems obvious. To the European with the self imposed mission of civilizing Africa, anything not Christian (or Islamic, a grudging concession was sometimes made to the Muslims), must be of the devil. By what criteria had he arrived at the conclusion that this must be a religious dance? To anybody who had taken the pains to casually enquire (to be fair, a few Europeans did attempt to, but their number was negligible and their motives mixed), the performer was either a professional entertainer earning his living within the cultural dictates of his society, or a parade phase of a community festival. But Hunter's aim, and many others like him was not to explore objectively, but to erode the cultural base and deny the humanity of a people. To do otherwise would have negated the colonial presence in Africa, contradicted the oft stated reasons and exposed the actual drive behind colonization—political and economic ambition and domination.

No religion is nurtured in the abstract, and neither Christianity nor Islam its inspired off-shoot,8 has escaped from the various influences of surrounding cultures. While polytheism with its rich concept of the sacred conveniently builds in the use of dance as a legitimate and proper form of reaching the divine, monotheism, with a much narrower concept makes it easier to exclude dance. This is not saying that monotheistic religions automatically reject dance, for Judaism, an older monotheistic religion, uses dance extensively in worship. However, somewhere in the development of these two religions, they separated the physical body of a person; there emerged distinct separate entities—the flesh and its spiritual essence—the soul. Invariably, the dichotomy creates an opposition where the flesh is earthly, secular and impure, and the soul is spiritual, sacred and pure. Since the two are in reality one and the same mundane person, the attainment of the desired purified state for religious purpose in necessarily dependent on a deliberate suppression of the natural demands of the body. The body consequently must be denied and restricted, it must not be allowed to be unduly expressive, for this would be a triumph of the secular flesh. The attainment of spiritual purification depends on the mortification of the body.

Given its direct association with the body, and as the most expressive, physical human creativity, obviously dance has no place in this context. Since the verbal, especially the written form, is more exclusive, more internalized, and less physically demonstrative than dance, it becomes a much more compatible means as an intimate communication vehicle. Even though the church and the mosque exist as central and public gathering places for devotees, emphasis is on individual private internalization of the word as a means of purifying a person, or, more appropriately the soul, rather than in a collective bodily reception of the divine through dancing. The communal gathering place for worshippers is more of a sanctified space where the Word of God resides and which is guided by the officiating priest into a more sequestered liminal space—the soul of the worshipper. Thus in vivid contrast to the centrality of dance in African indigenous religions, there is a heavy reliance of the Word in both Christianity and Islam and its superimposition over the nonverbal, in particular, dance.

3.1 Dance and Christianity. Western cultural attitude towards the body and ultimately towards dance, further affect the Christian attitude towards dance and particularly its acerbic reactions to sacred dance in Africa. Davies points out that it was not so much Christianity *per se* that militated against dance but "more a product of the Western culture" (33). Central to the attitude of the Christian religion to dance are the cultural attitudes of the West to the body; there is a fundamental cultural bias and confusion about the body which strongly prejudices the use of dance in the sacred.

Cultural effects on Christian perceptions about dance can be found as early as during the formative years of Christianity in Rome. The religion blossomed as the Roman empire declined not only as a political power but also as it fell into grave moral decadence. Dance, always a visible aspect of culture, consequently became very much abused and degraded. Its reputation even as an art form fell so low as to merit severe censorship from leading non-Christian Roman scholars. The Christians, anxious to establish their religion as a paradigm of morality and holiness, enthusiastically endorsed the various secular injunctions against dancing and denounced it specifically in the practice of their religion.

As the religion spread to Europe encountering local deities and other cultural norms, the initial anti-dance attitude persisted, although instances occurred where exceptions were made. According to Davies, some form of dance-rites were allowed during certain church services and dancing featured prominently at many Christian processions throughout the Christendom in the Middle Ages (47-61). The nineteenth century also produced a sect—the Shakers where dancing was fully integrated into their form of worship, but they were isolated and largely misunderstood by other Christian sects (62-69). Nonetheless, denouncing dance remained essentially for Christians a means of identifying themselves as separate and distinct from the other religions and secular life. It came to represent what Christianity was not, and eventually emerged as the symbol of all social evils—undiscipline, immorality and sin. Philip Stubbes, a 16th-century moralist who recognized "thankful dancing or spiritual rejoicing" (162), still denounced dancing as

> an introduction to whoredome, a preparative to wantonnes, a provocation to uncleaniness, and an introite to al kind of lewdness . . . It stirreth up the motions of the flesh, it introduceth lust, it inferreth bawdrie, affordeth ribalderie, maintaineth wantoneness . . . (166).

It is a symbolism regularly reinforced by a cycle of the moral and social decadence in Europe (again as in ancient Rome, the reflection of a crumbling ruling class). By the end of the sixteenth century, for example, the lascivious life style of the aristocracy with the associative social injustice and the emerging bourgeoisie gave rise to a particularly ascetic branch of Christianity—the Puritans. Reacting to social excesses, the Puritans became very strict and stern in their religious and personal lives. Dance especially was conceived solely in terms of gratification of the flesh leading to the total damnation of the soul. Ironically, the Shakers who believed in dance as a glorification of the Lord emerged from the Puritans.

It was at this period, that intensive Christian evangelism spread to Africa, bringing with it its puritan values. It was also at this time that various communities in Europe left their shores in protest against the general excesses and highhandedness of the ruling class to settle in the Americas in search of a "true" and "pure" form of Christianity which upholds high morality and socio-political justice. Unfortunately, the guiding democratic spirit of the Puritans did not accompany the introduction of Christianity to Africa, rather cultural arrogance and intolerance and a high notion of racial superiority were its mates. These attitudes were grounded in the Age of Enlightenment and Reason, the secular elements and philosophical enquiries that also characterized Europe at this time. It was a period when anything that could not be subjected to prevailing theories and be proved, was non-existent or at best sub-human (sub-European). The Cartesian separation of the mind from the body, and the super-imposition of the cognitive mind over the emotional body, further reduced the significance of the body. It became purely an emotional husk, divorced from the intellect-reason and therefore of no use to human civilization. Dance, the art of the body consequently became a purely physical activity below the new real humanity, and following on the Darwinian theory of evolution, it was discarded as a people ascended in civilization.

The association with the dance culture in Africa was clear. It was taken as conclusive evidence of their illogicality and incapability of reflexive thinking; if the Europeans were to successfully 'civilize' the Africans, their penchant for dancing had to be eradicated. Christianity which already had its own prejudice against dance was one of the weapons of the European "civilizing" crusade.

By mid-19th century, many African converts had received full clerical training and were serving as missionaries in various parts of Africa, particularly West Africa which had been very inclement to the Europeans causing high European mortality rates. The African missionaries first hand knowledge of the theology gave them more confidence in the religion, and enabled them to distinguish between the Christianity of the Bible and European-influenced Christianity. Ayandele's classic work on Christian missionary activities in Nigeria clearly demonstrates how this impacted on the direction of the religion in Africa (see 175-280) and the emergence of what is referred to here as "Africanised Christianity".

First, the Africans began to notice discrepancies between biblical injunctions and the various practices of the church hierarchy and discovered to their indignant shock that the much touted moral superiority of the white man was a myth. Europeans were found to be as equally weak in flesh as any other human being and committed fraud, adultery, fornication, and drunkenness. But most damaging to the reputation of the church was the condonation or blatant cover up for the white men guilty of these crimes by the church, while Africans were always subjected to degrading punishment. Another source of discontent was the color discrimination policy (C.M.S. 1879), where experienced and better qualified Africans were routinely placed under unqualified and untrained Europeans. Ayandele reports that by the end of the century, European Christianity had become thoroughly discredited and was described as a "dangerous thing," "an empty and delusive fiction" (263).

The seething resentment against European highhandedness and the "unscriptural" Christianity brought to Africa led the African Christian leaders to begin to review their own acceptance and practice of Christianity especially in comparison with the ways their forebears worshipped. They discovered that the intensity of devotion and religious fervor which characterized the devotees of traditional religions were missing among African Christians. They therefore resolved to go back to their African roots "to study their religion in order to see how much features of indigenous worship could be grafted on the 'pure milk of the Gospel'" (264, see also Lagos Weekly Record). This was a radical step which, at one level, injected a new form of life and respect to indigenous African religions, and at the other, revolutionized the form of Christianity in Africa, and subsequently the rest of the world.

The result of these researches, in conjunction with the cumulative anti-white feelings, "secession" from the European Church missions and it was most pronounced in West Africa, the center of the rebellion. The first to break away was the native Baptist Church in April 1888, from the American based Baptist mission in Nigeria, followed in 1891 and 1901 by the United Native African Church and the African Bethel Church respectively. By 1914, there was an impressive proliferation of African Churches especially in Nigeria (196, 201-5). Although religion centered, their cause was so popular and took on such strong political fervor that they were referred to as "nationalists". While the popularity of these churches was due in part to the high nationalistic (anti-white) feelings of the time, it was also largely due to the presence of those "features of indigenous worship" infused into the system of worship-specifically singing, drumming and dancing, all rhythmic elements that help to heighten the worshipers' perception of, and collective union with God. These, more than anything else, sustained the African churches amidst various efforts by the European church missions to see them collapse, particularly after the nationalistic sentiments moved out of the churches into full politics even up to the present time.

A number of churches such as the Cherubim and Seraphim (C-&S), Celestial and the African Apostolic faith churches were also established during this time but outside the core of the "nationalistists" movement. They were founded not as splinter groups from the European missions but independently by Africans who had not received any special theological training apart from reading and believing the Bible. Initially they totally rejected the Africanization of Christianity, criticizing what they regarded as the "pagan revisionism" of the splinter groups, especially their sponsorship of dramatic performances based on the stories of local deities. The bible served as their sole point of reference and inspiration. Three important features of worship they took from the bible are i) praising God with music and dance, ii)prophesying and iii) speaking in tongues (possession). In fact the C&S sect was founded in 1914 after a fourteen year old girl, Miss Akinsowon, had a vision instructing her on the directions of a new church very different from those already in existence. Their lack of a formal background in the European orthodox structure of worship afforded them the freedom to experiment with different forms of worship. Today, they are closest to the indigenous African system of worship in dance styles, prayer forms, composition of lyrics and in the use of musical instruments.

As in other churches, the Word remained the tenet of the religion but these new African churches have successfully blended both the Word and the dance in Christian worship. Bible readings, preaching and other verbal exhortation are regularly interspersed with gusty singing, lively clapping and ecstatic dancing. Possession, the climax of the worship occurs usually after a prolonged sing-dance session where the spirit of God is exhorted to descend amongst them. However, since the deity being exhorted here is the ultimate and Supreme God, and not a nature or an anthropomorphic god, His features are not known. Rather than manifesting "characteristics" of God through dance, the spirit of God (the Word) descends on the anointed (mediums) in visions or prophesies which may be rendered in 'tongues'.

Thus, as Africans became more confident of the significance of their cultural forms, the more Christianity adapted to the culture of its environment, and dance gradually reestablished itself as an important means of worship. The cultural innovations greatly endeared many

Africans who had felt alienated by the rather dull, uninspiring form of worship in European Orthodox churches but had stayed on because of the promise (or threat) of the afterlife. In the new churches they found religious upliftment and devotional piety. Even the African bishops who remained within the European missions attempted to introduce some music that encouraged rhythmic bodily expressions but the Europeans quickly put a stop to it.

3.2 Islam and the Representation of Human Forms in Art. Islam came into Africa not expressly as a religious crusade or with the righteous attempt to civilize non-believers, rather it came with the Saharan caravan trades through north Africa and the Arab slave-trade on the east coast of Africa. Nonetheless, even without the Jihad or the European vocation of "civilizing" the Africans, the effect of Islam on the African way of life and culture is no less devastating or total. In many superficial ways, it soon adapted to the local religions and the Imams settled amongst the people, intermarrying with them and eventually becoming *bona fide* citizens of authority.

This appearance of accommodation ultimately ensured the perfect assimilation of the new religion by the indigenes. Pressures to change to the ways of the "faith" and doing away with "practices of the unbelievers", were exerted from within families and "indigenous authorities" in the societies. Almost unobtrusively, Islamic practices became deeply entrenched, often times taking the garb of local customs, thus making it difficult to really distinguish Muslim culture from African cultures. Consequently, many indigenous creative expressions lost their originality or even disappeared altogether. Since the Islamic religion categorically forbids any human representation as an artistic expression, art forms such as dance, drama and sculpture, which capture the essence of humans, suffered the most. The contemporary concept of tashe performance among the Hausa people of Nigeria and its derivative among the Yoruba will serve as a relevant illustration.

During the month of Ramadan, the Muslim fasting period, a public procession is used to wake up Muslims, especially the women, to prepare the pre-dawn meal that precedes the day's fasting. Among Hausa Muslims, it is known as *tashe* (wake up). Its origin, however, predated Islam, it had existed in ancient Hausa society as a form of comic drama satirizing social deviants and preaching cultural ethics. Islam later appropriated the play within its context using it to the advantage of its dogma. As has been pointed out by Odekunle, but for its moralistic tone and adaptability in Islam, it would have been wiped out like other indigenous artistic expressions (2-3). Except for a few inserted

Muslim characters such as the Imam, it is still not a religious drama, having kept its pre-Islamic form, function and content, but now it is no longer performed outside the Ramadan period. The attempt to present tashe as a legitimate Islamic practice includes equating it with the shadow puppet plays—a cultural pastime used in some Arab countries as light entertainment to relieve the long Ramadan days. Odekunle further points out that the most popular tashe piece is called *Kayi rawa kai mallam Kayi rawa* "the learned cleric denies to have danced" (5-6). This is a revealing piece about the reaction of the people to an important aspect of the religion. It is obviously a satire of the Islamic anti-dance posture.

It is the Islamic concept of *tashe* that was adopted by the Yoruba Muslims who call it *ji were* (wake up quick). Also performed by young adults, it survives only as musical exhortations waking up the faithful. Despite the Islamic strict injunction against representational arts including dance, *ji were* music has inspired social music and dances such as *sakara* and *apala*. But the process of appropriation is clear. By the time *tashe* moved out of its area of origin it had become a full Islamic affair, such that the social dances it inspired were, until recently, strictly forbidden to "good" Christians.

4. The State of Religious Dances in Contemporary Times

Dance is still a strong dynamic force in religious worships in Africa. After centuries of distortion, misrepresentation, and the various eradication tactics of the colonial forces, sacred dancing has survived not only in the indigenous religions where faithful devotees strive to keep them alive and meaningful against all odds in a differently paced society, it has also "appropriated" and become integral to the religions that initially sought its destruction. In fact, very importantly, it survived the brutal uprooting from its nurturing source in Africa during the European slave trade and subsequent attempts to stamp it out on the European slave plantations in the Americas. Its deep-rooted significance as worship transcended all obstacles and it survived keeping its religion alive in the Brazilian *candombles*, the Cuban *bembe* and the *orisa* shrines in the U.S. These religious dances still prevail, adapting and creating new styles in radically different situations and influencing many more.

The influence of African religious dances extend beyond the continent or in the African religions that survived the Atlantic crossing. Its influence is strongly evident among Africans in the Diaspora converted to Christianity; the "Gospel" form of worship in African-American churches with clapping, singing, "shouts", and spiritual, ecstatic body movements are firmly rooted in African worship forms. Long regarded with suspicious curiosity and even at times with outright hostility by the Europeans, such forms of "charismatic" worships are becoming acceptable in many Christian churches worldwide.10 While they may not be in the exact form of African ecstatic religious dancing, many contemporary non-denominational Christian worships now found in many parts of the world have come to embrace more bodily expressive form of service—gestures, and rhythmic swaying to the accompaniment of lively percussion music rather than the traditional organ music. Even churches still within the orthodox church system have begun introducing significant changes to incorporate more expressive body movements. In Nigeria for example, both the Catholic and the Anglican churches became alarmed at the rate they were losing members to the Celestial churches while not making significant new converts, and so started going "charismatic" in the 1980's. Many religious sects are becoming "converted" to the idea that dance is a legitimate spiritual form of worship. The affecting influence of the religious dances of Africa cannot be denied; once denounced as heathenish and barbaric, they are now validated as fully devotional and spiritual means of communicating with God. These are the dynamics of African sacred dances.

Notes

1. For a fuller discussion of African cosmology and rituals, see Soyinka: *Myth, Literature and the African World*, 7-12, 45-54.
2. See Davies, *Liturgical Dance*, 124.
3. Thompson's *African Art in Motion* demonstrates the importance of movement to African plastic arts.
4. The analysis which follows is made in reference to minor deities assisting the Supreme Deity hence, the small letters used when referring to them as "deities" or "gods". The majuscule letter is used when their proper names are mentioned. Generally, the Supreme God remains an abstract conception of Power, as such, He or She is represented neither in nature nor in icons.
5. The possessions are unprovoked because the person involved would not have been performing the progression dance towards possession and need not have been a devotee of the deity in fact.
6. Sango was once a ruler of the powerful Oyo empire of West Africa. According to history, he was forced to abdicate because of his insatiable

thirst for wars and also because one of his experiments in attracting electricity form lighting went wrong resulting in a fire that destroyed almost half his kingdom.

7. See also Thompson, *Yoruba Gods and Kings*, 81.

8. Certain social codes are observed here so the privilege is not misused. While the citizens including non devotees are compelled to give, it is within their right to any unreasonable or malicious demands. Should they refuse, it is disaster for the *whole* community.

9. The Quar'an states that in one of his travels, the holy prophet Mohammed was inspired by the monotheism of Christianity and on returning to his native land began preaching against the polytheism of his people.

10. In 1990, the percentage of charismatic/pentecostal Christians is given as 21.4% of the world's total Christians, source: The Lausanne Statistical Task Force for the 1990 Pentecostal Convention in America. Although I doubt if the African charismatic Christians are included in this survey, this is still a remarkable number for a movement that did not begin to get recognition from the church hierarchy until the 1960s.

Works Cited

Ayandele, E. A. *The Missionary Impact on Modern Nigeria*. London: Longman, 1966.

C.M.S. (Church Missionary Society) CA1/25 (e), Cheetham to Wright, May 16, 1879; quoted in Ayandele 196.

Davies, J. G. *Liturgical Dance*. London: SCM Press, 1984.

van Genep, Arnold. *The Rites of Passage*. London: Routledge & Kegan Paul, 1960, reprinted. (1909).

Hunter. "The Ju-Ju Dancer." *Dancing Times*, (August 1931): 427.

Lagos Weekly Record, 28 November 1891.

Lagos Weekly Record, 27 July 1895.

Lagos Weekly Record, 27 March 1897.

Odekunle, Lantana Ladi. "The Development of 'Tashe' Drama in Hausaland" paper presented at SONTA 4th Annual Convention O.A.U. Ile-Ife April 23-26, 1987. Unpublished.

Soyinka, Wole. *Myth, Literature and The African World*. London: Cambridge University Press, 1976.

Stubbes, Philip. *Anatomy of the Abuses in England*, 1583 (ed. F. J. Furnival, New Shakespeare Society) quoted in Davies 31.

Thompson, Robert F. *African Art in Motion*. Los Angeles: UCLA Press, 1974.

—. *Black Gods and Kings*. Bloomington: Indiana University Press, 1976.

Turner, Victor and Edith Turner. "Religious Celebrations" in *Celebration*, pp. 201-219. Ed. Victor Turner, Smithsonian Institution Press, Washington, 1982.

THE ZIMBABWEAN DANCE AESTHETIC: SENSES, CANONS, AND CHARACTERISTICS

▲▲▲▲▲▲▲▲▲▲▲▲▲▲▲▲▲

Kariamu Welsh Asante

Introduction
The African Aesthetic

According to art historian Susan Vogel, "the aesthetic is fundamentally moral" (Vogel, 1986:15). The word for beauty and good is usually the same in many African languages. "This word usually means well made, beautiful, pleasing to the senses, virtuous, useful, correct, appropriate, and conforming to customs and expectations and stands in contrast to the word meaning vicious, useless, illmade, unsuitable" (Vogel, 1986:15). Vogel correctly points out the symbiotic connection between beauty and good that is so prevalent in African societies. This fusion of beauty and good does not denote a lack of distinction between the two. It is instead an indication of the perennial multiplicity of concepts that occupy equal status and dominance. Vogel continues by stating that "It becomes clear, however, that a real understanding of African Art and African value systems lies in the very recognition that the two concepts overlap" (Vogel, 1986:15).

The Zimbabwean dance is typical of this recognition as it is commonly defined in form and content. "Good/aesthetic expresses two sources of African aesthetic: the aesthetic form of a work (its external appearance) and its aesthetic content (the signification of something good)" (Vogel:15). Moral perfection in the African aesthetic as articulated by Thompson is the cornerstone to understanding the African aesthetic. The material manifestation of the art form will always be imperfect but the content, if functional, will achieve moral perfection and that is where the value is placed.

This article will examine Robert Farris Thompson's canons as one approach to analyze the aesthetic features of Zimbabwean dance. Familiar characteristics of the African dance have now been identified as key elements of a dance aesthetic delineated by Thompson. Implicit in a dance aesthetic is its movement constitution that is based upon its belief and value systems. While not every dance is specifically functional, every dance serves a function even though that function may be fluid. I have demonstrated that with both the *Jerusarema* and *Muchongoyo* dances. The *Jerusarema* and *Muchongoyo* dances represent two different and distinct traditions of dance in Zimbabwe. As such I was able to isolate the aesthetic features of those dances and then demonstrate the commonalities between the two dances. At the core of their commonality is rhythm! Rhythm has been identified by a concordance of scholars as central to any understanding or codification of an African aesthetic and so I have made this construct with rhythm as the bridge that connects the aesthetic intradisciplinary and interdisciplinary. Thompson's canonical theory provides a framework with which to examine the African dance. It also allows enough flexibility so that dances of different regions can be accommodated and consequently examined.

Aesthetic Characteristics of the *Jerusarema* and *Muchongoyo* Dances

Classifying the *Jerusarema* and the *Muchongoyo*

The *Jerusarema* and the *Muchongoyo* dances are an absolute product of culture, environment, and circumstances. This combination allows it to be categorized according to several classification systems: (1) Stearns' (1979) system in Jazz Dance, (2) Curt Sachs' (1937) scheme in *World History of Dance*, and (3) Zora Neale Hurston's characteristics of Negro expression in the *Sanctified Church*.

Marshall and Jean Stearns (1979) have outlined six characteristics of African dance:
(1) African style is often flat-footed and favors gliding, dragging, or shuffling steps;
(2) African dance is frequently performed from a crouch, knees flexed,

and body bent at the waits;

(3) African dance generally imitates animals in realistic detail;

(4) African dance places great importance on improvisation and satire, and allows for freedom for individual expression. This characteristic makes for flexibility and aids the evolution and diffusion of other African characteristics;

(5) African dance is centrifugal, exploding outward from the hip. The leg moves from the hip instead of from the knee;

(6) African dance is performed to a propulsive rhythm that gives it a swinging quality.

The Stearns' analysis of the characteristics of African dance has laid a foundation for further expansion and development. It is necessary to read Kunene's (1981) description of African dance and its relationship to the earth in order to put Stearns' first characteristic into perspective. In *Anthem of the Decades*, Kunene (1981) speaks of the "cosmological approach" to the earth. The African dance steps that the Stearns call "gliding, dragging or shuffling" relate to the union of man and the earth. The stamping of the ground with the feet is regarded as a sacred act celebrating this relationship. Indeed, according to Kunene, the Zulu, another southern African people, consider the internal echoes of the earth as one of the most powerful symbols of growth. We can only conclude that the divergence of views as to what constitutes heaven and/or paradise between the African and the European is related to the social attitudes toward the earth. One regards the earth as a friendly and benevolent world whereas the other considers the earth as a "hostile environment from which man must escape to a sky-heaven" (Kunene, 1981). To a large degree this explains the intimate relationship of African dance and the earth; from the Nigerian stomp to the Ghanaian squat to the Dunham *kaiso* walk to the shuffling movements of the *Adowa* to the slow drag of the African-Americans, to the *samba* of the African-Brazilians, the feet embrace the bountiful ground to draw from it additional power and sound. Zimbabwean dance reflects this relationship of the feet and earth in both the *Jerusarema* and *Muchongoyo* dances.

Rhythm As Text In the *Jerusarema* and *Muchongoyo* Dances

Dancing and drumming are rich artistic activities that play central roles in many traditional cultures in Africa. In this study the focus is on the forms of rhythmic expression vis-à-vis a textual and structural order. They are manifested in oral historical records, as agents of synthesis and harmony, and as possible indications of cultural dynamics. Most of my material is drawn from the Shona and Ndebele cultural traditions but other African traditions also support my observations and conclusions. My approach is oriented towards traditional customs generally shared by African cultures. However, I recognize that it is inappropriate and inaccurate to generalize about African culture in an absolute manner.

African dance and drum traditions are two distinct expressions of the same entity: namely rhythm. Both dancing and drumming require accompaniment. One, dancing demands physical involvement and the other, drumming demands human participation. In other words the requisite tool of both dancing and drumming is the human body. This requirement is demonstrative of the ontological order and structure of the African worldview. The significance of the anthropocentric artistic and creative ethos is both practical and philosophical. At the core of African culture is a humanistic philosophy that serves the people while serving the deities.

Rather than the material separation of the arts from each other and the physical distinctions between the played and the player, African culture relies upon holistic integration that subsumes an organic relationship. What is important to comprehend about any African culture and specifically Shona and Ndebele culture, is the permeation of the lifeforce throughout the entire cosmology as a recognizable and acknowledged presence. It cannot be overemphasized that this omnipresent force is a viable and active part of reality and consequently, real!

As a real and rational entity it (rhythm) is permanently ensconced in a tradition that is dynamic and vital. What strikes the so-called Western world as metaphysical and intangible is in fact concrete and tangible. This understanding negotiates and resolves all phenomenon both naturally and supernatural. If one is able to conceptualize rhythm as text, then both dance and drumming can be viewed as a dual unity. Text then provides structure that is dynamic and documentable. Unlike written text, this text is distinguished by it's "oral" quality even when this oral quality is manifested as visual, kinetic or sensory. The value of recognizing text in this manner is to focus on an entire cultural phenomenon that would otherwise be misunderstood, misinterpreted and disregarded. What lessons can we learn about the way that we categorize information and knowledge? Indeed, the task is formidable when we consider that deciding what and how to classify and categorize is just as important as the actual interpretation of the data. Contextually, dancing and drumming are the same, although perceived differently, they both emanate from the same foundation; namely rhythm! Therefore the categories of music and dance must be discarded when entering a discussion about African culture. Any discussions that center around separations or distinctions would automatically evolve around the question of sacredness or profaneness.

However one chooses to examine traditional African cultures, one must always be prepared to reevaluate the literature. This reevaluation and reexamination if you will, requires a worldview or mind-set that is predicated on holism and unity, rather than distinctions and separations. There are many distinctions and separations to be sure, but those distinctions are internal and interrelated within the entity as opposed to outside of it. As one continues to examine the *Jerusarema* dance, the approach can vary according to what is being observed. What is constant however is the idea that the *Jerusarema* is comprised of its movements and rhythms and even when examined separately, the other component must always be considered for its impact and interrelatedness. Analysis of African dance and music must be performed holistically or the interpretation is invalid.

Rhythm remains the central core to any expression of African culture and consequently the center of any analysis that is conducted. The difficulty then is organization of the information that the text offers. The challenge is the interpretation of not only the information but the interpretation of the organization. That will provide the discipline with a solid foundation that will engender more research and documentation. I'm not suggesting that we discard other ways of looking at African arts but that other perspectives are included that add to the overall understanding of the dances. The *Jerusarema* dance is an example of how perspectives impact upon the understanding of the dance. I have already stated that it is a traditional dance meaning that it is generational and recognizable by the community. The *"Jerusarema"* is a griotic and commemorative dance in that is was originally performed by very young children, women, and elderly men as a diversionary tactic in a time of imminent assault. It then made a transition into a classical commemorative dance used for social, ceremonial and honorific occasions. How to describe the *Jerusarema* then? It can be recognized by its steps but never to be confused with just being them! It can be acknowledged by its dancers but never to confuse the dancers with the dance! It can be witnessed by its rhythms but again never to be confused as just or only music!

Here is the classic paradigm for examining the African dance, the inclusion of rhythmic text as central to the structure of the dance.

A reorganization of perceptions must be actualized here before any true understanding can be effected. It would be irresponsible to even imply that this is a simplistic formula for the examination and observation of the African dance, however there must be a foundation from which to see, and consequently analyze the material. Rhythm acts as the pervasive and identifying agent in both African dance and music. In most cases, the rhythm identifies the text as well as the context! The *Jerusarema* dance is recognized by the Shona community by its rhythm. Neither the movements or rhythm alone would be sufficient enough to create a framework that would encompass the meaning of the event. Yet, it is clearly the rhythm that dominates and manipulates the movements as well as the context. This duality of rhythm and movement demonstrates a continuity that is cyclical as well as linear. The intensity of the rhythm signals where the entire community is a specific point of any event or commemoration. The rhythm also assists in identifying who is present, particularly the presence of dignitaries, strangers and spirits. The movements themselves do not change, but the rhythm provides the framework that instructs the choreography, the performers and the audience. This structure allows for an optimal freedom of expression and yet holds the continuity of tradition and dynamics in place. Complex as it sounds, this phenomenon is indeed repeated in every form and institution in African society. Because music and dance are generally associated as interrelated and interconnected in Western societies, another relationship that is even more intimate is difficult to imagine. The distinction is that rhythm and movement are not only inseparable but many times indistinguishable. In essence, the desired product must be indistinguishable if the optimal response is to be generated. That response can be pleasurable, spiritual or both. Again this structure permits both the sacred and the profane within the same body of rhythm, yet clearly identifiable by it's context and text. Remarkably, this sophisticated oral tradition lends itself to a myriad of interpretations and conclusions. What is so clear to the people living the culture boggles the minds of people studying the culture. Part of the confusion comes from perspective and part of the confusion comes from perception.

Information rendered by the rhythm is layered and exists at different levels. This means of course that you are never privy to all of the information because each layer generates another layer and so on. How to tackle the impossible task? One's perspective is crucial to furthering one's own understanding as well as others'. I doubt that the goal should be to master all of the knowledge about a particular subject but rather to master an understanding of the context and text. Once one is able to master an understanding, then, in a real sense, the observer becomes a participant. Participation merely implies that there is an organic involvement that cannot be realized without the involvement of self. This immediately places a responsibility on the observer/participant that is self-regulating and self-liberating. It is self-regulating in that once active participation is achieved the vantage point automatically changes and the person is bounded by the inner circles values. It is self-liberating in that the process of involvement and empathic interaction furthers the self.

Perception and perspective operate together, although as separate entities. One's perspective governs one's perception; in other words, what you see is what you think you see! The African dance is a good example in examining the relevance of perception and perspective. If one sees movement of specific body parts then the vision is geared towards what value is placed not only on the movement itself but the value that is placed on the specific body parts. In Western society there is often a tendency to equate a specific body part with a particular meaning. When the pelvis is accentuated or articulated for instance, that movement is often perceived as having sexual symbolism. One is then blinded by a preconceived meaning when the only basis for the activation of that belief is the movement of the pelvis. Example or not, the point must be made that movement is not detached from the value system that is placed on the instrument of movement; the body. Which of course brings us again to the issue of rhythm, movement and the body.

The percussive element of most traditional African dances only exacerbates the preconceived image of any body moving but particularly a body moving to drums, the most primal of all sounds. It would be negligent of me not to mention the racial aspect of this picture that I'm drawing. Clearly the added dimension of a "black" body invokes further stereotypes that have no basis in reality. Although it is not the purpose of this paper to discuss the racial implications of the positioning of African dance and music, it must be acknowledged that racism extends to the artistic and creative world as well.

Given the difference between movement and sound, there are bound to be differences and distinctions. The articulation of those differences are not central to this discussion, but rather, those features that belong to the "collective" dance and are shared by all the people who use them rather than individual virtuoso movements; "the essential" as opposed to accessory (Saussure, 1966:14).

When the examination of the full implications of rhythm as text is completed, the entire field of African dance and music will be reorganized and refocussed. Obviously this is no small task but it is one that must be completed if there is any real interest in knowledge of all cultures. For too long scholars have been studying the dances and music of Africa as if they were two distinct and separate entities when one has to look no further than the art form itself to see the perpetual blurring of the two areas. Dance is not music and music is not dance, others may argue, but again that is a determination that comes out of a specific perspective and cannot accommodate this different paradigm. Once one is comfortable with the idea that other viable paradigms exist, then perhaps some meaningful dialogue can be established and continued. This challenge exists for all areas of knowledge and all spheres of learning. The context of rhythm is just as significant as the notation of rhythm in as much as it establishes a foundation for analysis and theory.

In the *Jerusarema* dance of Zimbabwe, the percussive rhythms are interspersed with episodic displays of silence. The picture is incomplete until the movement is introduced. Without the rhythm and the movement in tandem, there can be no dance with the name of *Jerusarema*. Indeed, if you were to try to describe the movements without the rhythms, you would meet with some confusion as the dance nor the rhythms are conceptualized in that way. For the same reason one cannot mix and match movements and rhythms that are not normally together. It is a very clear system that does allow artistic expression in the guise of spontaneity, but also demands historical and cultural integrity. The artistic freedom that we in the West hold so dear is not an issue for the traditionalists. Rather they see themselves as "Keepers of the Traditions" and take pride in the fact that they have been able to maintain the dances and rhythms as the ancestors gave it to them. This noble attitude is rewarded by the community who depend on the traditionalists to maintain and to know when information is needed or a dispute arises regarding the dance that needs an informed resolution.

The work of ethnomusicologists, concentrating on analysis and sounds of the rhythms, has not yet begun to explain the phenomenon of rhythm and movement in tandem. Dance historians are more inclined to find the origins of the dance and to place emphasis on the first documentation of that work as opposed to the qualities and characteristics of the dance itself. Art historians are likely to assess the history as well as the structure, line, and composition of the artwork as a material artifact. Theologians find themselves extracting the spiritual meaning and religious history out of the music, dance and art. All of these scholars well intentioned have helped to divide and separate an entity that was never meant to be studied in that fashion. the institutionalization of these divisions have made it difficult for the necessary and inevitable reemerging of the above mentioned. I say necessary and inevitable because scholarship is already headed towards the examination of subjects from an internal perspective otherwise known as centrism. The academic community would only gain from such an exercise. And the world community would not only gain from this perspective but they would abolish so much of the ignorance and biases surrounding other cultural and artistic experiences.

As historical reservoirs, dance and music form a complex document that can be read in many different ways. Symbols, proverbs, adages and icons all reside in the dance and music. One has to know what the search is for and what the results mean. It is in the musical and movements symbols that the full rendering of the text can be actualized. The function of treating the entire text is to keep the connections and interrelationships as well as the intrarelationships intact. These elements interact in a way that is interdependent. How much or how little one can research from extracting one element from the rest is fairly clear. Fragmentation occurs and the study of the parts obscures the knowledge of the whole. This predisposition to truncating in order to decipher meaning and structure has created a large body of knowledge, that while useful, is very limited in its overall scope. The dance and music contain references to that and can be distinguished and then defined but only if the premise is focussed and centered. A combination of rhythms and movements that are inappropriate may be more than just a manner of being mistaken but making a tragic judgement. Therefore, how one looks at the material in question determines how successful and accurate the results of that observation will be.

In proposing a theoretical framework for examining the music and dance of traditional African societies and specially Shona society, I have meant to further ways that research can be carried out that without disrupting or disrespecting the knowledge being studied. There is a saying that "Codes are meant to be broken", but in order to effectively study the codes of culture then one must adopt the adage that "Codes are meant to be understood." Rhythm is manifested physically in the dance and is usually accompanied by action, activity or an active phase. Consequently, motion is manifested rhythmically in the music and is generally accompanied by sound, silence or an active pause. The physicality of both rhythm and motion is not only paramount to understanding the interrelationship but is consistent with the cosmological ordering of dual unity. This partnership, if you will, unites structurally and philosophically all of the aspects of dance and rhythm. In decoding the dances of Africa in order to read the "text," one must be very careful not to confuse the process of decoding with the process of interpretation. One cannot assume for instance that the information revealed is information understood. Decoding is the first step in the overall process and should be clearly distinct from all others functions concerning interpretation and analysis. Subsequent steps would be rendered ineffective unless the decoding process is in compliance with the context of the work. For instance, in decoding a dance one would ascertain data about the dance such as: meaning of dance, music accompanying the dance, costuming or dress, movements sequences, whereas in interpretation and analysis the decoding information would be used to facilitate the next process. Decoding is a more structured process that precedes the interpretation and analysis process which is more contextualized and subjective.

Aesthetic "Senses" of the *Jerusarema* and *Muchongoyo*

The analysis of African aesthetics that I have isolated in the Zimbabwean dance are the seven senses, outlined here: (1) Polyrhythm, (2) Polycentrism, (3) Curvilinear, (4) Epic Memory, (5) Texture, (6) Repetition, and (7) Holism. There has been a distinction between senses and characteristics of African dance. Among some characteristics are collective signature and creativity, theme, and uniformity. In my view, the senses refer to those qualities that make up the integral composition of the dance, while characteristics refer to those qualities that the dance itself performs in and of itself. These qualities are projected by the dance. Characteristics are commonly found in African dance with the qualities I have indicated, but these characteristics alone do not constitute the makeup of the dance. The senses undergird all of the dances regardless of theme, ethnicity, and geography. In this way, the senses like Thompson's canons help to identify what can be described as the African dance aesthetic.

The *Jerusarema* and *Muchongoyo* dances are *polyrhythmic* in sound and *polycentric* in movement. The rhythm is a basic 6/8 with a 5/4 on the *mukwas* and the constant vibrations of the leg rattles. As the dancers perform, the movement is centered in the torso area with waist, hip, and pelvis concentration until the movement explodes outward, thus fulfilling the Stearns' (1979) sixth characteristic and Thompson's multiple meters and ephebism canons.

In an article entitled "Native Dancing: A Wasted Asset," Hugh Tracey (1940) extolled the virtues of the *Jerusarema* and continued that the dances of Mashonaland are "athletic performances requiring much skill and physical energy." Tracey is talking about the ephebistic qualities of the *Jerusarema* that is a common characteristic of African dance.

Structurally, both the *Jerusarema* and *Muchongoyo* dances are *curvilinear.* The motions are circular and patterns may pass through 45° and 90° angles but do not pose or position themselves at 45°, 90°, or 180° degrees. The movements of the dance are rounded even when directed or accented. The *Jerusarema* and *Muchongoyo* are essentially a line dances in formation, but the shape of the movements are actually curvilinear.

The *epic memory* sense is a thematic one but in a very different perspective from what one is normally used to thinking. The African dancer remembers all others who danced the dance and why. The story behind the dance is not so important as who danced it, before whom was it danced, and is it now being danced well. Inasmuch as the experience sense is ancestral memory and involves ancestral connections, it is extremely significant because of its relatedness to spirituality, ethos, and empathy. *Jerusarema* dancers do not take individual credit for creativity, although they do take individual credit for virtuoso performances. The maker of the dance is usually an ancestor, spirit, or god; therefore, even as the dance is changed or modified, it is only a change on the Master Plan and not an act of creation itself. However, one may take praise for one's performances because those performances are tributes to the ancestors or manifestations of ancestors' will.

In a discussion of African artistic traditional music and dance in *Music in African Cultures*, J.H. Kwabena Nketia (1966:48) writes, "Every musical (dance) played (danced) in community life has a tradition behind it, a tradition which governs its mode of performance, its repertoire ... as well as tradition that governs the context in which it should be played (danced)." Those spectators familiar with these traditions expect to recognize them in practice and may be disturbed if there are serious departures, for there is enjoyment in the renewal of experience. Creative additions or innovations are tolerated if they reinforce this pleasure. Nketia (1966:48) also sees this experience as being interpretative:

> By interpretation we do not mean just the artistry evident in the performance of a given piece, but simply the concrete realization of a tradition in a way and manner acceptable to a traditional audience, and which may show the extent of the performer's correctness of memory and fidelity to tradition as well as the creative

imagination he brings into it. ... It cannot be overemphasized that in traditional society a great premium is placed on the renewal of experience.

The *texture* or *dimensionality* sense in the *Jerusarema* and *Muchongoyo* is a reverberation. It happens because of the first and second senses, polyrhythms and polycentrism. The texture sense is the extra-shape vibration that happens in the movement of the waist and hips. The multiple thrusting of the hips and the multiple spiraling of the waist give off a surrounding sound and motion that is indivisible from the movement.

Repetition is a distinct characteristic of the African aesthetic. It is not the refrain or chorus but the intensifying of one movement or one sequence or the entire dance until spiritual satisfaction has been reached, ecstasy, euphoria, and exhaustion. Time is a factor, but enough time rather than a set amount of time. Repetition is present in the *Jerusarema* and *Muchongoyo* dances. The *Jerusarema* dance, itself consists of two main movements, one for the men and one for the women, and yet the dance can go on for hours without being boring and without varying too much from the two basic steps. It is the same for the *Muchongoyo* dance; often it is not until the dance has been repeated numerous times is there any satisfaction for the audience and spectators.

There are four levels to the repetition in dance. Ruth Stone has devised a system for music that is also useful for the dance. I have kept her basic formula but the elaboration on the dance are mine.

Stone's Formula

(1) relatively simple repeating patterns:
(2) less simple and usually repeating patterns:
(3) simple and usually repeating pattern:
(4) complex and often varying pattern.

Revised Formula

(1) relatively simple repeating patterns: shuffle steps, time steps and side to side steps
(2) less simple and usually repeating patterns: combination of shuffle, timesteps and side to side movements
(3) omitted
(4) combinations, movements that match the rhythms of the drums in literally and then they repeat.

The final sense is holism and it has been previously stated in this article that the dance is part of an integral whole. Not only is the dance interconnected to the music and the drama, but it is linked to societal events and ceremonies.

Gerhard Kubrick states "motional prominence of the pelvis is considered a diagnostic trait of the movement style of the Southern Zaire/Angola Region" (Kubrick, 1978). This would place the *Jerusarema* with its hip and pelvis emphasis into the Central African Bantu Category. The chief characteristic of the Southern African Bantu Category is foot stomping and reliance on the percussive quality of the stomp, stamp, or clap, all done with the foot. It is not the only characteristic of Southern African Dance, but it is a distinguishing one. As Kubrick understands "there is a good deal of stylistic spillover across the presumed dance-style areas."

The *Jerusarema* is an example of the controversy over what is a "traditional dance." What "shapes" traditional dance? Historical, ecological, religious, cultural, political, and social changes are the various signatures written on the fabric of the dance. The essence of the dance remains unchanged even though the steps, costumes, music, and percussive instruments may undergo change. I have stated several changes in the Jerusarema that have not altered the nature of the dance itself, despite the fact that those elements were not present in the dance one hundred years ago. The *hoshos*, for example, are now made of soft drink cans instead of gourds, cloth skirts have replaced the *mbakiza* skirts, and the women no longer dance bare-breasted. These changes, while acknowledged, are incapable of changing the "motional" aspect of the dance of the polycentric quality of the dance or the actual steps of the *Jerusarema*.

Robert Farris Thompson in his discussion of ephebism, the youthful quality of African dance, refers to the individual aspects as vital aliveness, high intensity, speed and drive: "These are some of the facets of artful muscularity and depth of feeling that characterize the dance of the continent" (Thompson:6).

Ephebism certainly is a dominant quality in the *Muchongoyo* Thompson goes on to say, "People in Africa, regardless of their actual age, return to strong youthful patterning whenever they move with the steams of energy which flow from drums or other sources of percussion. They obey the implications of vitality with the music and its speed and drive." That explains the presence of a sixty-four-year-old man and a fourteen-year-old boy, both dance the *Muchongoyo* in the National Dance Company of Zimbabwe and there being no discernible difference between them. People would often come up to me, as director of the company, after a performance and ask which one was the sixty-four-year-old? He was fairly easy to pick out offstage but while he was dancing he was indeed "young."

The actual movements in the *Muchongoyo* number about five or six depending on the performers. The stamping step is the clear signature movement and that step when varied with rhythm and nuances can be repeated without ever appearing monotonous. Dramatic gestures and countenances are integral to the *Muchongoyo*. The mimetic element is as essential to the dance as the stamping. Acting out the exhilaration of the military drills and the expectation of competition, the face, hands and arms become extremely expressive. The hands twist and turn, giving directions if they are the hands of a common soldier. Even the singular action of lifting the knee up, sending it down with the full sole of the foot into the ground is enhanced by variations. In the pause of breath before the knee comes up, there is either a powerful contraction of the pelvis or a swing of the leg to the back before it rises thrusting the knee up to the chest. The *Muchongoyo* movement, that is, the *kutshongolo'* step is strong in terms of weight, vertical in regards to space and heavy in relationship to quality.

That is, the more the attitude of the movement "favors descent", the more the total weight of the body is brought to bear on the ground, and is perceived to be successfully executed. It is vertical in terms of space in that the movement essentially moves up and down and not from side to side. The posturing is to dialogue (in motion) while ascending, and to accent or descent. This creates a sense of many climaxes in the dance each time the dancers hit the ground which is always in unison.

The *Muchongoyo* is dynamic in its use of rhythm as a projector of strength and power even in the denouement. As the movement subsides, it retains an awesomeness and fierceness which maintains the dynamism. Furthermore, the sound made from the *Muchongoyo* step is an organic part of the movement, and is relied upon for rhythm and for rhythm and force. The two noted rhythms that accompany the dance are low-keyed in relationship to the whistle, the stamping sound, and the singing of the women.

The dance historically is performed by males yet there is female participation. Women are used primarily as musicians, playing the *hoshos* and singing alongside the men. They move constantly while singing, improvising their movements or using the standard movements of shuffling from one side to the other without lifting their feet from the ground. This movement is in direct contrast to the high knee lifts of the men. The movement that the women do while singing is related to a similar movement by African-Americans called the "shout" step (Hurston, 1979). It is so named because it was identified as taking place in church when devotees would "feel" the spirit and "shout". The movement of the Zimbabweans and the African-Americans are exactly parallel, as the entire body is involved with the weight of the torso and legs being driven into the feet as they shift from side to side.

The shuffle step is right out of the "tradition." It, too, sends the energy into the earth and not away from it; the goal is for the feet to always maintain contact with the earth. It takes considerable skill to keep both feet on the ground as you shuffle, maintain the rhythm and travel, all at the same time. The kick that the men do in the *Muchongoyo* adheres to the same principle and compensates for the raising of the leg so high by using speed to facilitate the return of he foot to the ground and therefore minimizes any break between the earth and body. Putting their hands to their foreheads in alternation as they shift from left to right, the women will sometimes move out of the chorus line in single file and dance around the drummer and male dancers until they return to their original positions.

Thompson's theory embraces an holistic view of African culture. His main studies have been in the Yoruba culture and have since broadened to include African retentions in the Americas. "African criticism enriches, in these cases, our sense of definition. By definition I mean the identification and characterization of expressive media which, like African dancing, might pass largely unanalyzed through the filter of western scholarship" (Thompson, 1973:19). Ladd supports Thompson's thesis by making this statement: "Aesthetic and ethical concepts are distinct from purely descriptive, empirical concepts in that they a) are open-textured, b) are multi-functional, c) involve criteria, d) are essentially contestable, and e) employ persuasive definitions" (Ladd, 1973:418).

Thompson, Ladd and Sieber have each constructed systems that help to enunciate aesthetic qualities of the dance/art. The following outline paraphrases a system that Roy Sieber had devised originally for the visual arts (Sieber, 1973:433), I have substituted the word "dance" for the word "art".

Dance is man made
Dance exhibits skill
Dance exhibits order (pattern, design)
Dance conveys meaning
Dance is the product of conscious intent
Dance is effective

Dance conveys a sense of unity, wholeness

Response is immediate

Perhaps Thompson, Ladd and Sieber have singled out the obvious but their outlines convey the basic foundation of all African dances. Ladd and Seiber's outlines are important because of their non-specificity in contrasts to Thompson's canons of African dance. Ladd and Sieber's outline applies to all dance and Thompson's canons applies to African dances. Blacking in a discussion about ballet dancers makes a statement that is apropos for African dancers as well. John Blacking offers this insight: I suggest that these contrasts are compatible with the transcendental aims of dance.

> To be effective in society, dance must mediate between nature and culture in human existence and so be transcendental in context. The intelligence of feeling should inform all action, and the insight and intuition that are nurtured by "artistic" experience are essential for the quality of life; but sequential linear processing of information is required for many of the techniques of the living .-.. witness how frequently outstanding dancers seem to "be danced" (Blacking, 1985:72).

Indeed, there is an expression that says "You have got to dance, dance!" In other words, dance has got to get hold of the dancer in order for the dancer to really dance and audiences are keenly aware of the dancers that are being "danced."

Viewed from Western traditions of realism and naturalism, African dance seems to be busy and frenzied with an emphasis on the head and torso. This is in direct opposition to the western tradition in dance that features the legs and arms as prominent. The dance body in African dance features long torsos and short legs, arms often flexed or *akimbo*, knees bent and feet parallel and flat on the ground. Rhythm, stance, expression and gesture combine in a layered fashion to create the phenomena known as African dance.

> The point of African dancing in many parts of the continent, at least, is for various parts of the body each to accompany one of the rhythms of the orchestra so that the poly-rhythms in the orchestra are reproduced by the dancer's body. The head moves in one rhythm, the shoulders in another; the arms in still another. Once the viewer has learned to see and feel the polyrhythms in the dance as it reflects the music, he can appreciate that African dancing

demands great precision and allows great freedom of expression to the dancers (Bohannon & Curtin:83).

The statement by Bohannon and Curtin, while general, is all the more valuable for its generalization. It supports my thesis that the most pervasive and dominant of all the characteristics of African dance is the polyrhythmic/polycentric aspect. Repeatedly it has been stated that you cannot separate the music and the dance and that the interdependent nature of each one on the other makes any isolated study of one incomplete. Bohannon and Curtin make the point that:

> Undoubtedly the most dramatic of the special attributes is its polyrhythmic structure. Polyrhythms are complex combinations of fairly simple but different rhythms, all played concurrently. Western music has the "classic" situation of "two against three"— the triplets played two "full value" notes during the same time span. Rarely, in Western music, a third rhythm may be added. In African music, on the other hand, five such rhythms are common, and as many as a dozen at a time have been recorded (Bohannon & Curtin:81).

In this study, the case has been made for the interpretation of rhythm and movement in tandem so that the underlying foundation of polyrhythms which support the music and the dance. The multiplicity of rhythms and movements all occurring simultaneously is the single most prominent characteristic of the *Jerusarema* and *Muchongoyo* dances. It is my contention that this statement is also true for most African dances.

Note

The Nigerian stomp and the Ghanaian squat are stylized movements from the *Umfundalai* dance technique. These two movements are part of the core movements of the *Umfundalai* technique, which I created in 1971.

Works Cited

Armstrong, Robert Plant. *Wellspring: On the Myth and Source of Culture.*
Berkeley: University of California Press, 1975.
Blacking, John. "Movement, dance, music, and the Venda girls' initiation
cycle" in *Society and the Dance*, ed. Paul Spencer. London: Cambridge

University Press, 1985.

Bohannon, Paul and Phillip Curtin. *Africa and the Africans*. Garden City: The Natural History Press, 1971.

Hurston, Zora Neale. *The Sanctified Church*. San Francisco: Turtle Press, 1979.

Kealiinohomoku, Joann. "A Comparative Study of Dance as a Constellation of Motor Behavior Among African and United Negroes." M.A. thesis, Northwestern University, 1965. Reprinted in *CORD Dance Research Annual VII 1976*.

Kunene, Masisi. *Anthems of the Decades*. London: Heineman, 1981.

Nketia, Kwabena. *Music in African Cultures*. Legon: University of Ghana, 1966.

Opoku, Albert Mawere. "The Dance in Traditional African Society," *Research Review* 7.1 (1970):1-7.

Saussure 1966.

Sieber, Roy. "Approaches to Non-Western Art," in *The Traditional Artist in African Societies*, ed. Warren d'Azevedo. Bloomington: Indiana University Press, 1973.

—. "Traditional Arts of Black Africa," in *Africa*, eds. Phyllis Martin and Patrick O'Meara. Bloomington: Indiana University Press, 1986.

Thompson, Robert Farris. "Dance Sculpture of the Yoruba: Its Critics and Contexts." Unpublished Diss. Yale University, 1965.

—. "Aesthetics in Traditional Africa." *Art News* 66.9 (1968): 44-45.

—. *African Art in Motion*. Los Angeles: University of California Press, 1974.

Vogel, Susan Mullin. *Aesthetics of African Art*. New York: The Center for African Art, 1986.

A BIBLIOGRAPHIC ESSAY AND SELECTED BIBLIOGRAPHY OF AFRICAN DANCE

▲▲▲▲▲▲▲▲▲▲▲▲▲▲▲▲▲

Glendola Yhema Mills

There have been several annotated and strict bibliographies that have served historians, cultural analysts, dance historians, and critics of African dance for decades. Among the notable ones are Margaret Thompson Drewal and Glorianne Jackson's collaboration on *Sources on African and African-Related Dance*, Alice J. Adamczyk's *Black Dance: An Annotated Bibiography;* Herbert O. Emezi's *A Bibliography of African Music and Dance: The Nigeria Experience;* Fred R. Forbes', Jr. Dance: *An Annotated Bibliography, 1965 - 1982;* and L.J.P. Gaskin's, *A Select Bibliography of Music in Africa.* This bibliography has several goals:

1. To list entries that do not specifically focus or refer to dance but have some significant dance content;

2. To demonstrate the areas and regions in which more research needs to be done;

3. To complement and sometimes duplicate with more accurate information entries from the aforementioned bibliographies.

The overlapping of some entries is necessary because it illustrates the wealth of information that can be gleaned from literature that appears obtensively about a different subject matter, i.e. music, religion, theater, and history. In this selected bibliography, which contains new entries and recent entries, my contention is that all information should be reexamined from more specific and particular Afrocentric perspectives.

In this bibliography, Africa is spoken of as a continental entity which means that North Africa, which is generally omitted from discussions of African dance, is considered a part of the continent cultur-ally and politically. Certain terms, because of their pejorative meanings in the nineteenth and twentieth centuries, have been changed to terms that are more accurate except in cases of direct quotes. For example, I have substituted the terms *ethnic groups* for tribes, *societies of secrets* for secret societies and cults, and *indigenous* for primitive.

What makes an entry significant? The information that the entry refers to may only offer the name of the dance and the ethnic group. In research terms this is sparse information. In the case of African dance, it is vital because many of these entries provide clues that lead to additional documents and hopefully more complete information. Many primary sources used in African dance research like program notes, flyers, newspaper adverts and articles are useful sources for the purposes of this bibliography.

Many of the names of the dances that appear in the literature are anglicized or francophone versions of the indigenous dance names and so spellings may vary according to which colonial power occupied the country and translated the information. Names have also changed par-ticularly after independence when many nations wanted the names to properly reflect the language of the people. For example, the *Jerusarema* dance, as it is called in Zimbabwe, was originally named *Mbende* and the Shona people of Zimbabwe continued to call it that in the rural areas. Now throughout the country it is considered acceptable to call the dance *Mbende*. The *Mbende* dance is one of Zimbabwe's greatest cultural symbols and so it was important to reclaim the name along with the status of the dance and the country's independence.

An additional point to be made in reference to conducting African dance research is that there are numerous citations for African dances in which the dances are named by their descriptions. I have omitted these dance citations because most African societies have wedding dances, funeral dances, puberty dances, and celebration dances. It is necessary to reclaim the language of the dance in order to reclaim the dance. While all information is important in the research process, it is the name of the dance not the description that aids scholars in the location of more vital information.

Dance in Africa is complex, multifaceted and rich. Having said that, it is clear that the majority of dances in Africa are, for the most part, unknown to dance scholars and historians. It is also true that dance acts as a medium, facilitates the transition of life's passages (birth, death, puberty), and relays messages in African societies. This selected bibliography attempts to bring some of those documents together and to offer new interpretations of their text. During the last thirty years as the world witnessed African nationalism and the independence of many African countries, it also spawned an interest in those nations preserving and documenting their dances. As each African nation took center stage in the world arena, national dance companies were the natural cultural ambassadors for their respective nations.

Many questions arose from artists, scholars and historians that are still being answered today. How should we (audiences) look at the dances? Are they ritual dances? If so, how does one reconcile the idea of putting a ritual, which is usually sacred, into a secular forum such as a concert or on a stage? If these dances represent the traditional cultures of a myriad of African ethnic groups, what criteria should one use to critique the dances and in what medium? It may seem obvious that a critic's tool is the written word but that cannot be assumed in African dance.

Robert Farris Thompson, the art historian, discusses the process of constructive criticism in African dance. In most African communities, the critics are a part of the culture that they are reviewing. They know the dances kinetically, musically and culturally. Consequently, they can operate from a vantage point that is in harmony with the obligations of the performers. Everyone has a vested interest in the performance and criticism reflects the desire to correct, enhance, verify and not to destroy. Like the performers, the reviewer is also a performer and may very well at some juncture join the performance. This act, in and of itself, is significant because the reviewer's participation affirms the dance and its collective identity. The interaction between the reviewer and the dancers symbolize even more trust, security, and cultural solidarity; aspects that are operative in the music, songs, and movements but they may rarely find their way to the printed word.

It is my intention that this selected bibliography will generate additional interest in research in African dance culture. Valerie A. Briginshaw and Nadia Chilkovsky's African dance bibliographies provide facts for a more complete resource. Aning's bibliography is important because of the holistic approach he takes by combining African music and dance. For now my focus is on African dance because scholars normally ignore it or subsume African dance under music, theater and art.

This bibliography, albeit short, reflects the multidisciplinary nature of dance especially when discussed in Western intellectual discourses. African intellectual discourses does not include discussion of the dance in research except when they focus on dance or the arts in particular. This bibliography demonstrates the difficulty in researching African dance. There are several issues that have arisen in my own research that should be addressed in further research.

1) Because dance facilitates all phenomenom in Africa, it is impossible to research dance without examining the context in which the dance is discussed.

2) Dance can be viewed as art. However, it must be reintepreted as art in a holistic context because it is an intregal part of the society affecting all things and affected by all things.

3) African dance is fluid, it changes meaning and function without destroying the integrity of the dance.

4) African dance, as with all cultures, varies from group to group and there are generalizations that can be made but great attention must be paid to the individual qualities and particularity of the ethnic group.

5) African dance culture is just that. It cannot be limited to just the discussion of steps and movements. African dance culture encompasses dance, music, myth, theater, sculpture (masks and stiltwalking) and religion.

6) There is sacred dance in the sense that almost all African dances are connected to the ancestors and the pantheon of deities and their supreme being. But secular and non secular divisions are for the most part meaningless distinctions since the dances can be sacred for one event and secular for the next event.

7) The languages are also difficult because they are phonetically translated into English or French. Therefore depending on who is doing the translation, the name of the dance changes. In addition, the same dance may be performed by related ethnic groups who have different nationalities. These dances may be spelled differently and even pronounced slightly different but the dances remain essentially the same.

8) Terminology in describing the African dance can be confusing. Commonly, the terms ceremony (the formality observed on some important or proclaimed event for some community, public, or state occasion), masquerade (a celebration, dance or other social gathering of the community wearing masks and full body panoply, and other historical, or spiritual dresses), ritual (an ancient or established procedure for sacred events—a prescribed code of behavior regulating social conduct, as that exemplified by the touching or the shaking of hands in greeting) and festivals (a day or time of religious or other celebration,

marked by feasting, ceremonies, or other observances—a periodic commemoration, anniversary, or celebration) are used interchangeably.
Again because of the fluidity of the dances, they may well be performed in an individual context but that is rare. So a definition of the
aforementioned should be clarified for the researcher's use.

Festivals can incorporate rituals, ceremonies, and masquerades.
Rituals are most often seen in ceremonies.

Masquerades can be involved in all of the above and are used
accordingly to facilate the event that is being commerated.

9) Many pejorative terms and use of language cited in previous
bibliographies and sources have appeared so often and have become a
permanent part of the historical records. Writers should strive to use
the language of the people and not names that were assigned to them.
Researchers on African dance culture can make better use of the documents and their research if when they write they begin to exorcise or
contextualize those terms according to time periods and historical
events.

10) Many of the earlier books and articles have references to
nations and ethnic groups that have consolidated, changed or are extinct.
For instance, before independence many African nations had names
that the colonialists assigned to them. It was common to refer to African
nations by the names assigned to them by their colonial government
prior to 1950. In the 1950's as African nations began to gain their independence, many of the nations chose to reclaim ancient or historical
names for themselves. This trend continues into the 1990's. Nations
such as Burkina Faso still appear on many maps as Upper Volta.
Southern and Northern Rhodesia are now Zimbabwe and Zambia.
Tanzania was formerly Tanganyika and Zanzibar and Ghana was formerly the Gold Coast. The researcher faces another problem with the
countries that have nationalized city and street names. The city Harrare
in Zimbabwe was formerly Salisbury but the former name will still be
very prominent in most of the history books until the 1980's. The resort
city of Mutare was called Umtali by the Rhodesians as was the town
Maradellas which is now Maraderra in Zimbabwe. This is just a sample
of some of the names that have been restored to their original names or
have chosen a name that is reflective of the country's national character.
Many of the names of ethnic groups have changed as well. Although
colonialists certainly had a part in the mispronouncement of various
words in the myriad of African languages, as groups were thrown together
under the artifical nations, they also had difficulty pronouncing certain
sounds. The 'l' and 'y' were often problematic in the southern Africa area

with the settlers substituting the 'l' for the 'y' as in Muchongolo instead of the proper name of the dance Muchongoyo. In Mali, Guinea and Gambia, the native 'n'was changed to 'r' by outsiders so that the ethnic group Bambana was refered to in the literature as "Bambara."

A challenge that African scholars face across all disciplines however when researching African dance is the scrutiny of articles, books, and pamplets for any mention of dance. The word dance alone will not suffice. The name of the dance is a valuable lead and from there ethnic group, music, and event will help to begin the process of documenting the dance. Often times the dance and the music share the same name. In many African languages, the word for music and dance are the same with individual names designated for specific rhythms and movements as well as the event. So when the music is mentioned and the dance isn't, the music must be examined to it's ultimate conclusion which may be the dance.

Finally, a suggestion for future research and implications for further studies should be made. The categorization of African dance, music and theater should be renamed African performance arts. In this way, a bibliography can be broadened to include all of the entities that are so much a part of the African aesthetic phenomenon. In addition, any discussion or research on African performance arts must include masquerades, festivals, ceremonies, rituals and promenades which provide the context and venue in which the dances, music and dramas are performed. I am isolating the identification of the dance sources momentarily not only to establish their existence and prominence as viable entities but also to acknowledge the interdependence and interrelatedness of African dances with the aforementioned disciplines. African dance is beauty, motion, and a seamless bond with humanity and the ancestors.

This bibliography shares new information and a new perspective with which to access African dance more thoroughly. The technological transformation of the world has already affected traditions in Africa. It is important that scholars not only research African dance culture but that we find new ways to gather information. It is a formidable task but one that must be undertaken if we are to ever document as many of the dances as possible to increase our knowledge and expand our appreciation for African dance. For all its fury and passion, the dance heals, soothes and transcends all that is mundane. It is in that spirit that I wrote this essay.

A Selected Bibliography
of African Dance

Acogny, Germaine. *African Dance*. Dakar, Senegal: Les Nouvelles
  Editions Africaines, 1980. Acogny, a dance teacher who taught
  at Mudra, the dance school that Maurice Bejarat and Senghor
  began as a collaboration of the modern and traditional dance
  forms. Ms. Acogny describes African dance as lasting for hours
  at a time, sometimes accompanied by drums and words and
  always related to the religious worldview and cosmology.
  Acogny states "When we dance, we can bring our breathing,
  our heartbeat and the beat of our arms and legs into such unison, that we are as if literally beside ourselves, our personalities
  split in a trance." She stresses that modernism and tradition in
  Black Africa must be reconciled in spheres of song and dance.
  She identifies a synthesis of different dance influences as
  impacting her school and African urban society as never before;
  the variety of influences felt come particularly from
  India/Hindi dance, European, and African-American dance
  styles. She asks that indigenous modern African dance be
  developed in relation to the African urban context; "traditional
  dance is meaningful only within a given socio-cultural context." A traditional context which is rapidly disappearing. A
  dancer and physical education teacher, Acogny discovered her
  own peoples' dances in earnest as an adult. Her school explores
  indigenous native dance along with international styles of modern dance. Her description of African traditional dances is com-
  plemented by excellent photographs which accent rhythmic
  movement and presentation styles of contemporary, traditional
  dancing.
Adamczyk, Alice J. *Black Dance: An Annotated Bibliography*. New York:
  Garland Publishing Inc., 1986.
Adamson, Joy. *The Peoples of Kenya*. London: Collins and Harvill
  Press, 1973. Describes Njemps, Turkana, Kuria, Kamba, and
  Sanye dances.
African Research Committee Conference on the African Arts.
  "Report of the Dance Group." *African Studies Bulletin*, 14-18.
Agawu, V. Kofi. "Gi Dunu, Nyekpadudo, and the study of West
  African Rhythm." *Ethnomusicology* 30 (Winter 1986): 64-83, 54-
  57.

Alagoa, E. J. "Delta Masquerades." *Nigeria Magazine*, 93. Pictures of Acrobatic dancers of the Delta Masquerades.

—. "The Ju Festival." *Nigeria Magazine*, 11-16. Two ritual dances are described and illustrated.

Alaja-Browne, Afolabi. "The Origin and Development of Juju Music." *The Black Perspective in Music* 17.1-2 (1989): 55-72. Discusses how Nigerian dance rhythms have changed over time as well as the problems faced by Westernization.

Alladin, M. P. *Folk Dances of Trinidad and Tobago*. Maraval, Trinidad: n.p., 1974. Identifies and describes folk dances. Gives origins of dances such as the bong, calinda, shango, bele, and pique.

Almeida, Renato. *Danses Africaines en Amerique Latine*. Rio de Janeiro: MEC, Companha de Defesa Folklore Brasileiro, 1969. Discusses popular Latin American dances and their roots in Africa and Afro-American cults (p. 9).

Aloff, Mindy. Rev. of "Africa Oye!" *Art in America* 77 (July, 1989): 63. Discusses actual performances at French-African festival and the problems faced in presenting traditional dances out of context for Americans.

Andrews, George Reid. *The Afro-Argentines of Buenos Aires, 1800-1900*. Madison: University of Wisconsin Press, 1980. Afro-Argentine participation in and contribution to culture of Buenos Aires. Discusses condoubes, milongo, and the history of the tango.

Aretz, Isabel, Manuel Moreno Fraginals, and Leonor Blum. "Music and Dance in Continental Latin America, with the Exception of Brazil." *Africa in Latin America: Essays on History, Culture, and Socialization*. Holmes & Meier; UNESCO (1984): 189-226 & p. 342.

Asagba, Austin Ovigueraye. "Roots of African Drama: Critical Approaches and Elements of Continuity." *Kunapipi* 8.3 (1986): 84-99.

—. "Roots of African Drama: Critical Approaches and Elements of Continuity." *New Literature Review* 14 (1985): 47-57.

Assuncao, Fernando. "Aportaciones Para un Estudio Sobre los Origenes do la Zamacueca (Baile Popular Hispanoamericano de las Regiones Costeras de Pacifico)." *Folklore Americano* 17-18.16 (1969-70): 5-39. Surveys the African influence in the New World with emphasis on the Zamacueca dance of Peru (p. 15).

Awoonor, Kofi. *The Breast of the Earth*. New York: Anchor, 1976. African History, Culture, and Literature. Brief mention of Dance.

Baker, Richard E. St. barbe. "Dancing on the Equator." *The Dancing Times*, (Feb. 1924): 482-485. Descriptions and pictures of Kikuyu dances.

"Ballet in Mozambique." *Ballet-international*. Koln. 8.5 (May 1985): 50. Ballet entitled *The Hands*, dealing with the legends of the Makonde people, presented by the country's State Song and Dance Company.

Bansisa, Y. "Music in Africa." *Uganda Journal* 4 (1936). Brief summary about the functions of African dance on p. 111.

Barret, W.E.H. "Notes on the Customs of the Wagiriana." *Journal of the Royal Anthropological Institute* 41: 20-40. Descriptions of the Mchele dance and a dance for healing persons transformed by the spirits.

Basso, Ellen B. *A Musical View of the Universe: Kalapalo Myth and Ritual Performances*. Philadelphia: University of Pennsylvania Press: 1985.

Bauzo, Luis F. "Kubata: Cuban Cultural Authenticity in Music and Dance." *Caribe* 7.1-2: 36-38.

Bere, R. M. "Acholi Dances." *Uganda Journal* 1.1: 64-65.

Berger, R. "African and European Dance." *Nigeria Magazine* 92: 87-92.

Berliner, Paul. *The Soul of Mbira: Music and Traditions of the Shona People of Zimbabwe*. Berkley: University of California Press, 1978. 280 p., 16 color plates.

Bertonoff, Deborah. *Dance Towards the Earth*. On a Unesco grant in Ghana. Translated from the Hebrew by I.M. Lask. Alityros books, Tel-Aviv, 1963.

Bibliographic Guide to Dance: 1988. Dance Collection of the Performing Arts Research Center, NYPL. Printed yearly, listed by subject. Good reference especially for recorded visual works and unpublished papers.

Biebuyck, Daniel. "Nyanga Circumcision Masks and Costumes." *African Arts* 6.2 (Winter 1973): 20-25, 86-92, pictures.

Blacking, John. "An Introduction to Venda Traditional Dances." *Dance Studies* 2 (1977): 34-56. Jersey, Channel Islands, Centre for Dance Studies. Discussion of Givha Visa, Tshikona, spirit possession dances, Tshigombela, a girls' dance, Dzhombo, children's play dances, malende beer-songs, and initiation dances.

—. "An Introduction to Venda Traditional Dances." *Dance Studies*. Jersey, Channel Islands, Centre for Dance Studies. Discusses children's play dances, malende beer songs, initiation dances,

Giuha Visa, Tshikona, spirit possession dances, a girl's dance, Dzhombo.

—-. "Movement, Dance, Music and the Venda Girls' Initiation Cycle" in Spencer, Paul. *Society and the Dance: The Social Anthropology of Process and Performance*. Cambridge: Cambridge University Press, (1985): 64-91.

—-. "Songs, Dances, Mimes and Symbolism of Venda Girls Initiation Schools. Part IV, the Great Domba Song." *African Studies* 28: 215-266. Blakely, Thomas D. And Pamela A. R. Blakely. "So'o Masks and Hemba Funerary Festival." *African Arts*. 21.1 (November 1987): 30-37, 84-86. Important for understanding the performance context of dance in the Hemba Funerary festival.

Blassingame, John W. *The Slave Community*. New York: Oxford University Press, 1972.

Blixen, Karen. *Out of Africa*. London: Penguin, 1937. Descrip tion of Kikuyu dances.

Blum, Odette. "Dance In Ghana." *Dance Perspective* 56, (1973). New York, Winter 1978. Blum discusses dance in Ghana, describing specific dances, religious meanings and accompanying cultural and historical contexts. She writes this having spent two years in Ghana teaching Labonotation and modern dance. Dances traditionally take place outdoors, usually performed in a ring with a circle of onlookers. Every village has a set of instruments including xylophones, string instruments, horns trumpets, flutes, clappers, bells and rattles (consisting of calabash with encircling loosely-woven beads). According to Blum, compared to Western dance, Ghanaian dancing demonstrates ease downward (versus upward, held) energy, which emphasizes the "dancers" relationship with the earth; a posture of modesty and humility; ripples of body movement stemming from the relative ease, and interspersed or overlaid qualities of quickness, lightness and strength; as well as accelerations and decelerations. In the book's last section, Blum describes dances of four main groups: the Anlo Ewe, Ashanti, Dagomba, and the Lobis of Lawra with notations. She emphasizes the role of improvisation and spontaneous variation to tradition. Music in the Akan dances. Ghanaian dance still reflects and reaffirms the traditional structure and values of African villages, although new influences are introduced through touring and modernization.

Boas, Franziska. *The Function of Dance in Human Society*. 1944.

Reprint. New York: Dance Horizons, 1972. Includes a discussion of Dance in West Africa.

Bohannan, Paul and Phillip Curtin. *Africa and Africans.* 2nd. rev. ed. New York: Natural History Press, 1971. Brief discussion of dance and music included in section on African Arts.

Boone, Sylvia Ardyn. "Sources for the History of Black Dance: Egypt and the Middle East," unpublished seminar report, Yale University, 1972.

Bravmann, René A. "Gyinna-Gyinna: Making the Djinn Manifest." *African Arts* 10.3 (April 1977): 46-52.

—-. *Islam and Tribal Art in West Africa.* London: Cambridge University Press, 1974.

Campbell and Eastman. "Ngoma: Swahili Adult Song Performance in Context." *Ethnomusicology* 28.3 (Sept. 1984): 467-93. Ann Arbor, Michigan.

Cardona, Carlos Mota. "A Gift from Dakar." *The Feet* (June 1973): 12, 31. A review and description of the National Dance Company of Senegal's repertoire.

Carvalho, Jose Jorge de, Manuel Moreno Fraginals, and Leonor Blum. "Music of African Origin in Brazil." *Africa in Latin America: Essays on History, Culture, and Socialization.* Holmes & Meier; UNESCO (1984): 227-248, 342.

Cayou, Dolores Kirton. *The Origins of Modern Jazz Dance.* Palo Alto, California: National Press Books, 1971. Expansion of the above to include mention of societal changes, specific techniques, instructional planning, social and stage dance.

—-. "The Origins of Modern Jazz Dance." *Black Scholar 1*, 8 (June 1970): 26-31. This article traces the evolution of modern jazz dance from traditional African dance through slavery, minstrel shows, vaudeville, and ending in the dance styles of the 1930's. The author also addresses African dance characteristics.

Cerulli, Ernesta. "Peoples of South-West Ethiopia and Its Border land." In Daryll Ford, ed., *Ethnographic Survey of Africa.* London: Hazel, Watson and Viney, Ltd. 1956. Gives examples of the use of dance in several South-West Ethiopian Cultures.

Champion, Arthur M. "The Atharaka." *Journal of the Royal Anthropological Institute* 42: 68-90. Four dances are described: Kisboso, Nzungo, Mungeri, and Mboboi.

Chilkowsky, Nadia. "African Dance." *African Studies Bulletin* 2 (May 1962): 45-47.

Clark, Doris. "Memorial Service for an Ox in Karamoja." *Uganda*

Journal 16: 69-71. Brief descriptions on several Karamajong dances.

Clark, J. P. "Poetry of Urhobo Dances Udje." *Nigeria Magazines*, 87: 282-287, 1965.

Conquabre, Pierre. "African Dances." *Phylon*, Atlanta 5: 355-360.

Coplan, David B. "Ideology and Traditions in South African Black Popular Theater" in *Journal of American Folklore*, 99.392 (April-June 1986): 151-176.

Cosentino, Donald. Bk. Rev. *I Am Not Myself, The Art of African Masquerade* by Herbert M. Cole in *African Arts* 19.1 (November 1985): 81-82.

Crahan, Margaret E. and Franklin W. Knight, eds. *Africa and the Caribbean: The Legacies of a Link*. Baltimore and London: Johns Hopkins University Press, (1979): 80-100.

"Dance Types in Ethiopia." *Journal of International Folk Music Council 19*: 23-27.

"Dance Vrou." *Dance Magazine* (December 1962): 50. Describes ceremonial dance of welcome performed by the Baoule people.

"Dancers as Emissaries in Irigwe, Nigeria." *Dance Research Journal*, 32-35.

Darbois, Dominique. *African Dance*. Prague, (1972): 132. Mainly illustrations.

Dauer, Alfons M. "Transcribing African Music From Synchronized Film." *Dance Research Collage* (c1979): 143-156. New York: CORD.

Davis, Hassoldt. "Yho, the Sorcerer's Village." *Dance Magazine* (July 1953): 10-15.

DeCock, J. "Pre-theatre et Rituel: National Folk Troupe of Mali" *African Arts*. 1:3 (Spring 1968) 31-37 pictures (in French and English) Brief mention of the Mandiani dance performed by the National Dance Company of Mali.

Demery, Felix. "Dancing In Johannesburg." *The Dancing Times* (September 1935): 582-583.

Deren, Maya. "Drums and Dance." *Salmagundi*. 33/34 (1976): 193-209.

Dorsinville, Roger. *The Regulated World of Hinterland Dancing*. Monrovia, Liberia, 1970.

Doull, Alex. "Native Dances of Eastern Africa." *The Dancing Times* (May 1936): 131-132. Description of Beni dances.

Drewal, Margaret Thompson. "Films on Music and Dance in Southern Africa." *Dance Research Journal* CORD. New York

12.1 (Fall-Winter 1979-80): 30-33. Film reviews of nine films produced by the University of Pennsylvania Museum and the International Library of African Music: the Mbira series, the 1973 Mgodo series and Dances of Southern Africa, 1978.

—-. "Symbols of Possession: A Study of Movement and Regalia in an Anago-Yoruba Ceremony." *Dance Research Journal* 17 (Spring/Summer 1975): 15-24.

Drewal, Margaret Thompson and Henry John Drewal. "Gelede Dance of the Western Yoruba." *African Arts* 8.2 (Winter 1975): 36-45, 78-79, pictures, diagrams. Descriptive and informative account of the Gelede dance.

Duncan, Donald. "The Difference is the Purpose." *Dance Magazine*, 36 (December 1962): 48-51. The Ivory Coast engages Tom Skeleton, an American expert in ethnic staging, to prepare a national dance company.

Eibl-Eibesfeldt, I. "Ko-Bushmen (Kalahari): Trance Dance." *Qua Homo Gottengen* 24.3-4 (1973): 245-252.

Ellis, Havelock. *The Dance Of Life*. London: Constable, 1943.

Emery, Lynne F. *Black Dance In The United States From 1619-1970*. National Press Books, California 1972. Emery, Lynne Fauley, *Black Dance in the U.S. from 1619-Today*. Princeton, NJ: Princeton Books, 1989. Foreword by Katherine Dunham. The first comprehensive study of African-inspired dance in the United States. Short discussions of socio-cultural contexts in which these art forms arose are provided. "She analyzes," Dunham writes, "the entire complex of black dance, traces its origins and describes with remarkable lucidity and conciseness its social meaning in the area where it has been performed." Emery recognizes black dance's fundamental relationship to oral literature, music and poetry as part of African aesthetic expression. Emery explores the continuance of many African values and aesthetic traditions, attributing much of this continuity to the perpetuation of formalized ritual traditions, specifically at funerals, so preserving a heritage of community African ritual dance. She explores the relegation of Black dance and art performance to religious spirituality and ecstasy. She embraces black dance as a vital part of American creativity and points to its continuing ability to let us hear, African American culture, artistry, heritage and energy.

Enem, Edith. "Nigerian Dances." *Nigeria Magazine*, 115-116 (1975): 68-115. Eleven Classifications of Nigerian dance. (1)

Masquerade, (2) Maidens, (3) War, (4) Acrobatic, (5) Puppet
Theater, (6) Vocational, (7) Ritual, (8) Elders, (9) Creative, (10)
Social Entertainment and (11) Ceremonial.

Epstein, Dena J. "African Music in British and French America."
Musical Quarterly (January 1973): 61-91. Discussion of enslaved
Africans dance used to illustrate the various types of African
principles of music.

Erlmann, Veit. "Trance and Music in the Hausaboòrii Spirit
Posession Cult in Niger." *Ethnomusicology* 26.1 (January 1982):
49-58. Ann Arbor, Michigan. Analysis of possible factors that
contribute to inducing a trance state.

Euba, O. Akin and the Nanka Atilogu Dance Group. "Nanka
Atilogu Dancers." *African Arts* 5:2 (Winter 1972):60-61.
Highlights this company as the 1971 first place prize winners.

Everald, Jane. "African Dances." *The Dancing Times* (April 1944):
303-305.

Ferguson, I. "Dancers of the Ivory Coast." *African Music.*

Fernandez, James. "Dance Exchange in Western Equatorial Africa."
Dance Research Journal 8 (Fall/Winter 1976): 1-7. Discusses the
exchange of certain elements of the dance and the consequences of this exchange in Western Equatorial Africa. He
observes the Pahouin peoples or Yaounde Fang speakers of
Northern Gabon, Southern Cameroons and Equatorial Guinea.

Fodeba, Keita. "African Dance and the Stage." *World Theatre*
7.3:164-178.

Forbes, Fred R. Jr. *Dance: An Annotated Bibliograhy 1965-1982.* New
York & London: Garland Publishing, Inc., 1986.

Foss, Perkins. "Festival of Ohworu at Evwreni." *African Arts* 6:4
(Summer 1973): 20-27, 94, pictures.

Fulahn. "Swing Music: New Discoveries in Drum Rhythms." *The
Dancing Times* (May 1938): 154-157. Relationship of drum
rhythms to various African dances.

Gann, Lewis H. et al. *Africa and the World: An Introduction to Sub-
Saharan Africa from Antiquity to 1840.* Scranton: Chandler
Publishing Co. (1972): 94. Explains the importance of dance as
an African art form.

Gaskin, L.P.J. *A Select Bibliography of Music in Africa.* London:
International African Institute, 1965. Offers over 35 general
listings of African dance and over 275 listings arranged geographically including both periodical listings and books.

Gebauer, Paul."Dances of Cameroon." *African Arts* 4.4 (Summer

1971): 85-115, pictures, drawings. The relationship between the sculpture and dance of the Cameroons is described. Cameroonian culture depends upon the maintenance of traditional dance forms and recognition of its importance.

Giorgetti, F. "Missions Christian Dances Among the Azade." *African Missionary Society Newsletter 2.*

Glaze, Anita J. "Dialectics of Gender in Senufo Masquerades." *African Arts.* 19.3 (May 1986): 30-39, 82-83, pictures.

Goines, Margaretta Bobo. "African Retentions in the Dance of the Americas." *Dance Research Monography One.* New York: CORD, 1973: 207-229. Discussion of the theory that Black dance in Latin America and the Caribbean have retained more of the African influence than other regions touched by the diaspora. Examination of common traits in the role of dance in African societies and in Haiti, Cuba, Surinam and Brazil.

Gollanex, Victor. *The Music of Africa.* London: 1975. Ill. Contains chapters on interrelations between dance and music and dance and drama.

Gorer, Geoffrey. *Africa Dances: A Book About West African Negroes.* New York: W. Norton and Co., 1962; first 1935. 245 pgs. (L.C.) Written in 1934, *Africa Dances* has been a seminal work about African dance. It has become so in spite of its perjorative tone and strong religious overtones. Geoffrey Gorer, an anthropologist, acknowledges in his new introduction that the study is dated. Gorer confirms that the African dance differs from ethnic group to ethnic group and that there were professional dancers in the village. Finally, he makes the statement that dance is the greatest art of Africa. "The West African expresses every emotion with rhythmical bodily movement. With each group distinct in costume, movement, and tempo."

—. "The Function of Dance." *Salmagundi.* special dance issue. 33/34 (1976): 175-192.

—. "Out of Africa." In *The Dance Has Many Faces*, edited by Walter Sorrell, New York: World, 1951. One chapter containing general comments on African dance.

Götrick, Kacke. Rev. of *Art and Female Power Among the Yoruba* by Henry John Drewal and Margaret Thompson Gelede Drewal, in *Research in African Literatures*, 16 (Fall 1985): 449-452.

Green, Doris. "African Oral Tradition Literacy" in *Journal of Black Studies* 15 (June 1985): 405-25. Ms. Green examines dance, music, and oral tradition and their relationship with each other in African societies.

Gulliver, Pamela. "Dancing Clubs of Nyasa." *Tanganyika Notes and Records UI* 41 (1955): 58-59.

—. "Dancing Clubs of Nyasa." *Tanganyika Notes* 41 (December 1955):58-59.

Hall, R. de Z. "The Dance Societies of the Wasukuma as Seen in the Maswa District." *Tanganyika Notes* 1 (March 1936): 94-96.

Hallpike, C. R. *The Konso of Ethiopia: A Study of the Values of a Cushitic People.* Oxford: Clarendon Press (1972): 32-33. The dances of the Konso people are described in the context of gender roles and the typical structures of such dances are mentioned.

Hampton, Barbara. "Music and Ritual in the Ga Funeral." In *Yearbook of the International Folk Music Council* 14 (1982): 75-105. This article explores the ethnomusicology of folk dance, and song in the funeral rites tradition of the Ga in Ghana, Africa.

Hanna, Judith Lynne. "African Dances as Education." *Impulse* (1965): 48-52. Illustrated; includes bibliography.

—. "African Dance Research: Past, Present and Future." *African Journal* 11.1-2 (1980): 42-51.

—. "African Dance and the Warrior Tradition." In a special issue, "Warrior Tradition in Modern Africa." Ali A. Mazrui, ed., *Journal of African and Asian Studies* 12 (1977): 1-2.

—. "Dance Field Research: Some Why's and African Where-fores." (abstract) *Research in Dance* (1967): 82-84. Discusses need for in-depth analyses of sociocultural contexts of dance.

—. "Dance Odyssey and Theory." *New Dimensions in Dance Research.* New York: Conferences on Research in Dance, 1974. Reiterates premise that dance is linked to the life of a society by affecting cultural patterns, tension management, goal attainment, adaptation, and integration.

—. "Dance and Social Structure: The Ubakala of Nigeria." *Journal of Communications* 29.4 (1979): 184-191.

—. "Field Research in African Dance: Opportunities and Utilities." *Ethnomusicology* 12.1 (January 1968): 101-106. Illustrates several approaches to African dance research.

—. "Functions of African and American Negro Secular Dances: Parallel Answers and Research Quotations." *Black Dance* (November 1967).

—. "The Highlife: A West African Urban Dance." In *Dance Research Monograph One* (Committee on Research in Dance Manual V), edited by Patricia A. Rowe and Ernestine Stodell, New York: n.p,n.d.; 138-152.

—-. "The Interrelations of African Music and Dance." *Journal of the International Folk Music Council* 17.2: 91-101.

—-. "Nkwa di iche iche: Dance-plays of Ubakala." *Presence Africaine* 65.1 (1968): 13-38.

—-. "Warrior Dances: Transformations Through Time." *To Dance is Human* (c1979): 179-198. Austin: University of Texas Press.

Hanna, W.J. & Hanna, Judith L. "The Social Significance of Dance in Black Africa." *Civilizations* 21 (1971): 238-241.

Harper, Peggy. "Dance In A Changing Society." *African Arts* 1.1 (Autumn 1967):10-13; 76-77; 79-80, pictures. Discusses how dance reflects the life of of the people in Nigeria. This article has broad implications for understanding the transformation of traditional cutlure in contemporary Africa.

—-. "A Festival of Nigerian Dances." *African Arts* 3.2 (Winter 1970): 48-53, pictures. Describes several dances performed for various reasons including seasonal agricultural festivals, funeral celebrations, entertaining visitors, installation of an Emirand important chief. Among the dances discussed are the Miango and Takai dance and the Gelede Masquerade.

—-. "The Role of the Dance in the Gelede Ceremonies of the Village of Ijio." In *Odu* (4 October 1970). I have not seen this article however, I believe its title reveals that it contains some discussion on African dance.

—-. *Studies in Nigerian Dance, #2, The Miango Dancers.* Ibadan Nigeria: Caxton Press, 1966. Made to accompany an 11 minute film available from the Institute of African Studies, U. of Ibadan, Nigeria. (L.C. Ref) Dances of the Nigerian Irigwe (a Hausa community) are danced primarily by men; when dancing together in a shared space, males and females dance separately. Dancers accompany themslves vocally and chorally interact with the audience/community participants as well as the drums. Performers sometimes wear rattling bracelets or bands of beads, beans and stone to accent danced rhythms. Specific dances mark different occasions in the nature of the human life cycle. As of 1968, dances traditionally performed for important visitors accommodated tourists with money, who could sometimes pay chiefs to see dances. This patronage impacted on the costumes, purpose, styles and meanings of dances, making them an economic commodity rather than a ritual, communal event.

Hart, W. A. "Limba Funeral Masks." *African Arts* 22.1 (November 1988): 60-67, 99, pictures. Discusses different dancers who perform during different phases of a funeral ceremonies.

Herrick, Allison Butler et al. *Area Handbook for Uganda*. Washington, DC: U.S. Government Printing Office (1968): 153-55. Describes several dances such as the "leaping dance" and funeral dances. Also explores the age when people can officially take part in village dances.

Hight, Gladys. "Safari Through Africa." *Dance Magazine*, (October 1948): 22-25. Description, with illustration of trip to Africa and dance ceremonies in the Congo.

Hill, Peter. "Tribal Dances in Kenya's Nyanza Province." *East African Annual* (1949-50): 57-59.

Hinckley, Priscilla Baird. "The Dodo Masquerade of Burkina Faso." *African Arts* 19.2 (February 1986): 74-77, 91, pictures. Focuses on how the children's game known as Dodo masquerade "has become a means by which youths express their new sense of being powerful and up-to-date." Article also briefly discusses the transformation of the Dodo.

Hinde, Sydney Langford and Hildegarde Hinde. *The Last of the Masai*. London: Hernemann, 1901.

Huet, Michel. *The Dance, Art, and Ritual of Africa*. Trans. From French by Jean-Louis Paudrat. New York: Pantheon Books, (1978): 241.

Imperato, Pascal James. "Contemporary Adapted Dances of the Dogon." *African Arts* 5.1 (Autumn 1971): 28-34, 68-72, pictures.

—. "The Dance of the Tyiwara." *African Arts* 4.1 (Autumn 1970): 8-13, 71-80, pictures. Descriptive account of the Dance of Tyi Wara of the Bamana and Maninka of Mali.

Imperato, Pascal James and Shamir, Marli. "Bokolanfini: Mud Cloth of the Bamana of Mali." *African Arts* 3.4 (Summer 1970): 32-40, pictures.

Ingrams, W. H. "The People of Makunduchi, Zanzibar." *Man*. 68.

Jackson, Irene V. *More Than Drumming: Essays on African and Afro-Latin Music and Musicians*. Westport, CT: Greenwood Press, 1985. This book contains ten essays by various authors. Some deal directly with music, but the majority offer a look at music and dance in relationship to each other. Touches on aspects of dance such as ritual, expression, drama, rhythm, and spirit. Some illustrations.

Jahn, Janheinz. *MUNTU: An Outline of the New African Culture*. New York: Grove Press, 1961. Originally published in German, this is an important book about neo-African culture and it remains current. Values, traditions, modes of communication and inter-action, posture, religion, language, philosophy, literature, art, music, and dance are all discussed. Jahn explores African cultural values, by referring to a Rwanda (Bantu) philosophical framework first posited by theologian Alex Kagame. Jahn distinguishes Western and African dancing traditions as primarily tied to differences in rhythm, posture, steps, and gesture which essentially relate to meaning in African culture and so cannot be reproduced as African dance without the accompanying cultural and religious framework and intent. He makes the distinction that performance without the cultural bedding makes African dances those of display for an audience instead of group events essentially involving the whole community.

Jones, A. M. "African Music: The Mganda Dance." *African Studies* 4.4 (December 1945). Good description with illustrations of trip to Africa and dance ceremony in the Congo.

Jones, A. M. and L. Kombe. *The Icila Dance Old Style: A Study in African Music and Dance of the Lala Tribe of Northern Rhodesia*. London: Longmans Green - Africa Music Society, 1952. Specific descriptions of the Icila dance contained in Chapter one, pages 1-15.

July, Robert W. *An African Voice: The Role of the Humanities in African Independence*. Durham: Duke University Press, 1987. Chapter Five, "African Dance" is about dance, music and their combination in African culture. July seems to be trying to prove the existence of specific African cultures even though Africa has long been influenced by Europeans through colonization. This chapter does not have descriptions of dances, but does describe its place in culture.

Kaemmer, John E. "Social Power and Musical Change Among the Shona." *Ethnomusicology* (Winter 1989): 31-45. Little dance description, but discusses attitudes towards traditional dance and how they have been historically changed in relationship to politics.

Kaeppler, Adrienne L., ed. *Reflections and Perspectives on Two Anthropological Studies on Dance*. New York: CORD Dance Research Annual, VII, 1976. 161 pages, diagrams, theoretical intent, interpretation, and original bibliographies of the pub-

lished 1965 academic works. (I.U.) Two seminal works of
dance ethnology—or the anthropology of dance—presented in
original form with authors' more contemporary, 1976 reflections. The two studies are: "A Comparative Study of Dance as
a Constellation of Motor behaviors Among African and U.S.
Negroes," by Joann Kealiinohomoku and "The Dance of the
Taos Pueblo," by Donald Brown. Dance, closely related to
music, is a stylized behavior which retains traditions more thoroughly—because of its stylized exaggeration and increased
uniqueness—than daily routine movement. "It is evident that
analysis of dance, when used to supplement other anthropological studies, promises to be a useful tool for research concerning the processes of change, resistance to change, acceptance of
change, and reinterpretations" of a cultural tradition.

Kamlongera, Christopher. "An Example of Syncretic Drama from
Malawi: Malipenga." *Research in African Literature* 17 (Summer
1986): 197-210.

—. "The Growth of Popular Theater in East and Central Africa" in
New Literature Review 13 (1984): 17-28.

Kauffman, Robert A. "African Rhythm: A Reassessment." *Ethno
musicology* 24 (September 1980): 393-415.

—. "Tactility as an Aesthetic Consideration in African Music." 251-
253. In Blacking, John and Kealiinohomoku, Joann W. (eds.),
Tax, Sol (pref.) *The Performing Arts, Music and Dance.* New York:
Mouton; (1979): Xxii, pp. 344.

Kealiinohomoku, Joann Wheeler. "Ethnic Historical Study." In
*Dance History Research: Perspectives from Related Arts and
Disciplines* (1970): 86-97. New York: Committee on Research in
Dance. A comparison of the similarities in black American
dance and the dances of Western Africa.

Kenyatta, J. *Facing Mount Kenya.* London: Secker and Warburg, 1938.

Kerr, D. and M. Nambote. "The Malipenga Mine of Likoma Island"
in *Critical Arts: A Journal of Media Studies* 3.1 (1983): 9-28. This
article explores the ethnomusicology and folk dance elements
of the Malipenga mine on Lake Malawi on Likoma Island in
Southern Africa.

Kinney, Esi Sylvia. "Africanisms in Music and Dance of the
Americas." In *Black Life and Culture in the United States*, edited
by Rhonda L. Goldstein. New York: Thomas Crowell (1971):
49-63.

Kirk-Greene, A.H.M. Review of: *The First Dance of Freedom: Black*

Africa of the Postwar Era, by Martin Meredith in *International Affairs* 61 (Spring 1985): 332-333. This article covers the history of African government and politics from 1945-1960 and 1960 to the present as well as a discussion on dance in relation to current political changes.

Kubik, Gerhard. *Dance, Art, and Ritual of Africa*. New York: Random House,1978.

—-. "Pattern Perception and recognition in African Music." 221-249, In Blacking, John and Kealiinohomoku, Joann W. (eds.), Tax, Sol (pref.), *The Performing Arts: Music and Dance*. New York: Mouton, (1979): xxii, 344, ill.

—-. "Patterns of Body Movement in the Music of Boys' Initiation in South-East Angola." In John Blacking, ed., *The Anthropology of the Body* (pp. 253-74). London: Academic Press, 1977.

Kuper, Hilda. "Celebration of Growth and Kingship: Incwala in Swaziland." *African Arts* 1.3 (Spring 1968): 56-59, 90, pictures.

—-. *The Swazi, A South African Kingdom*. New York: Holt, Rinehart and Winston, (c1963).

Ladzekpo, C. Kobla and Hewitt Pantaleoni. "Takaola Drumming." *African Music* 4.4 (1970).

Lambert, H. E. "The Beni Dance Songs." *Swahili* 33.1 (1962). Good description of these dances, which spread over parts of East, Southern, and Central Africa at the beginning of the twentieth century. Many song text reproduced.

Leib, Elliot and Renee Romano. "Reign of the Leopard: Ngbe Ritual." *African Arts* 18.1 (November 1984): 48-57, 94-96, pictures. A detailed description of the Ekpe (Efik) peoples in the Cross River region and their masked dance forms. Descriptive accounts of dance and music provided.

Lerner, Rose. "Tribal Dancing Among the Bantu." *The Dancing Times* (June 1935): 253-254.

Lewis-Williams, J. D. "A Dream of Eland: An Unexplored Component of San Shamanism and Rock Art" in *World Archaeology* 19 (October 1987): 165-177. Among the subjects covered in this article were: San (African people), trance, rock drawings, Shamanism, Elands in art and dancing in art.

Locke, David. *Drum Gahu!: A Systematic Method for an African Percussion Piece*. Crown Point IN: White Cliffs Media Company, 1987. Instruction and study techniques for the Gahu drum, West African dance music, and cultural specifics of the Ewe people. 142 pp., ill.

—. "Drums of West Africa: Ritual Music of Ghana." *Ethnomusicology* 23.2 (May 1979): 366-367. Middletown, Conn. Review of recording of Ewe dance drumming and music of the Blekete cult during actual religious ceremonies.

—. "Principles of Offbeat Timing and Cross-Rhythm in Southern Ewe Dance Drumming," in *Ethnomusicology: Journal of the Society for Ethnomusicology* 26.2 (May 1982): 217-245. This article explores the subjects of ethnomusicology, folk music, and drum music in Africa and specifically among the Ewe group in Guinea, West Africa. Timing and rhythm are very specifically explored.

Lokko, Sophia D. "Ghana: The Twin Cult of the Asre." *The Drama Review* 23.2 (June 1978, occult and foreign issue): 89-93. Describes Ghanaian ritual dances.

Lonsdale, Steven. "The Choreography of the Hunt" and "The Final Season: The Dance of Death." *Animals and the Origins of Dance* (1981): 54-69 and 11328. London: Thames and Hudson.

Mackay, M. and A. Ene. "The Atilogwu Dance." *African Music*, 20-23. Description of this dance from Eastern Nigeria.

Mark, Peter. "Dance Masks in Motion," unpublished report, Yale University: 1973.

—. "Ejumba: The Iconography of the Diola Initiation Mask" in *Art Journal* 47 (Summer 1988): 1399-1146. "Mark talks of the different African rites and ceremonies existing and especially the role of the mask in these ceremonies."

Mazrui, Ali. "African Dance and the Warrior Tradition." (Special issue: "The Warrior Tradition in Modern Africa," ed. Ali A. Mazrui.) *Journal of African and Asian Studies* 12 (1977): 1-2. Includes some articles that discuss dance as part of the warrior tradition.

Middletown, John. "1921 - The Dance Among the Lugbara of Uganda." *Society and the Dance: The Social Anthropology of Process and Performance*, ed. Paul Spencer. Cambridge, England, New York: Cambridge University Press, 1985, pp. 165-82. 224 pp., 1 leaf of plates, ill.

Mitchell, J. C. *The Kalela: Aspects of Social Relationships Among Urban Africans in Northern Rhodesia* (Rhodes Livingston Papers #57). Manchester, England: Manchester University Press, 1956. Monograph which includes detailed discussion and description of the Kalela dance.

Monts, Lester P. "Dance in the Vai Sande Society." *African Arts* 17.4

(August 1984): 53-59. An essay on the role of dance in the Vai
Sande society of Liberia with focuses on folklore, religious
activity, rites, and ceremony. Visual component "Vai Tombo
Music and Dance in Liberia." Santa Barbara: Television
Services, University of California, 1985.

Moyana, Tafirenyika. "Muchongoyo: A Shangani Dance." *African
Arts* 9.2 (January 1976): 40-42, 80, pictures. Describes the
Muchongoyo dance, which is possibly the most popular cultural activity among the Ndau, as evidence of the Nguni
legacy.

Mubitana, Kafungulwa. "Wiko Masquerades in a Zambian Town."
African Arts 4.3 (Spring 1971): 58-61, pictures.

Murray, Jocelyn, ed. *Cultural Atlas of Africa.* New York: Facts on File,
1981. (McCabe Ref.) A book with very brief introductions to
individual nations as well as to cultural unities. The section on
Music and Dance reflects a limited study of African Dance. 240
pp., ill.

Newman, Anita F. "The Bridge Between Physical and Conceptual
Reality: The Trance Experience of the !Kung Bushman" in
UCLA Journal of Dance Ethnology 3 (Fall/Winter 1979-1980): 1-
7. This article investigates folk dance in trance and folk medi-
cine of the !Kung Bushman of the Kalahari Desert in South
Africa.

Nicholls, Robert W. "Igede Funeral Masquerades." 17.3 (May 1984):
70-76, 91-92, pictures.

—-. "Music and Dance Guilds in Igede," 91-117, In Jackson, Irene
V. (ed.) *More Than Drumming: Essays on African and Afro-Latin
Music and Musicians.* Westport, CT: Greenwood, (1985): xv,
207.

Nketia, J. H. Kwabena. *Drumming in Akan Communities of Ghana.*
London: Thomas Nelson, 1963. 212 pp., ill.

—-. "Possession Dances in African Society." *Journal of the
International Folk Music Council* 9 (1957): 4-9.

Nwabuobu, Emeka. "Folklore and Education: Dance as the Mirror
of Human condition, with Particular Reference to the Birnin
Kebbi People of Sokoto State of Nigeria." *Dance Notation
Journal* 2.1 (Spring 1984): 18-30.

Nyrop, Richard, et al. *Area Handbook for Rwanda.* Washington, DC:
U.S. Government Printing Office (1969): 103. The traditional
dances of the Tutsi, a Rwandan ethnic group, were often
related to their primary interests of cattle and war. Both the tra-

ditional and present day theater dances are often expressions of emotion, desires, and thanksgiving related to weddings, births, harvests, and hunting.

Nzekwu, Onoara. "Ibo Dancing." *Nigeria Magazine* 73: 35-45.

Okonkwo, F.I. "Igeri Ututu: An Igbo Folk Requiem Music Dance Ritual." In *The Performing Arts: Music and Dance*, John Blacking and Joann Kealiinohomoku, eds. New York: Mouton, (1979): 84-121.

—-. "National Festival Week-Dancers." *Nigeria Magazine*, 1965.

Opoku, Albert M. "The African Dancer as a Person." *Impulse* (1961) pp.27-28.

—-. "Choreography and the African Dance." *University of Ghana Institute of African Studies Research Review* 3 (1): 53-59.

—-. Opoku, Albert M. and Willis Bell. *African Dances: A Ghanaian Profile, Pictorial Excerpts from Concerts of Ghanaian Dances.* Legon: Univ. Of Ghana, Institute of African Studies, 1965. 40 pp., chiefly illustrated. (L.C.) Photographs do point to the distinct importance of: dynamism, asymmetry and angularity, gesture, imitation, costumes and instruments in dance. "To us, life, with its rhythmic cycles, is dance. The dance is life expressed in dramatic terms." The book links the multi-level use of space and simultaneous distinct body movements of African dance to the complexity of life patterns embodied by the dancers. There is very little text; some photos do look staged to/for camera, but the joy, vitality, group participation and complexity of these dances is clear. Individual dances are specified with descriptive captions beneath.

Ottenberg, Simon. "Afikpo Masquerades: Audience and Performers." *African Arts* 6.4 (Summer 1973): 33-35, 94.

—-. "The Beaded Bands of Bafodea." *African Arts*. 25.2 (April 1992): 64-75, 98-99, pictures. Discusses dance in relation to the function of beaded bands. Dance is placed into the context of girls' and boys activities before during and after initiation activities.

—-. *Masked Rituals of Afikpo, the Context of an African Art.* Seattle: University of Washington Press, 1975. 229 pp., 8 leaves of plates, ill.

Ottenberg, Simon and Linda Knudsen. "Leopard Society Masquerades: Symbolism and Diffusion." 18.2 (February 1985): 37-44, 93-95, 103-104, pictures. Includes discussion of dance.

Pantaleoni, Hewitt. "Three Principles of Timing in Anlo Dance

Drumming." *African Music* 5: 50-63.

Peek, Philip M. "Isoko Artists and Their Audiences." *African Arts.* 58-60, 91, pictures. Discusses dance within the structures of interaction between the artist and the audience. Peek notes that "Overall, it appears that the majority of artist-audience interactions among the Isoko are rather straightforward transactions...dancing seems to be the most highly charged artistic event, while traditional carving draws the least interaction."

Pern, Stephen. "Masked Dancers of West Africa: The Dogon." Amsterdam: Time-Life Books, 1982. Quality photos and brief text discussing the life style and culture of the Southern Mali people. A book of the "Peoples of the Wild" series with text in the form of a personal account."

Primus, Pearl. "Africa." *Dance Magazine* 33 (March 1958): 43-49, 90.

—-. "Africa Dance." In *Headway: A Thematic Reader.* Lois A. Michel, ed. New York: Holt, Rinehart, and Winston, 1970. Pp. 193-199.

—-. "African Dance." In *Presence Africaine 1961.* Special Edition. New York: Standard Press and Graphics, Inc., 1963.

—-. "African Dance: Eternity Captured." *Caribe* 7.1-2 (1983): 10-13.

—-. "Dance as a Cultural Expression." *The World Today in Health, Physical Education, and Recreation.* C. Lynn Vendien and John Nixon, eds. Englewood Cliffs, N.J.: Prentice-Hall, Inc., 1968. Pp 18-26.

—-. "Dreams and the Dance." *Monograph 8.* New York: Journal of the American Academic of Psychotherapist, September 1964

—-. "Earth Theatre in Africa." *Monthly Magazine.* Brooklyn, New York: Brooklyn Institute of Arts and Sciences. February 1951.

—-. "Living Dance Of Africa." *Dance Magazine,* June, 1946.

Prins, A.H.J. *The Coastal Tribes of the North Eastern Bantu.* London: International African Institute, 1952.

Ranger, Terrence O. *Dance and Society in Eastern Africa 1890-1970: The Beni Ngoma.* Berkeley: University of California Press, 1975. 170 pp., maps. Discussion of the evolution of Beni Ngoma dance and society.

Ravenhill, Phillip L. "An African Triptych: On the Interpretation of Three Parts and the Whole (The Goli Masquerade of the Wan)." *Art Journal* 47 (Summer 1988): 88-94. Discusses masks and costumes from the Ivory Coast and how they were used in funeral rites and other ceremonies.

Ridgeway, William. *Dramas and Dramatic Dances of Non-European Races in Special References to the Origin of Greek Tragedy.*

Cambridge, England: Cambridge University Press, 1915. Small section on African dance and drama.

Robbins, Larry J. and M. E. Robbins. "A Note on Turkana Dancing." *Ethnomusicology* 15: 231-235.

Roberts, Thomas Duval, et. al. *Area Handbook for Liberia.* Washington, D.C.: U.S. Government Printing Office (1972): 47, 127-128. Explains that music and dance are the most common means of self expression of the Liberian people. There is mention of north eastern stilt dancing which is slowly vanishing.

Rood, Armistead P. "Bete Masked Dance: A View from Within." *African Arts* 2.3 (Spring 1969): 35-43, 76, pictures.

Royce, Anya Peterson. *The Anthropology of Dance.* Bloomington IN: Indiana University Press, 1977. 238 pp. including index and bibliography, ill. This book does try to integrate material on African culture and dance according to several traditions— Ashante, Bisa, Nguni, Wolof, Xhosa, and Zande albeit very briefly. Royce is primarily concerned with identification, and establishing a comprehensive base for the anthropology of dance.

Saighoe, Francis A. Kobina. "Dagaba Xylophone Music of Tarkwa, Ghana: A Study of Situational Change." *Current Musicology* 37/38 (1984): 167-175.

"The Senegambian Horned Initiation Mask: History and Provenance."

The Art Bulletin 69 (December 1987): 626-640. Discusses African masks and the rites and ceremonies in which they are used.

Shack, William A. "The Central Ethiopians: Amhara, Tigrina, and Related Peoples." In Daryl Forde, ed., *Ethnographic Survey of Africa.* London: Lowe and Brydone, Inc. (1974): 115. Gives a brief explanation of the form and purpose of the mwara waram (funeral dance of the Gurage).

Shostak, Marjorie. *Nisa: The Life and Words of a !Kung Woman.* Cambridge MA: Harvard University Press, 1981. 402 pp., ill. Shostak, an anthropologist who did her fieldwork in the 1970's, presents her observations with the account of one woman's stories as representative of the traditional culture. Dances are described within a cultural context; medicine trances, spiritual, healing dances, menstruation ceremonies, women's drum dance are the ones discussed.

Sithole, Elkin Thamsanga. "Ngoma Music among the Zulu" in Blacking, John and Kealiinohomoku, Joann W. (eds.), *The*

Performing Arts: Music and Dance. New York: Mouton, 1979. This article covers subjects like ethnomusicology, Ngoma folk dance, music, and song among the Zulu in Natal South Africa.

Skeleton, Thomas R. "Staging Ethnic Dance - The Dance And The Dancers." *Impulse*; International Exchange In Dance (1963-64): 64-74.

Sow, Alpha I. *Introduction to African Culture*, Paris UNESCO, 1979. Chapter One (pp. 33-83), "Form and Expression in African Arts" by Ola Balogun includes discussion of visual art and dance as communicative art. In this chapter, dance is discussed in the second category.

Spencer, Anne M. "Ritual and Ceremony in African Life." (The Newark Museum, New Jersey—new permanent collection). *African Arts* 18.4 (August 1985): 84.

Spencer, Frank. "Dancing in West Africa." *The Dancing Times.* (December 1945): 106.

Standifer, James A. "The Tuareg: Their Music and Dances" in *Black Perspective in Music* 16 (Spring 1988): 45-62. Standifer writes of the Tuareg people of Southwest Libya. Specifically he concentrates on those of Ghat which is known as the "Dancing City." Standifer finds important the assimilated Arab and African traditions in the culture of the Tuareg people. He goes on to describe the differences between male/female musical practices and dances such as the Targi Dance and the Sword Dance. The article also includes an appendix on Tuareg musical instruments.

Stephen, Martin et al. *Dancers of Mali.* Dunetz & Lovett.

Stevens, Phillips Jr. "The Nupe Elo Masquerade." *African Arts* 6.4 (Summer 1973): 40-43, 94.

Stobel, Margaret. "Women's Wedding Celebrations in Mombasa, Kenya" in *African Studies Review* 18 (December 1985): 35-45. Stobel examines the change and progression of dance within wedding ceremonies.

Story, Sommerville. "Arab Dancing Girls." *The Dancing Times* (March 1936): 759-762.

Sunkett, Mark Ellis. *Mandiani Drum and Dance Forms and Aspects of African-American Aesthetics.* Diss. University of Pittsburgh, 1994.

Thompson, Robert Farris. "An Aesthetic of the Cool: West African Dance," in Hill, Errol (ed.), *The Theater of Black Americans: A Collection of Critical Essays.* New York: Applause (1987): 99-111. In this article Thompson discusses American literature, Afro-

American dramatists, and African folk music and dance in West
Africa.

—. *African Art in Motion: Icon and Act*. Los Angeles: University of
California Press, 1974. Ill. And plates.

—. "African Dancers at the Fair." *Saturday Review*, 47 (July 25,
1964): 37-39. Thompson dispels the "bigoted assumptions"
and "cliché notions" Westerners have of African dance by
explaining the true aspects of African dance. Thompson
explores the notions of "Apart Dancing," "Total body movement," "Dances of derision," and "Posture." Photos included.
His article is an encouragement to look more with knowledge
at the dances of the Sudan at the World's Fair.

Tracey, Hugh. "African Music and Dancing." *Empire* 44.6 (1982):
252-254.

—. *Chopi Musicians, Their Music, Poetry and Instruments*. London:
Oxford University Press, 1970.

—. *African Dances of the Witwatersrand Gold Mines*. Johannesburg:
African Music Society, 1952. 156 pp., ill. (L.C.) Tracey, a recognized authority on the dances and music of Southern Africa
people, describes twelve dances of twelve different ethnic
groups.

Turner, Edith L. B. *The Spirit and the Drum: A Memoir of Africa*.
Tuscon: University of Arizona Press, 1987. 165 pp., port. Focuses on
rites, ceremonies, social life, and customs of the Ndembu people.

—. "Zambia's Kankanga Dances: The Changing Life of Ritual" in
Performing Arts Journal 10.3 (1987): 57-71. In this article Turner
writes of Zambian women's dance in religion and in folklore.
She pays particular attention to the subject of puberty rites in
the lives of the Ndembu people.

Udoka, Arnold. "Ekong Songs of the Annang." *African Arts* 18.1
(November 1984): 70+.

Vadasy, Tibor. "Ethiopia Folk Dance II: Wallo and Galla." *Journal
of Ethiopian Studies* 11.1 (1973): 214-231.

Van Onselen, Charles. *Chibaro: African Mine Labour in Southern
Rhodesia, 1900-1933*. London: Pluto Press, 1976. 326 pp., maps.
This book is about the forced labor in Southern Rhodesian
mines. In the labor camps, men developed dancing groups.
This enabled them to associate with men from their own society while, for the mine owners, it maintained tribal differences
so that they did not have to fear that all the workers would join

together and revolt against the dehumanizing cond
mining. As these dance societies continued, they inc
other functions such as burial societies and eventually
a sort of aid society amongst the workers for moral and
support. It describes the meaning of dance within the su
ture of early twentieth century Southern Rhodesian mine
ture.

Vidal, T. "Lagos State Music and Dance." *African Arts* 9.2 (Januar
1976): 35-39.

Vrydagh, P Andre. "Makisi of Zambia." *African Arts* 10.4 (July 1977):
12-19, pictures. Discusses the Makisi performed for ceremony
of circumcision.

Waite, Gloria. "Spirit Possession Dance in Eastcentral Africa," in
UCLA Journal of Dance Ethnology 4 (Spring 1980): 31+. Folk
dance, and spirit possession dance in East Central Africa with
respect to folk medicine was the major theme of this article.

Warren, Lee. *The Dance of Africa: An Introduction.* Englewood Cliffs,
N.J.: Prentice Hall, 1972. Includes dance instructions, with
illustrations by Harris Petie. Describes many African dances
and discusses their origin and their significance as a reflection
of various aspects of African life.

Wells, Liz. "Thusa! Celebrating the Creative Spirit of Black South
Africa: Four Photographers Amid the Music and Dance."
British Journal of Photography (August 18, 1988): 135. Wells is
able to provide what is often lacking in descriptions of African
dance and music—the images. Descriptions of dance are often
technically accurate but difficult for the reader to visualize
"Thusa!" over comes this common problem.

Welsh Asante, Kariamu. "Commonalities in African Dance: An
Aesthetic Foundation." in Asante, Molefi Kete and Welsh-
Asante, Kariamu (eds.), *African Culture: The Rhythms of Unity.*
Westport, CT: Greenwood, (1985): 71-82.

—. The Creation of the National Dance Company of Zimbabwe:
Report to the Ministry of Education and Culture. Harare:
Zimbabwe, (1982).

—. "The Jerusarema Dance of Zimbabwe." *Journal of Black Studies*
15 (June 1985): 381-404. Discusses traditional dances and functions of the Shona peoples of Zimbabwe.

—. *Zimbabwean Dance: An Aesthetic Analysis of the Jerusarema and
Muchongoyo Dances.* Diss. New York University, 1993.

Wetl, Peter. "Masked Figure and Social Control: The Mandinka

'onal African Institute 41 (1971): 279-
'n dances, rituals and their place in

.niel. "Black Dance: Its African
." Minority Voices 1.2: 73-80. An essay
that africanisms have been transplanted
.t not transformed.
ne Dance of The Bedu Moon." African Arts 2.1
968): 18-21, 72, picture, drawings, diagram.
.d and Rev. J.S. Steemers, and J.E.K. Kumah.
.odae: Come and Dance!" African Arts 3.3 (Spring
.970):36-39, pictures. Description of the dance and why it is
performed for the Okosi (gods) and special funeral occasions.
Yoshida, Kenji. "Masks and Secrecy Among the Chewa." African Arts
26.3 (April 1993): 34-45, 92.

ions of
rporated
became
hysical
ocul-
ul-

eral articles on African dance and theater.

Myriam Evelyse Mariani is a Professor of Dance in the School of Physical Education at the Federal University of Minas Gerais (UFMG), Brazil, where she has taught since 1975. Dr. Mariani (Ph.D., University of Wisconsin) also coordinates the Masters Program in Physical Education as well as conducting dance research and directing seminars, workshops, and concerts throughout Brazil. Her work has also been presented in Canada, Germany, and the United States.

Glendola Yhema Mills is an Assistant Professor specializing in the Umfundalai dance technique in the Department of African American Studies at Temple University. Ms. Mills is the Associate Director for the Institute for African Dance Research and Performance and the Managing Editor of the *International Journal of African Dance*. Her research to date focuses on the African and African American aesthetic and dance with an emphasis on the image of dance in literature and popluar culture forms. Ms. Mills is also interested in the role, meaning, and significance of movement and its forms in Black family life. In addition to her research interest, she is a principal artist and dance master with Kariamu and Company—Traditions.

Sir Rex Nettleford is a Full Professor at the University of the West Indies, Jamaica, where he edits *Caribbean Quarterly* and directs the School of Continuing Studies. He is also the founder, Artistic Director, and principal choreographer of the National Dance Theatre Company of Jamaica. A Rhodes Scholar, Rex Nettleford is a leading Caribbean intellectual and renaissance figure who was Cultural Advisor to the Prime Minister of Jamaica.

Robert W. Nicholls is an Assistant Professor of Educational Technology at the University of the Virgin Islands, St. Thomas. He has written several articles on African music and dance.

Pearl Primus (November 29, 1919–October 29, 1994) was born in Trinidad and went on to become an African dance pioneer and a renowned choreographer and teacher. Primus traveled the South, observing the lifestyles of the common people, living with sharecroppers and visiting Black churches. It was that experience that inspired much of her subsequent choreography. Dances like *Strange Fruit* became classics, because of her bold statement of social protest.

CONTRIBUTORS

Omofolabo Soyinka Ajayi is an Associate Professor at the University of Kansas where she teaches literature, dance, theory, and criticism in Women's Studies and the Theatre Department. Also a dancer/choreographer, she has a book forthcoming on Yoruba dances with Temple University Press. Her other publications appear in *Dance Resear Journal*, *Semiotics*, *Journal of Dramatic Theory and Criticism*.

Felix Begho received his Ph.D. from New York University. Begh choreographer and researcher in dance theory, has published se articles on dance, including "Black Dance Continuum: Reflectio the Heritage Connections Between African Dance and Afro-Ame Jazz Dance."

Doris Green is an ethnomusicologist and a certified tea Labanotation. She is a pioneer in ethnochoreographology, th tific study of the art of representing dances symbolically, toget its music of a particular race or cultural group through Labanot Greenotation. She is the creator of the GREENOTATION s writing African music aligned with dance in a single score. recipient of three CUNY Faculty Research awards and was of the Fulbright award for Ivory Coast and the Gambia.

Katrina Hazzard-Gordon, a Henry E. Rutgers Research Associate Professor and Chair of Sociology at Rutgers Camden, is the founder and Director of the Diaspora D and Research Group. Dr. Hazzard-Gordon's most rece is *Jookin': The Rise of Social Dance Formations in African-A*

Esilokun Kinni-Olusanyin teaches in the Departm Arts at University of Ibadan, Ibadan Nigeria and he